Concentrate

Free online study and revision support

Visit the online resource centre at:

www.oup.com/lawrevision/

Take your learning further:

➤ Multiple-choice questions

➤ An interactive glossary

➤ Outline exam answers

➤ Flashcards of key cases

➤ Download our free ebook, *Study and Exam Success for Law Students,* which includes:

• Guidance on how to approach revision and prepare for exams

• Guidance on how to use a statute book

'I always buy a Concentrate revision guide for each module and use the online resources. The **outline answers are particularly helpful** and I often use **the multiple choice questions to test my basic understanding** of a topic'

Alice Reilly, Cardiff University

'The Online Resource Centre has been **exceptionally useful.** In my first year, I used the resources to **quiz myself,** to test **my knowledge and understanding of cases,** and **to pick up extra pointers that could give me a few extra marks'**

Kelly Newman, University of Exeter

consolidate knowledge > focus revision > maximise potential

I would like to thank my daughter Rebecca, a former law student, for her advice and observations during the writing of this book.

Contract Law
Concentrate

2nd edition

Jill Poole

Deputy Dean, Aston Business School
Professor of Commercial Law, Aston University

OXFORD
UNIVERSITY PRESS

OXFORD
UNIVERSITY PRESS

Great Clarendon Street, Oxford, OX2 6DP,
United Kingdom

Oxford University Press is a department of the University of Oxford.
It furthers the University's objective of excellence in research, scholarship,
and education by publishing worldwide. Oxford is a registered trade mark of
Oxford University Press in the UK and in certain other countries

First edition 2013

Impression: 1

Published in the United States of America by Oxford University Press
198 Madison Avenue, New York, NY 10016, United States of America

British Library Cataloguing in Publication Data

Data available

Library of Congress Control Number: 2015933302

ISBN 978-0-19-872972-3

Printed in Great Britain by
Ashford Colour Press Ltd, Gosport, Hampshire

New to this edition

This edition covers the key changes of relevance to Contract law introduced by the Consumer Rights Act 2015. These changes (see Chapter 5) relate to sale and supply law in the context of consumer contracts – and, in particular, the implied promises made by the trader (and corresponding statutory rights of the consumer). Certain pre-contract information supplied by the trader in a B2C contract may also become terms. Other significant developments include the important changes to consumer law governing unfair contract terms with the enactment of a single regime governing B2C contracts in Part 2 of the Consumer Rights Act 2015 and the separation of the legislative regulation of exemption clauses in B2B contracts within UCTA 1977 (see Chapter 6). The government indicated that this legislation (which received royal assent in March 2015) would be brought into force by October 2015 (and the current Unfair Terms in Consumer Contracts Regulations 1999 revoked), so this book reflects the enacted law.

The other statutory amendment of note is achieved by the Consumer Protection Amendment Regulations 2014, SI 2014/870, which adds a system of civil 'rights to redress' for consumers in B2C contracts in relation to 'misleading actions' (misrepresentations) under the CPRs 2008 and excludes the possibility of these consumers recovering damages under s. 2 MA 1967.

New case law added in this edition includes: *Marks and Spencer plc v BNP Paribas Securities Services Trust Co (Jersey) Ltd* (2014) (implied terms in fact and *Belize*); *Kudos Catering (UK) Ltd v Manchester Central Convention Complex Ltd* (2013) (construction in a commercial context); *Overy v Paypal (Europe) Ltd* (2012) (meaning of 'consumer' for the purposes of the unfair terms legislation) and the decision of the Court of Appeal in *Makdessi v Cavendish Square Holdings BV* (2013) (penalties).

Contents

Table of cases   viii
Table of legislation   xvii

1   Agreement   1

2   Agreement problems   29

3   Enforceability criteria   46

4   Privity and third party rights   73

5   Terms and breach of contract   97

6   Exemption clauses and unfair contract terms   120

7   Remedies for breach of contract   141

8   Contractual impossibility and risk: Frustration and common mistake   163

9   Misrepresentation   187

10   Undue influence   208

Glossary   A1
Index   A5

Table of cases

A to Z Bazaars (Pty) Ltd v Minister of Agriculture 1974 (4) SA 392; 1975 (3) SA 468 (South Africa) . . . 14–15

Achilleas, The *see* Transfield Shipping Inc. v Mercator Shipping Inc.

Adam Opel GmbH v Mitras Automotive (UK) Ltd [2008] EWHC 3205 (QB); [2008] Bus LR D55 . . . 54

Adams v Lindsell (1818) 1 B & Ald 681; 106 ER 250 . . . 13

Addis v Gramophone Co. Ltd [1909] AC 488 . . . 153

AEG (UK) Ltd v Logic Resource Ltd [1996] CLC 265 . . . 127

Ailsa Craig Fishing Co. Ltd v Malvern Fishing Co. Ltd [1983] 1 WLR 964 . . . 128

Alaskan Trader, The *see* Clea Shipping Corp. v Bulk Oil International Ltd

Alder v Moore [1961] 2 QB 57 . . . 158

Alderslade v Hendon Laundry Ltd [1945] 1 KB 189 . . . 129

Alfred McAlpine Construction Ltd v Panatown Ltd [2001] 1 AC 518 . . . 90, 91, 92, 94, 96

Allcard v Skinner (1887) LR 36 ChD 145 . . . 210, 214

Amalgamated Investment & Property Co. Ltd v John Walker & Sons Ltd [1977] 1 WLR 164 . . . 176, 184

Anglia TV v Reed [1972] 1 QB 60 . . . 149

Antons Trawling Co. Ltd v Smith [2003] 2 NZLR 23 (Court of Appeal of New Zealand) . . . 69

Appleby v Myers (1867) LR 2 CP 651 . . . 178

Atlantic Baron, The *see* North Ocean Shipping Co. Ltd v Hyundai Construction Co. Ltd

Atlas Express Ltd v Kafco [1989] 1 All ER 641 . . . 54

Attica Sea Carriers Corp v Ferrostaal Bulk Reederei GmbH, The Puerto Buitrago [1976] 1 Lloyd's Rep 250 . . . 115

Attorney General of Belize v Belize Telecom Ltd [2009] UKPC 10; [2009] 1 WLR 1988 . . . 108, 117

Attwood v Small (1838) 6 Cl & F 232 . . . 193

Avery v Bowden (1855) 5 E & B 714; 119 ER 647 . . . 115

Avraamides v Colwill [2006] EWCA Civ 1533; [2007] BLR 76 . . . 81

B & S Contracts & Design Ltd v Victor Green Publications Ltd [1984] ICR 419 . . . 54

Bacardi-Martini Beverages Ltd v Thomas Hardy Packaging Ltd [2002] EWCA Civ 549; [2002] 2 All ER (Comm) 335 . . . 135

Bainbrigge v Browne (1881) LR 18 ChD 188 . . . 210

Baird Textiles Holdings Ltd v Marks & Spencer plc [2001] EWCA Civ 274; [2002] 1 All ER (Comm) 737 . . . 35, 51, 70

Balfour v Balfour [1919] 2 KB 571 . . . 51, 52

Balmoral Group Ltd v Borealis (UK) Ltd [2006] EWHC 1900 (Comm); [2006] 2 CLC 220 . . . 135

Banco de Portugal v Waterlow & Sons Ltd [1932] AC 452 . . . 151

Bank of Montreal v Stuart [1911] AC 120 . . . 210

Bannerman v White (1861) 10 CB NS 844; 142 ER 685 . . . 102, 112, 117

Barclays Bank plc v Fairclough Building Ltd [1995] QB 214 . . . 151

Barry v Davies (t/a Heathcote Ball & Co.) [2000] 1 WLR 1962 . . . 25

Barton v County NatWest Bank Ltd [1999] Lloyd's Rep Bank 408 . . . 194

Bell v Lever Brothers Ltd [1932] AC 161 . . . 169–70, 170, 185

Beswick v Beswick [1968] AC 58 . . . 88, 94, 95, 141, 144

Bettini v Gye (1876) LR 1 QBD 183 . . . 112

Bisset v Wilkinson [1927] AC 177 . . . 191

Blackpool & Fylde Aero Club Ltd v Blackpool Borough Council [1990] 1 WLR 1195 . . . 24

Boulton v Jones (1857) 2 H & N 564; 157 ER 232 . . . 41

Bowerman v Association of British Travel Agents Ltd [1996] CLC 451 . . . 19, 51

BP Exploration Co. (Libya) Ltd v Hunt (No. 2) [1979] 1 WLR 783 . . . 181, 186

Brennan v Bolt Burdon [2004] EWCA Civ 1017; [2005] QB 303 . . . 171

Brimnes, The see Tenax Steamship Co. Ltd v The Brimnes (Owners)

Brinkibon Ltd v Stahag Stahl GmbH [1983] 2 AC 34 . . . 16

British Crane Hire Corp Ltd v Ipswich Plant Hire Ltd [1975] QB 303 . . . 107

British Steel Corporation v Cleveland Bridge & Engineering Co. Ltd [1984] 1 All ER 504 . . . 30, 35, 44, 144

British Westinghouse v Underground Electric [1912] AC 673 . . . 151

Britvic Soft Drinks v Messer UK Ltd [2002] EWCA Civ 548; [2002] 2 Lloyd's Rep 368 . . . 135

Brogden v Metropolitan Railway Co. (1877) LR 2 App Cas 666 . . . 10

Butler Machine Tool Co. Ltd v Ex-Cell-O Corporation (England) Ltd [1979] 1 WLR 401 . . . 10, 25, 26

Byrne & Co. v Van Tienhoven & Co. (1880) 5 CPD 344 . . . 19, 27

C & P Haulage Co. Ltd v Middleton [1983] 1 WLR 1461 . . . 150, 161

Carlill v Carbolic Smoke Ball Company [1893] 1 QB 256 . . . 19, 20, 27, 51

Casey's Patents, Re [1892] 1 Ch 104 . . . 57

CCC Films v Impact Quadrant [1985] 1 QB 16 . . . 151

Cehave NV v Bremer Handelsgesellschaft GmbH, The Hansa Nord [1976] QB 44 . . . 112, 117

Cellulose Acetate Silk Co. Ltd v Widnes Foundry (1925) Ltd [1933] AC 20 . . . 156, 157, 159

Cenargo Ltd v Izar Construcciones Navales SA [2002] EWCA Civ 524; [2002] CLC 1151 . . . 157

Central London Property Trust Ltd v High Trees House Ltd (High Trees House) [1947] KB 130 . . . 66, 67, 68, 71

Chandler v Webster [1904] 1 KB 493 . . . 178

Chapelton v Barry U.D.C. [1940] 1 KB 532 . . . 125, 126, 139

Chappell & Co. Ltd v Nestlé Co. Ltd [1960] AC 87 . . . 56

Chartbrook Ltd v Persimmon Homes Ltd [2009] UKHL 38: [2009] 1 AC 1101 . . . 42

Cheese v Thomas [1994] 1 WLR 129 . . . 213

CIBC Mortgages plc v Pitt [1994] 1 AC 200 . . . 212, 214

City and Westminster Properties (1934) Ltd v Mudd [1959] Ch 129 . . . 103

Clarke v Dickson (1858) 120 ER 463 . . . 197

Clea Shipping Corp. v Bulk Oil International Ltd, The Alaskan Trader [1984] 1 All ER 129 . . . 115

Clef Aquitaine SARL v Laporte Materials (Barrow) Ltd [2001] QB 488 . . . 193

Co-operative Insurance Society Ltd v Argyll Stores (Holdings) Ltd [1997] 2 WLR 898 . . . 144

Collins v Godefroy (1831) 1 B & Ad 95 . . . 58

Combe v Combe [1951] 2 KB 215 . . . 67

Cooper v Phibbs (1867) LR 2 HL 149 . . . 167, 168

Couchman v Hill [1947] KB 554 . . . 103, 112

Countess of Dunmore v Alexander (1830) 9 S 190 . . . 14

Countrywide Communications Ltd v ICL Pathway Ltd [2000] CLC 324 . . . 35

Couturier v Hastie (1856) 5 HL Cas 673; 10 ER 1065 . . . 167, 168, 184

Crossley v Faithful & Gould Holdings [2004] EWCA Civ 293; [2004] 4 All ER 447 . . . 117

CTN Cash and Carry Ltd v Gallaher Ltd [1994] 4 All ER 714 . . . 53

Cundy v Lindsay (1878) LR 3 App Cas 459 . . . 40, 44

Curtis v Chemical Cleaning & Dyeing Co. [1951] 1 KB 805 . . . 125

Table of cases

✱✱✱✱✱✱✱✱✱✱✱✱

D & C Builders Ltd v Rees [1966] 2 QB 617 . . . 68, 72

Darlington Borough Council v Wiltshier Northern Ltd [1995] 1 WLR 68 . . . 91, 94

Daulia Ltd v Four Mill Bank Nominees Ltd [1978] Ch 231 . . . 22

Daventry District Council v Daventry and District Housing Ltd [2011] EWCA Civ 1153; [2012] 1 WLR 1333 . . . 42

Davis Contractors Ltd v Fareham UDC [1956] AC 696 . . . 176, 185

Denny, Mott & Dickson v James B. Fraser & Co. Ltd [1944] AC 265 . . . 174

Derry v Peek (1889) LR 14 App Cas 337 . . . 195

Dick Bentley Productions Ltd v Harold Smith (Motors) Ltd [1965] 1 WLR 623 . . . 102, 117

Dickinson v Dodds (1876) LR 2 ChD 463 . . . 19

Dimmock v Hallett (1866) LR 2 Ch App 21 . . . 191, 194

Director General of Fair Trading v First National Bank plc [2001] UKHL 52; [2002] 1 AC 481 . . . 137, 138, 140

Dolphin & Maritime & Aviation Services Ltd v Sveriges Angfartygs Assurans Forening, The Swedish Club [2009] EWHC 716 (Comm); [2009] 1 CLC 460 . . . 79–80

Downs v Chappell [1997] 1 WLR 426 . . . 199, 200

Doyle v Olby (Ironmongers) Ltd [1969] 2 QB 158 . . . 199

Dunbar Bank plc v Nadeem [1998] 3 All ER 876 . . . 213

Dunlop Pneumatic Tyre Co. Ltd v New Garage & Motor Co. Ltd [1915] AC 79 . . . 157, 159, 162

Dunlop Pneumatic Tyre Co. Ltd v Selfridge & Co. Ltd [1915] AC 847 . . . 55, 76, 84, 95

East v Maurer [1991] 1 WLR 461 . . . 199, 200, 202, 203, 207

Ecay v Godfrey (1947) 80 Lloyd's Rep 286 . . . 102, 190

Edgington v Fitzmaurice (1885) LR 29 ChD 459 . . . 192, 193, 207

Edwinton Commercial Corporation v Tsavliris Russ (Worldwide Salvage and Towage) Ltd, The Sea Angel [2007] EWCA Civ 547; [2007] 2 Lloyd's Rep 517 . . . 174, 177

Entores Ltd v Miles Far East Corporation [1955] 2 QB 327 . . . 15, 16, 17, 27

Equitable Life Assurance Society v Hyman [2002] 1 AC 408 . . . 108

Erlanger v New Sombrero Phosphate Co. (1878) LR 3 App Cas 1218 . . . 197

Errington v Errington & Woods [1952] 1 KB 290 . . . 21, 28

Esso Petroleum Co. Ltd v Mardon [1976] QB 801 . . . 102, 192, 200

Eugenia, The see Ocean Tramp Tankers Corporation v V/O Sovfracht

Eurymedon, The see New Zealand Shipping Co. Ltd v A. M. Satterthwaite & Co. Ltd

Farley v Skinner (No. 2) [2001] UKHL 49; [2002] 2 AC 732 . . . 154, 160, 162

Felthouse v Bindley (1862) 11 CB (NS) 869; 142 ER 1037 . . . 12, 25

Fercometal SARL v Mediterranean Shipping Co. SA, The Simona [1989] AC 788 . . . 114

Fibrosa SA v Fairbairn Lawson Combe Barbour Ltd [1943] AC 32 . . . 178

Fisher v Bell [1961] 1 QB 394 . . . 7

Foakes v Beer (1884) LR 9 App Cas 605 . . . 60, 64, 71

Foley v Classique Coaches Ltd [1934] 2 KB 1 . . . 34

Frederick E. Rose (London) Ltd v William H. Pim Junior & Co. Ltd [1953] 2 QB 450 . . . 42

Gamerco SA v I.C.M./Fair Warning (Agency) Ltd [1995] 1 WLR 1226 . . . 179, 180, 184, 186

George Mitchell Ltd v Finney Lock Seeds Ltd [1983] 2 AC 803 . . . 134, 135

GHSP Inc. v AB Electronic Ltd [2010] EWHC 1828 (Comm); [2011] 1 Lloyd's Rep 432 . . . 25

Gibbons v Proctor (1891) 64 LT 594 . . . 20

Gibson v Manchester City Council (CA) [1978] 1 WLR 520 . . . 25, 26

Gibson v Manchester City Council (HL) [1979] 1 WLR 294 . . . 6

Gillatt v Sky Television Ltd [2000] 1 All ER (Comm) 461 . . . 34

Glasbrook Bros. v Glamorgan CC [1925] AC 270 . . . 58

Golden Strait Corporation v Nippon Yusen Kubishika Kaisha, The Golden Victory [2007] UKHL 12; [2007] 2 AC 353 . . . 146

Goodchild v Bradbury [2006] EWCA Civ 1868; [2007] WTLR 463 . . . 210

Gordon v Selico Co. Ltd (1986) 278 EG 53 . . . 191, 192

Gould v Gould [1970] 1 QB 275 . . . 52

Grainger & Son v Gough [1896] AC 325 . . . 7

Gran Gelato Ltd v Richcliff (Group) Ltd [1992] Ch 560 . . . 204

Granville Oil & Chemicals Ltd v Davies Turner & Co. Ltd [2003] EWCA Civ 570; [2003] 1 All ER (Comm) 819 . . . 134

Great Peace Shipping Ltd v Tsavliris Salvage (International) Ltd [2002] EWCA Civ 1407; [2003] QB 679 . . . 170, 171, 183, 185

Griffith v Brymer (1903) 19 TLR 434 . . . 168, 175, 184

Grogan v Robin Meredith Plant Hire [1996] CLC 1127 . . . 125, 126, 127

H. Parsons (Livestock) Ltd v Uttley Ingham & Co. Ltd [1978] 1 QB 791 . . . 153

Hadley v Baxendale (1854) 9 Exch 341; 156 ER 145 . . . 151, 152, 160, 161

Halpern v Halpern [2007] EWCA Civ 291; [2007] 3 WLR 849 . . . 198

Hamilton Jones v David & Snape (a firm) [2003] EWHC 3147 (Ch); [2004] 1 WLR 924 . . . 154

Hammond v Osborn [2002] EWCA Civ 885; [2002] WTLR 1125 . . . 211

Hansa Nord, The see Cehave NV v Bremer Handelsgesellschaft GmbH

Harris v Nickerson (1873) LR 8 QB 286 . . . 7

Hartley v Ponsonby (1857) 7 E& B 872 . . . 62

Hartog v Colin & Shields [1939] 3 All ER 566 . . . 38

Harvela Investments Ltd v Royal Trust Co. of Canada (CI) Ltd [1986] AC 207 . . . 23

Hayes v Dodd [1990] 2 All ER 815 . . . 154

Hedley Byrne & Co. Ltd v Heller & Partners Ltd [1964] AC 465 . . . 200, 201, 202, 204, 205

Henthorn v Fraser [1892] 2 Ch 27 . . . 12

Herne Bay Steam Boat Co. v Hutton [1903] 2 KB 683 . . . 175, 185

Heywood v Wellers [1976] QB 446 . . . 154

Hi-Lite Electrical Ltd v Wolseley UK Ltd [2011] EWHC 2153 (TCC); [2011] BLR 629 . . . 151

HIH Casualty & General Insurance Ltd v Chase Manhattan Bank [2003] UKHL 6; [2003] 1 All ER (Comm) 349 . . . 130

Hillas & Co. Ltd v Arcos Ltd (1932) 147 LT 503 . . . 31

Hirachand Punamchand v Temple [1911] 2 KB 330 . . . 65

Hochster v De La Tour (1853) 2 E & B 678; 118 ER 922 . . . 114

Holwell Securities Ltd v Hughes [1974] 1 WLR 155 . . . 13, 27

Hong Kong Fir Shipping Co. Ltd v Kawasaki Kisen Kaisha Ltd [1962] 2 QB 26 . . . 112, 117, 118

Horsfall v Thomas (1862) 1 H & C 90 . . . 192, 193

Houghton v Trafalgar Insurance Co. Ltd [1954] 1 QB 247 . . . 128

Hounslow LBC v Twickenham Garden Developments Ltd [1971] Ch 233 . . . 116

Household Fire and Carriage Accident Insurance Co. Ltd v Grant (1879) LR 4 ExD 216 . . . 13, 27

Howard Marine & Dredging Co. Ltd v A. Ogden & Sons (Excavations) Ltd [1978] QB 574 . . . 202

Howe v Smith (1884) LR 27 ChD 89 . . . 158

Hutton v Warren (1836) 1 M & W 466 . . . 107

Huyton SA v Peter Cremer GmbH & Co. [1999] 1 Lloyd's Rep 620 . . . 54

Hyde v Wrench (1840) 3 Beav 334; 49 ER 132 . . . 9, 10, 26

Table of cases

✴✴✴✴✴✴✴✴✴✴✴✴

Inntrepreneur Pub Co. v East Crown Ltd [2000] 2 Lloyd's Rep 611 . . . 104

Interfoto Picture Library Ltd v Stiletto Visual Programmes Ltd [1989] QB 433 . . . 127, 140

Investors Compensation Scheme Ltd v West Bromwich Building Society (No 1) [1998] 1 WLR 896 . . . 129

Isabella Shipowner SA v Shagang Shipping Co. Ltd, The Aquafaith [2012] EWHC 1077 (Comm); [2012] 2 All ER (Comm) 461 . . . 116

J. Evans & Son (Portsmouth) Ltd v Andrea Merzario Ltd [1976] 1 WLR 1078 . . . 104, 118

J. Lauritzen AS v Wijsmuller BV, The Super Servant Two [1990] 1 Lloyd's Rep 1 . . . 177

J. Spurling Ltd v Bradshaw [1956] 1 WLR 461 . . . 127

Jackson v Horizon Holidays Ltd [1975] 1 WLR 1468 . . . 89, 155

Jackson v Union Marine Insurance Co. Ltd (1874) LR 10 CP 125 . . . 173

Jarvis v Swans Tours [1973] QB 233 . . . 154, 155

Jobson v Johnson [1989] 1 WLR 1026 . . . 156

Jones v Padavatton [1969] 1 WLR 328 . . . 52

Jones v Vernon's Pools Ltd [1938] 2 All ER 626 . . . 51

Joscelyne v Nissen [1970] 2 QB 86 . . . 42

Keates v Cadogan (1851) 10 CB 591 . . . 191

King's Norton Metal Co. Ltd v Edridge, Merrett & Co. Ltd (1897) 14 TLR 98 . . . 41

Koufos v Czarnikow Ltd, The Heron II [1969] 1 AC 350 . . . 152

Krell v Henry [1903] 2 KB 740 . . . 168, 175, 184, 185

Kudos Catering (UK) Ltd v Manchester Central Convention Complex Ltd [2013] EWCA Civ 38; [2013] 2 Lloyd's Rep 270 . . . 130

Kyle Bay (T/A Astons Nightclub) v Underwriters Subscribing Under Policy Number 019057/08/01 [2007] EWCA Civ 57; [2007] 1 CLC 164 . . . 171

L. Schuler AG v Wickman Machine Tool Sales Ltd [1974] AC 235 . . . 113, 118

Leaf v International Galleries [1950] 2 KB 86 . . . 170, 197

Les Affréteurs Réunis SA v Leopold Walford (London) Ltd [1919] AC 801 . . . 87

L'Estrange v Graucob Ltd [1934] 2 KB 394 . . . 125

Lewis v Averay [1972] 1 QB 198 . . . 42, 45

Linden Gardens Trust Ltd v Lenesta Sludge Disposals Ltd (St Martins Property Appeal, St Martins Property Corporation Ltd v Sir Robert McAlpine Ltd) [1994] 1 AC 85 . . . 89, 90, 91, 92, 94, 96

Liverpool City Council v Irwin [1977] AC 239 . . . 108, 110, 118

Lloyds Bank Ltd v Bundy [1975] QB 326 . . . 210, 214

London Drugs Ltd v Kuehne and Nagel International Ltd (1993) 97 DLR (4th) 261 . . . 86, 93

Long v Lloyd [1958] 1 WLR 753 . . . 197, 198

Luxor (Eastbourne) Ltd v Cooper [1941] AC 108 . . . 21, 22, 28

McArdle, Re [1951] Ch 669 . . . 57

McRae v Commonwealth Disposals Commission (1951) 84 CLR 377 (Australia) . . . 144, 149, 161, 166, 168

Makdessi v Cavendish Square Holdings BV [2013] EWCA Civ 1539; [2013] 2 CLC 968 . . . 156, 157

Manchester Diocesan Council for Education v Commercial & General Investments Ltd [1970] 1 WLR 241 . . . 12

Maritime National Fish Ltd v Ocean Trawlers Ltd [1935] AC 524 . . . 177

Marks and Spencer plc v BNP Paribas Securities Services Trust Co (Jersey) Ltd [2014] EWCA Civ 603; [2014] 2 P&CR DG16 . . . 117

May & Butcher Ltd v R [1934] 2 KB 17n . . . 33, 34

Mediterranean Salvage and Towage Ltd v Seamar Trading and Commerce Inc., The Reborn [2009] EWCA Civ 531; [2009] 1 CLC 909 . . . 108

Mendelssohn v Normand Ltd [1970] 1 QB 177 . . . 128

Merritt v Merritt [1970] 1 WLR 1211 . . . 52

Metropolitan Water Board v Dick Kerr & Company Ltd [1918] AC 119 . . . 166, 175

Monarch Airlines Ltd v London Luton Airport Ltd [1997] CLC 698 . . . 129

Mondial Shipping and Chartering BV v Astarte Shipping Ltd [1995] CLC 1011 . . . 16

Moorcock, The (1889) LR 14 PD 64 . . . 108

Morgan v Manser [1948] 1 KB 184 . . . 173

National Carriers Ltd v Panalpina (Northern) Ltd [1981] AC 675 . . . 174

National Westminster Bank Plc v Morgan [1985] AC 686 . . . 210

Naughton v O'Callaghan [1990] 3 All ER 191 . . . 202, 203

New Zealand Shipping Co. Ltd v A. M. Satterthwaite & Co. Ltd, The Eurymedon [1975] AC 154 . . . 59, 74, 81, 85, 86, 95

Nickoll & Knight v Ashton, Edridge & Co. [1901] 2 KB 126 . . . 173

Nicolene Ltd v Simmonds [1953] 1 QB 543 . . . 32

Nisshin Shipping Co. Ltd v Cleaves & Co. Ltd [2003] EWHC 2602 (Comm). [2004] 1 Lloyd's Rep 38 . . . 80, 87, 95

North Ocean Shipping Co. Ltd v Hyundai Construction Co. Ltd, The Atlantic Baron [1979] QB 705 . . . 55

O'Brien v MGN Ltd [2001] EWCA Civ 1279; [2002] CLC 33 . . . 126, 127

Ocean Marine Navigation Ltd v Koch Carbon Inc., The Dynamic [2003] EWHC 1936 (Comm); [2003] 2 Lloyd's Rep 693 . . . 116

Ocean Tramp Tankers Corporation v V/O Sovfracht, The Eugenia [1964] 2 QB 226 . . . 176, 177

Office of Fair Trading v Abbey National plc [2009] UKSC 6; [2010] 1 AC 696 . . . 137

Olley v Marlborough Court Ltd [1949] 1 KB 532 . . . 126

Omak Maritime Ltd v Mamola Challenger Shipping Co., The Mamola Challenger [2010] EWHC 2026 (Comm); [2011] Bus LR 212 . . . 149, 150, 161

Oscar Chess Ltd v Williams [1957] 1 WLR 370 . . . 102

Overy v Paypal (Europe) Ltd [2012] EWHC 2659 (QB), [2013] Bus LR D1 . . . 130

Pankhania v Hackney London Borough Council [2002] EWHC 2441 (Ch); [2002] NPC 123 . . . 192

Pao On v Lau Yiu Long [1980] AC 614 . . . 53, 54, 57, 59, 70

Parker v Clark [1960] 1 WLR 286 . . . 52

Partridge v Crittenden [1968] 1 WLR 1204 . . . 7

Payne v Cave (1789) 3 Term Rep 148 . . . 18

Payzu Ltd v Saunders [1919] 2 KB 581 . . . 151

Peek v Gurney (1873) LR 6 HL 377 . . . 193

Peekay Intermark Ltd v Australia & New Zealand Banking Group Ltd [2006] EWCA Civ 386; [2006] 2 Lloyd's Rep 511 . . . 125

Perry v Sidney Phillips & Son [1982] 1 WLR 1297 . . . 154

Pharmaceutical Society of Great Britain v Boots Cash Chemists [1953] 1 QB 401 . . . 7

Philips Hong Kong Ltd v AG of Hong Kong (1993) 61 BLR 41 . . . 157

Phillips v Brooks Ltd [1919] 2 KB 243 . . . 42

Photo Production Ltd v Securicor Transport Ltd [1980] AC 827 . . . 129, 134, 140

Pilkington v Wood [1953] Ch 770 . . . 151

Pilmore v Hood (1838) 5 Bing NC 97 . . . 193

Pinnel's Case (1602) 5 Co Rep 117a . . . 64

Post Chaser, The see Société Italo-Belge pour le Commerce et L'Industrie SA (Antwerp) v Palm and Vegetable Oils (Malaysia) Sdn Bhd

Poussard v Spiers (1876) 1 QBD 410 . . . 111

Progress Bulk Carriers Ltd v Tube City IMS LLC [2012] EWHC 273 (Comm); [2012] 1 CLC 365 . . . 54

Puerto Buitrago, The see Attica Sea Carriers Corp v Ferrostaal Bulk Reederei GmbH

R v Clarke (1927) 40 CLR 227 (High Court of Australia) . . . 20

R. W. Green Ltd v Cade Brothers Farms [1978] 1 Lloyd's Rep 602 . . . 136

Table of cases

✱✱✱✱✱✱✱✱✱✱✱✱

Raffles v Wichelhaus (1864) 2 H & C 906; 159 ER 375 . . . 36, 37, 44

Reardon Smith Line Ltd v Hansen-Tangen [1976] 1 WLR 989 . . . 117

Reborn, The see Mediterranean Salvage and Towage Ltd v Seamar Trading and Commerce Inc.

Redgrave v Hurd (1881) LR 20 ChD 1 . . . 190, 193, 194, 204, 206

Regalian Properties plc v London Dockland Development Corporation [1995] 1 WLR 212 . . . 35

Regus (UK) Ltd v Epcot Solutions Ltd [2008] EWCA Civ 361; [2009] 1 All ER (Comm) 586 . . . 135

Robinson v Davison (1871) LR 6 Ex 269 . . . 173

Robinson v Harman (1848) 1 Exch 850 . . . 146

Rose & Frank Co. v J. R. Crompton & Brothers Ltd [1925] AC 445 . . . 51

Routledge v Grant (1828) 4 Bing 653; 130 ER 920 . . . 18

Royal Bank of Scotland plc v Etridge (No. 2) [2001] UKHL 44; [2002] 2 AC 773 . . . 212, 214

Royscot Trust Ltd v Rogerson [1991] 2 QB 297 . . . 202

RTS Flexible Systems Ltd v Molkerei Alois Muller GmbH & Co. (UK Production) [2010] UKSC 14; [2010] 1 WLR 753 . . . 30, 35

Ruxley Electronics and Construction Ltd v Forsyth [1996] 1 AC 344 . . . 148, 160

Ryan v Mutual Tontine Westminster Chambers Association [1893] 1 Ch 116 . . . 144

St Martins Property Corp. Ltd v Sir Robert McAlpine & Sons Ltd see Linden Gardens Trust Ltd v Lenesta Sludge Disposals Ltd

Saunders v Anglia Building Society [1971] AC 1004 . . . 43

Scammell & Nephew Ltd v Ouston [1941] AC 251 . . . 31

Schawel v Reade [1913] 2 IR 81 . . . 101, 102

Schebsman, Re [1944] Ch 83 . . . 87

Scriven Brothers & Co. v Hindley & Co [1913] 3 KB 564 . . . 37

Scruttons Ltd v Midland Silicones Ltd [1962] AC 446 . . . 85, 86, 93

Sea Angel, The see Edwinton Commercial Corporation v Tsavliris Russ (Worldwide Salvage and Towage) Ltd

Selectmove Ltd, Re [1995] 1 WLR . . . 64, 70

Shanklin Pier v Detel Products Ltd [1951] 2 KB 854 . . . 86, 104

Shell UK Ltd v Lostock Garage Ltd [1976] 1 WLR 1187 . . . 109

Shogun Finance Ltd v Hudson [2003] UKHL 62; [2004] 1 AC 919 . . . 30, 31, 36, 40, 42, 43, 44

Shuey v US 23 L Ed 697 (1875); 92 US 73 . . . 22

Siboen and the Sibotre, The [1976] 1 Lloyd's Rep 293 . . . 55

Smith New Court Securities Ltd v Scrimgeour Vickers (Asset Management) Ltd [1997] AC 254 . . . 199, 202, 203, 207

Smith v Eric S. Bush [1990] 1 AC 831 . . . 131, 132

Smith v Hughes (1871) LR 6 QB 597 . . . 38, 44, 170

Smith v Land & House Property Trust Ltd (1884) LR 28 ChD 7 . . . 190, 192, 194, 206

Snelling v John G Snelling Ltd [1973] 1 QB 87 . . . 52

Société Italo-Belge pour le Commerce et L'Industrie SA (Antwerp) v Palm and Vegetable Oils (Malaysia) Sdn Bhd, The Post Chaser [1982] 1 All ER 19 . . . 67

Solle v Butcher [1950] 1 KB 671 . . . 171, 183

South Caribbean Trading v Trafalgar Beheer BV [2004] EWHC (Comm) 2676; [2005] 1 Lloyd's Rep 128 . . . 62

Spencer v Harding (1870) LR 5 CP 561 . . . 7, 23

Spice Girls Ltd v Aprilia World Services BV [2002] EWCA Civ 15; [2002] EMLR 27 . . . 191

Standard Chartered Bank v Pakistan National Shipping Corp. (Nos. 2 & 4) [2002] UKHL 43; [2003] 1 AC 959 . . . 204

Sterling Hydraulics Ltd v Dichtomatik Ltd [2006] EWHC 2004 (QB); [2007] 1 Lloyd's Rep 8 . . . 126

Stevenson, Jacques & Co. v McLean (1880) 5 QBD 346 . . . 9

Stilk v Myrick (1809) 2 Camp 317; 6 Esp 129 . . . 60, 61, 62, 70, 71

Sudbrook Trading Estate Ltd v Eggleton [1983] 1 AC 444 . . . 34

Super Servant Two, The see J. Lauritzen AS v Wijsmuller BV

Surrey County Council v Bredero Homes Ltd [1993] 1 WLR 1361 . . . 145

Swedish Club, The see Dolphin & Maritime & Aviation Services Ltd v Sveriges Angfartygs Assurans Forening

Tamplin v James (1880) LR 15 ChD 215 . . . 37

Tatem Ltd v Gamboa [1939] 1 KB 132 . . . 176

Taylor v Caldwell (1863) 3 B & S 826 . . . 173

Tekdata Interconnections Ltd v Amphenol Ltd [2009] EWCA Civ 1209; [2009] 2 CLC 866 . . . 10

Tenax Steamship Co. Ltd v The Brimnes (Owners), The Brimnes [1975] QB 929 . . . 16, 17

Thomas v BPE Solicitors (a firm) [2010] EWHC 306 (Ch) . . . 16, 18

Thomas v Thomas (1842) 2 QB 851 . . . 56

Thomas Witter Ltd v T.B.P. Industries Ltd [1996] 2 All ER 573 . . . 195, 197, 198

Thompson v London, Midland & Scottish Railway [1930] 1 KB 41 . . . 126

Thornton v Shoe Lane Parking Ltd [1971] 2 QB 163 (CA) . . . 126, 127, 140

Tinn v Hoffman & Co. (1873) 29 LT 271 . . . 11

Tool Metal Manufacturing Co. Ltd v Tungsten Electric Co. Ltd [1955] 1 WLR 761 . . . 68

Transfield Shipping Inc. v Mercator Shipping Inc., The Achilleas [2008] UKHL 48; [2009] 1 AC 61 . . . 153, 160

Trentham Ltd v Archital Luxfer [1993] 1 Lloyd's Rep 25 . . . 25, 34

Tsakiroglou & Co. Ltd v Noblee Thorl GmbH [1962] AC 93 . . . 173, 176

Tweddle v Atkinson (1861) 1 B & S 393; 121 ER 762 . . . 76, 77, 94

Universe Sentinel, The see Universe Tankships Inc of Monrovia v International Transport Workers Federation

Universe Tankships Inc of Monrovia v International Transport Workers Federation, The Universe Sentinel [1983] 1 AC 366 . . . 54

Vesta v Butcher [1989] AC 852 . . . 151

Victoria Laundry (Windsor) Ltd v Newman Industries Ltd [1949] 2 KB 528 . . . 153, 159, 161

W. J. Alan & Co. Ltd v El Nasr Export and Import Co. [1972] 2 QB 189 . . . 67

W. L. Thompson Ltd v Robinson (Gunmakers) Ltd [1955] Ch 177 . . . 147

Walford v Miles [1992] 2 AC 128 . . . 32, 44

Walton Harvey Ltd v Walker & Homfrays Ltd (1931) 1 Ch 274 . . . 176

Waltons Stores (Interstate) Ltd v Maher (1988) 164 CLR 387 (High Court of Australia) . . . 69, 70

Ward v Byham [1956] 1 WLR 496 . . . 58

Warlow v Harrison (1859) 1 E & E 309; 120 ER 925 . . . 25

Warren v Mendy [1989] 1 WLR 853 . . . 144

Watford Electronics Ltd v Sanderson CFL Ltd [2001] EWCA Civ 317; [2001] 1 All ER (Comm) 696 . . . 134

Watts v Morrow [1991] 1 WLR 1421 . . . 148, 154

Wenkheim v Arndt (1873) 1 JR 73 (New Zealand) . . . 14

White and Carter (Councils) Ltd v McGregor [1962] AC 413 . . . 115, 116, 119, 143

White v Bluett (1853) 23 LJ Ex 36 . . . 56

White v John Warwick & Co. Ltd [1953] 1 WLR 1285 . . . 124, 129

William Sindall plc v Cambridgeshire County Council [1994] 1 WLR 1016 . . . 166, 183, 204

Table of cases

****

Williams v Carwardine (1833) 5 C & P 566; 172 ER 1101 . . . 20

Williams v Roffey Bros. [1991] 1 QB 1 . . . 47, 48, 53, 60, 62, 63, 64, 66, 67, 69, 70, 71

Williams v Williams [1957] 1 WLR 148 . . . 58

With v O'Flanagan [1936] Ch 575 . . . 191, 206

Woodar Investment Development Ltd v Wimpey Construction UK Ltd [1980] 1 WLR 277 . . . 89, 94, 155

Workers Trust and Merchant Bank Ltd v Dojap Investments Ltd [1993] AC 573 . . . 158

Wright v Carter [1903] 1 Ch 27 . . . 210

Yates Building Co. Ltd v Pulleyn & Sons (York) Ltd (1975) 237 EG 183 . . . 11

Yuanda (UK) Co. Ltd v WW Gear Construction Ltd [2010] EWHC 720 (TCC); [2011] Bus LR 360 . . . 133

Table of legislation

UK legislation

Consumer Rights Act 2015 . . . 97, 98, 99, 113, 120, 121, 122, 131, 134, 139, 143, 149
  Part 1, Chp 2 (ss.3–32) . . . 106, 110
  s.3(4) . . . 105
  s.5 . . . 105
  s.6 . . . 105
  s.9 . . . 106
  s.9(1) . . . 169
  s.9(2)–(4) . . . 106
  s.10 . . . 106
  s.11 . . . 107, 169
  s.11(4) . . . 169
  s.13 . . . 107
  s.17 . . . 107
  ss.19–24 . . . 113
  s.23(3) . . . 149
  s.23(4) . . . 149
  s.48 . . . 105,
  s.49 . . . 107, 110, 113, 124
  s.50 . . . 107, 113
  s.51 . . . 33
  s. 54 . . . 114
  s.55 . . . 114
  s.56 . . . 114
  Part 2 (ss.61–76) . . . 130, 136–8
  s.62 . . . 120, 136
  s.62(1) . . . 138
  s.62(4) . . . 137
  s.62(5) . . . 137
  s.63(1) . . . 137
  s.64(5) . . . 136
  s.65 . . . 130, 138
  s.65(4) . . . 124
  s.67 . . . 138
  s.71 . . . 139

Sch.2, Part 1 . . . 137
Sch.4 . . . 93
Contracts (Rights of Third Parties) Act 1999 . . . 73, 74, 77, 78, 80, 81, 83, 155
  s.1 . . . 73, 74, 81, 82, 83, 86, 93, 94
  s.1(1) . . . 78, 79, 82
  s.1(1)(a) . . . 78, 79
  s.1(1)(b) . . . 78, 79, 80, 95
  s.1(2) . . . 78, 79, 80, 81, 86, 95
  s.1(3) . . . 81, 86
  s.1(5) . . . 78
  s.1(6) . . . 78
  s.2 . . . 83
  s.2(1) . . . 82
  s.2(2) . . . 82
  s.2(3) . . . 82
  s.2(4)–(7) . . . 83
  s.4 . . . 83
  s.5 . . . 83
  s.7(1) . . . 83
Law of Property (Miscellaneous Provisions) Act 1989
  s.1(2) . . . 55
  s.1(3) . . . 55
Law Reform (Contributory Negligence) Act 1945 . . . 151, 204
Law Reform (Frustrated Contracts) Act 1943 . . . 164, 178, 179, 181, 183, 184
  s.1(2) . . . 178, 180, 181, 182, 183, 184, 186
  s.1(3) . . . 180, 181, 182, 184, 186
Misrepresentation Act 1967
  s.2 . . . 188, 203
  s.2(1) . . . 100, 187, 195, 196, 201, 202, 203, 204, 205, 206
  s.2(2) . . . 195, 196, 197, 198, 203, 204
  s.2(4) . . . 203
Sale of Goods Act 1979 . . . 105
  s.2(1) . . . 104

Table of legislation

****

s.6 . . . 167
s.8 . . . 33
s.12 . . . 105
s.13 . . . 105, 110, 113, 132, 133, 169
s.13(2) . . . 106
s.14 . . . 113, 132, 133
s.14(2) . . . 105, 110, 132, 169
s.14(2A) . . . 105
s.14(2C) . . . 105
s.14(3) . . . 106
s.15 . . . 106, 113, 132, 133
s.15A . . . 113
s.23 . . . 198
s.50(3) . . . 147
s.51(3) . . . 146
Supply of Goods and Services Act 1982
ss.2–5 . . . 106
s.5A . . . 113
s.6 . . . 105
ss.7–10 . . . 106
s.9 . . . 125
s.10A . . . 113
s.13 . . . 106, 124
s.15 . . . 33
Unfair Contract Terms Act 1977 . . . 93, 120,
    122, 130, 131, 134, 139
s.1 . . . 124, 132
s.2 . . . 132
s.2(1) . . . 132, 138
s.2(2) . . . 132, 134
s.3 . . . 93, 132, 133, 134
s.6 . . . 133
s.6(1A) . . . 133, 134
s.7 . . . 133
s.7(1A) . . . 93, 133, 134
[s.7(3)] . . . 93
s.11 . . . 130, 132, 133, 134

s.11(1) . . . 134
s.11(4) . . . 135
s.11(5) . . . 134
s.13(1) . . . 132, 136
Sched.2(a) . . . 135
Sched.2(b) . . . 135
Sched.2(e) . . . 135

UK secondary legislation

Consumer Contracts (Information,
    Cancellation and Additional Charges)
    Regulations 2013 (SI 2013/3134) . . . 169
Consumer Protection (Amendment)
    Regulations 2014 (SI 2014/870) . . . 188,
    203, 205
Consumer Protection from Unfair Trading
    Regulations 2008 (SI 2008/1277) . . . 97,
    188, 195, 196, 203, 205
reg.5 . . . 201, 205
reg.6 . . . 201
reg.27E . . . 205
reg.27I . . . 205
Electronic Commerce (EC Directive)
    Regulations 2002 (SI 2002/2013)
reg.9(4) . . . 18
reg.11 . . . 17
reg.11(3) . . . 18
reg.12 . . . 7, 17
[Unfair Terms in Consumer Contracts
    Regulations 1999 (SI 1999/2083) . . . 136]

New Zealand legislation

Contractual Mistakes Act 1977 . . . 183

United States

American Restatement of Contract (2d)
    s 90 . . . 69

#1
Agreement

- Agreement is normally determined by the existence of **offer** and **acceptance**.

- Ensure you can distinguish **bilateral** and **unilateral agreements**. Bilateral (promise in exchange for promise). Unilateral (promise in exchange for act).

- An **offer** is a definite promise to be bound, without more, if the offeree agrees to the offer **terms** and must be distinguished from an **invitation to treat** which is an invitation to negotiate or make offers.

- All responses must be communicated in order to be effective. The correct communication rule must be used.

- **Acceptance** is the final and unqualified agreement to all the terms contained in the offer. It follows that adding or amending an offer term amounts to a **counter-offer** which itself constitutes an offer and is not an acceptance. A counter-offer also destroys the original offer so that it is no longer available for acceptance. **Counter-offers** must be distinguished from **requests for further information** before deciding whether to accept. Requests for further information do not have the effect of a counter-offer.

- Acceptance must be actually communicated (operates on receipt) although postal acceptances are effective on posting (operate on dispatch). **The postal rule** can be avoided and it may even be possible to overtake a postal acceptance with another communication.

- Actual communication in the case of non-instantaneous communications using instantaneous means (e.g. leaving messages on telephone answering machines) depends on who has the onus of communicating and the question of fault. In the case of

Key facts
★★★★★★★★★ ★

communications to businesses which are not instantaneous, the point when they become effective depends on what the parties would reasonably expect so that communication to the machine (business communications sent during office hours) will be actual communication. Communication on the next working day is to be anticipated where messages are sent to businesses outside office hours.

- **Revocation of an offer** can occur at any time before acceptance and in the context of unilateral offers this will generally mean before the offeree has started to perform.

- **Revocation of an offer must be communicated to the offeree** (although need not be communicated by the offeror) and communication via the same channel as the offer will suffice where the revocation relates to a unilateral offer to the whole world.

Introduction

Agreement is an essential ingredient of a contract. Traditionally an agreement is comprised of an offer and a corresponding acceptance. It sounds simple and *is* simple if you have a structured approach to identifying these different ingredients making up agreement and the relationship of these ingredients to one another.

What is a contract?

A contract is a legally enforceable agreement.

(a) There must be an agreement (Chapter 1 focuses on determining the existence of agreement and Chapter 2 looks at events that may prevent that agreement).

(b) It must be a legally enforceable agreement (Chapter 3). The question of WHO may enforce the agreement is then examined in Chapter 4.

The question for this topic:

Have the parties reached agreement?

Has Alex (A) made an offer to Becky (B)—to sell her his bicycle for £150—and has there been an acceptance of that offer by Becky?

There may be other related issues, for example:

Has Becky accepted Alex's offer before, having changed his mind about selling his bicycle, Alex revoked the offer?

In addition, there may be other potential agreements to sell the same bicycle to Charlie (C) or Daniel (D) so that you need to determine which agreement was the first to be made—and the effect this has on the position of the other people who allege that they are entitled to the bicycle.

Revision tip

Ask the correct question and use the correct terminology for this topic.

The terminology for agreement questions

We are seeking to determine *the existence of agreement* by assessing whether the **offeror's** (Alex in the example) offer or promise has been accepted by the **offeree** (Becky).

Introduction
****

Notice that there is no reference to the making of any *contract* as there are other elements to consider before coming to such a conclusion.

Think like an examiner

This book is structured to help you to focus from the outset on the types of questions typically set as assessments and to provide you with templates that you can adapt to address the assessment question set for you. This provides greater flexibility than one or two suggested solutions.

The topic of agreement is frequently assessed using one or more hypothetical problem scenarios so the primary focus of this chapter is on the approach to take to the various formats for problem questions covering agreement, highlighting the issues that tend to preoccupy the minds of examiners. There are limited topics that could justify an essay-style question (see p. 25, 'Key debates').

You should bear in mind that agreement is typically one of the first topics studied by students who may have little, if any, previous experience of the problem-style question. Examiners know this only too well and want to guide you gently using short problem scenarios.

Revision tip

It is also important to be pragmatic when thinking like your examiner. Agreement problem questions are easier to set than problem questions on some other topics. It is rare for this topic to be excluded from an examination paper and it usually takes the form of a problem question.

Structure for answering all problem questions on agreement

Examine each piece of correspondence or each action by the parties in chronological order and determine:

- whether as a matter of fact it is capable in law of operating either as an offer, acceptance, or revocation in the agreement process (FACT) and
- whether, and if so when, it has been effectively communicated (COMMUNICATION).

Both the factual and communication requirements must be fulfilled.

The communication question requires us to consider two further questions:

- **What is the relevant communication requirement?** This may mean, for example, that the offer, acceptance or revocation must have been actually communicated or that, if it is a letter of acceptance, it is effective and binding from the moment it is posted.
- **Has the correct communication requirement been complied with?**

The key distinction: Bilateral and unilateral agreements

In broad terms agreements will be one of two types:

- **Bilateral**
- **Unilateral**

Definition

Bilateral agreements: by far the most common in practice and consist of a promise in exchange for a promise. Bilateral means that both parties are bound on the exchange of promises, although there has yet to be any performance of those promises.

A typical sale of goods agreement is bilateral.

Practical example

Alex offers (or promises) to sell his bicycle to Becky for £150 and Becky accepts, thereby promising to pay £150. (We will use this as our example of a **bilateral agreement** and look at variations and additions to the facts throughout this chapter.)

Definition

Unilateral agreements: consist of a promise in exchange for an act. It follows that only one party is bound at the outset by a promise. The other's acceptance is the performance of the requested act.

For example, a typical unilateral agreement will involve an offer of a reward and may be phrased as an 'if' contract: I promise to pay £50 to anyone who finds and returns my lost dog.

Practical example

Daniel offers (or promises) a free watch to anyone who returns three tokens from the packets of cereal he manufactures, together with a cheque for £5. Emily accepts by returning the three tokens with her cheque for this amount. (We will use this as our example of a unilateral agreement and return to this example again later in the chapter.)

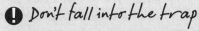 **Don't fall into the trap**

Making the correct distinction. It is not possible to accept a unilateral offer by promising to find and return the lost dog or by promising to collect and return the tokens and the cheque. By comparison, the agreement to sell the bicycle cannot be unilateral. Students sometimes suggest that a simple sale contract is unilateral by interpreting the act of paying for the ➡

> ➜ bicycle as the requested act. This is incorrect since as long as it is possible to accept by promising to buy (which it is in the example), the agreement will be bilateral.

Let us say that you have identified the scenario as involving reciprocal promises rather than a reward situation (bilateral: promise in exchange for an act) and now need to establish that these apparent reciprocal promises have resulted in agreement.

Scenario 1: Bilateral agreement

Step 1: Does the communication amount to an offer? Distinguish offers from invitations to treat.

To address this question you need to know what amounts to an offer in law so that you can determine whether the particular communication qualifies (i.e. is an offer in fact).

Definition
Offer: a definite promise to be bound, without more, if the offeree agrees to the offer terms.

It follows that on acceptance an agreement will result.

Definition
Invitation to treat: an invitation to others to make offers as part of the negotiating process.

It follows that the reply to an invitation to treat can be only, at best, an offer and may be no more than another invitation to treat.

How do we distinguish an offer from an invitation to treat?

In practice the analysis will tend to focus on which party the law considers should have control over the agreement process, i.e. which party should be making the acceptance.

Guidance questions for distinguishing offers and invitations to treat

- Is it possible to respond to the communication by saying 'yes' so that a concluded agreement will result? If not, it is likely that further negotiation is envisaged and the statement will be no more than an invitation to treat.
- The language used may lack the necessary firmness required to qualify as an offer, e.g. *Gibson v Manchester City Council* (1979): the Council had replied that it 'may be prepared to sell' the council house and had invited the plaintiff to complete an application form.

Scenario 1: Bilateral agreement

✳✳✳✳✳✳✳✳✳

There are recognized instances of invitations to treat in the context of bilateral agreements:

- **Advertisements, circulars and brochures:** *Partridge v Crittenden* (1968), justified the conclusion that the advertisement was an invitation to treat using the limited stocks argument (Lord Herschell in *Grainger & Son v Gough* (1896)), i.e. if a brochure constituted an offer, the acceptance would be the customer's order and the supplier would be bound to supply when his stocks were necessarily limited. The law considers that in a bilateral situation the supplier should have control over the making of the agreement.

❶ *Don't fall into the trap*

Since the position is different if the advertisement, circular or brochure is unilateral (i.e. they may be offers, p. 19, 'Unilateral advertisements'), it is vitally important to check whether the advertisement or brochure requests a promise (bilateral) or an act (unilateral).

- **Displays of goods in shop windows** (*Fisher v Bell* (1961)) **or on supermarket shelves** (*Pharmaceutical Society of Great Britain v Boots Cash Chemists* (1953)): in a shop the offer is made by the customer *(on presenting* the goods to the cashier and so communicating the *offer to buy) whereas the shop controls the making of the agreement* via its acceptance ('acceding to the sale' by moving the goods over the bar-code reader).

- **Retailers' websites**: these are probably invitations to treat, although as yet there is no definitive authority on this point. **Regulation 12 of the E-Commerce (EC Directive) Regulations 2002** *suggests* that the customer's order may well be the offer so that the website would be an invitation to treat.

- **Requests for bids or tenders** (*Spencer v Harding* (1870)): this is an invitation to treat since the requestor can then control the making of the bilateral contract to sell, buy or perform a service. The contract is awarded to the bidder selected by the person requesting the bids. It follows that **in general** there is no liability for failure to award the bilateral contract to the highest or lowest bidder or for any failure to consider a particular bid (although see p. 23, 'Tenders or bids' for exceptions).

- **Requests for bids at an auction or advertisement that an auction is to be held** (*Harris v Nickerson* (1873)): again, it is the auctioneer or advertiser who controls agreement by determining acceptance. The goods can be withdrawn from sale at a general auction, or an advertised auction can be cancelled, without incurring any liability (although see p. 24, 'Auctions "without reserve"').

Step 2: Was the offer communicated?

An offer must be **actually communicated** to the offeree(s) in order to be effective.

Scenario 1: Bilateral agreement
✸✸✸✸✸✸✸✸✸✸✸

> ### ✔ Looking for extra marks?
>
> The meaning of **actual communication** is invariably crucial in any hypothetical bilateral problem question and is considered in detail at pp. 15–18, 'Telephone and fax communications', since it is usually more of an issue in relation to acceptances and revocations of offers. Avoid referring to the need for 'communication' if you intend the specific meaning of 'actual communication'.

Communication of the offer is vital since a related principle concerning factual acceptance states that an offeree cannot accept an offer that she does not know about and she must act in response to an offer.

Step 3: Did the offeree accept that offer or was the offer withdrawn before acceptance?

Definition
Acceptance: the *final* and *unqualified* agreement to all the terms contained in the offer.

Step 4: Can the response to the offer constitute an acceptance in law?

There are three requirements to fulfil:

- The response must correspond with the exact terms in the offer (mirror-image rule).
- It must be a response to the offer, i.e. made with knowledge of the offer.
- As a general rule the response must follow any method for acceptance which has been prescribed in the offer (prescribed method).

Mirror-image rule

Is the response a mirror image of the offer or has the response amended or added new terms? Is it an acceptance or a counter-offer?

In order to constitute an acceptance a response must correspond with the exact terms in the offer.

If the offeree either (i) introduces a new term or (ii) amends a term in the offer, the response will be a counter-offer rather than an acceptance.

Practical example of a counter-offer

Alex offers to sell his bicycle to Becky for £150. Becky says that she will have the bicycle but won't pay more than £120 for it.

Hyde v Wrench (1840): two consequences follow from this:

(i) Becky's counter-offer (changing the price in her response) has destroyed Alex's original offer so that it is not possible for Becky to claim there is a binding contract by later agreeing to pay the full price of £150.

(ii) Becky's counter-offer is an offer which Alex can accept. If he does so, there will be a contract to sell the bicycle for £120.

However, these consequences will not follow if the response, whilst not yet constituting an acceptance, amounts to a **request for further information** (*Stevenson, Jacques & Co. v McLean* (1880)) rather than a counter-offer.

Distinguishing counter-offers and requests for further information before offeree makes up his mind whether to accept

Definition

Counter-offer: purports to be an acceptance but has either added a new term or, more usually, amended an existing term.

Definition

Request for further information: *asking* for more information or whether a particular means of performance will be possible before finally committing via acceptance.

Practical example of request for further information

Alex offers to sell his bicycle to Becky for £150 cash. Becky replies by asking whether Alex would be able to deliver the bicycle to her home.

Since Becky is not yet purporting to accept and is not seeking to modify an existing term, this is not a counter-offer. It follows that it does not destroy the original offer and Becky can accept by simply promising to pay £150. Similarly, in *Stevenson v McLean*, the offer was to sell at '40s net cash per ton' and the response asked *whether it would be possible* to pay 40s but have delivery over a two-month period.

If Becky had responded by agreeing to pay £150 for the bicycle and stating 'although it must be delivered to my home', she would be adding a new term so that Alex could decide whether to agree to this counter-offer.

Revision tip

Examiners are extremely fond of the acceptance, counter-offer, and request for further information distinction and you should know your definitions and be able to apply and illustrate them by reference to *Hyde v Wrench* and *Stevenson v McLean*.

Scenario 1: Bilateral agreement
∗∗∗∗∗∗∗∗∗∗∗

Battle of forms: The counter-offer analysis

This acceptance or counter-offer analysis is applied by English law to determine whether an agreement on the terms has resulted after the parties exchange their own (differing) standard terms and conditions.

Practical example

What if Axel Ltd makes an offer to Brandon Ltd to sell Brandon Ltd some manufacturing machinery? The offer states that it is made on Axel Ltd's terms and conditions, which shall prevail, and which contain a clause allowing for the price to be increased to reflect inflation between the date of the agreement and the date of delivery. Brandon Ltd purports to accept, but does so on its own terms and conditions which state that the price is fixed. The parties will probably believe that they have reached agreement, although they will disagree as to the applicable terms.

Have the parties reached agreement and, if so, whose terms govern?

In *Butler Machine Tool Co. Ltd v Ex-Cell-O Corporation (England) Ltd* (1979) the majority of the Court of Appeal (CA) applied *Hyde v Wrench* to this scenario so that, since the buyer (Brandon Ltd in the example) has altered the price term, the buyer is making a counter-offer. It follows that at this point there is no agreement between the parties. However, the counter-offer is itself an offer available to be accepted by the seller (Axel Ltd in the example). This acceptance, like all acceptances, can occur in one of two ways:

(i) by explicit agreement to the terms and conditions, and in *Butler Machine* this occurred because the sellers had completed and returned a tear-off slip at the bottom of the buyers' order stating that they accepted the buyers' order on the basis of its terms and conditions. Therefore the buyers' terms governed; **OR**

(ii) by conduct (*Brogden v Metropolitan Railway Co.* (1877)) so that if Axel Ltd said nothing in response to Brandon Ltd's order but simply delivered the machinery to Brandon Ltd, the agreement would be made on the basis of Brandon Ltd's terms (*Tekdata Interconnections Ltd v Amphenol Ltd* (2009)). Thus, the 'last-shot' frequently wins the battle of forms.

In *Butler Machine* Lord Denning MR reached the same overall conclusion as the majority, i.e. that the buyers' terms prevailed, but his analysis was very different because he considered that there could be agreement despite the existence of differences in the parties' terms and conditions as long as the parties were 'broadly in agreement' and there were no material differences. He then offered a number of solutions for determining the question of content (whose terms governed), e.g. last shot, first shot, or shots of both with gaps caused by irreconcilable differences to be replaced with reasonable implication.

The difficulty with this approach is that it effectively destroys the mirror-image rule as a requirement for the existence of acceptance since the essence of this rule is the interdependence of formation and content rather than its separation.

Respond to the offer

Acceptance must be made in response to the offer, i.e. with knowledge of the offer

It follows that cross-offers cannot result in agreement (*Tinn v Hoffman & Co.* (1873)).

Practical example of cross-offers

On Monday at 9 a.m. Alex posts a letter offering to sell his bicycle to Becky for £150. At the same time Becky posts a letter to Alex offering to buy his bicycle for £150. Objectively there is no agreement between the parties (i.e. it is not possible to say which is the offer and which the acceptance) despite the fact that subjectively Alex and Becky are in agreement.

This response principle has particular relevance in the context of unilateral (or reward) offers and will therefore be discussed further in this context.

Prescribed method of acceptance

If the offer prescribes the method of acceptance, will acceptance by a different method suffice as a factual acceptance?

Practical example of how this can arise

Alex offers to sell his bicycle to Becky for £150 and asks her to send an email to his home email address by the end of the day if she accepts. Becky sends an immediate fax acceptance to Alex's home fax.

(i) If the method prescribed in the offer was mandatory then it must be complied with so that the use of any other method prevents the 'acceptance' from operating as an acceptance. However, in order to conclude that a method was mandatory the offer must have made it clear that this method *must* be followed and that no other method will be permitted as an acceptance. Therefore simply prescribing the method of acceptance will not have this effect.

(ii) If the method was not mandatory (as in the practical example), any other method will suffice as long as it fulfils the purpose behind prescribing the method in a way which is no less advantageous. It is necessary to decide:

- What was the purpose in prescribing this method? It may be to benefit the offeror who wants a quick response in writing and so prescribed acceptance by email. On the other hand, it may be to benefit the offeree (and be inserted at the offeree's request), e.g. the use of a certificate of postage for a postal acceptance.
  - If the method was **to benefit the offeree** then the offeree can waive (give up) the benefit of this stipulation in his favour, e.g. by taking the risk of the ordinary post (*Yates Building Co. Ltd v Pulleyn & Sons (York) Ltd* (1975)).

Scenario 1: Bilateral agreement
✱✱✱✱✱✱✱✱✱✱✱

     – Alternatively, was the actual method used no less advantageous in fulfilling the purpose behind prescribing the method of acceptance? (*Manchester Diocesan Council for Education v Commercial & General Investments Ltd* (1970): stipulation for benefit of offeree which offeree could waive and/or the actual method used was no less advantageous to the offeror in terms of receipt of the acceptance.)

Practical example

A fax, assuming the machine is working correctly, may be just as effective as email in fulfilling the offeror's purpose for a quick response in writing. However, if Becky sent her email acceptance to Alex's work email the purpose in prescribing the method might not necessarily be fulfilled, e.g. the evidence may be that Alex was not in work on that day, assumed Becky was not interested when he received no message at home, and therefore sold the bicycle to Charlie. It is arguable that Becky's 'acceptance' in these altered circumstances would be ineffective.

> **Step 5: Was this acceptance communicated to the offeror? When was it communicated?**

The general rule is that **acceptances need to be *actually communicated* to the offeror**. There are some difficulties with the meaning of 'actual communication', e.g. will communication to the offeror's business premises suffice? Will communication to the offeror's fax machine or email server suffice or does the acceptance have to be seen by him? However, let us assume for the present that it means 'received' by the offeror (**'receipt rule'**).

Silence as acceptance

It follows from the receipt principle for communications that an offeror in a *bilateral contract* cannot (as a general rule) stipulate that silence will constitute acceptance (*Felthouse v Bindley* (1862)).

Practical example

If Becky is silent in response to an offer from Alex stipulating 'If I hear nothing from you by Friday I will assume that you want the bicycle at £150', there is no acceptance.

There are a number of exceptions and some interesting academic argument relating to acceptance by silence. These are considered further below as they lend themselves to essay-style questions.

The postal rule of acceptance

There is an important exception to the 'receipt rule' since, if the post is a proper method on the facts in order to communicate acceptance (*Henthorn v Fraser* (1892): if the parties are at a distance a postal acceptance is one *possible* method of acceptance unless the circumstances indicate that a quick response was required), acceptance is complete as soon as the letter is posted (**'dispatch rule'**) (*Adams v Lindsell* (1818)) and it is irrelevant that the acceptance letter is lost in the post and never arrives (*Household Fire and Carriage Accident Insurance Co. (Ltd) v Grant* (1879)). It follows that where the postal rule applies to the acceptance, the offeree is protected on posting and the risk that the acceptance may never arrive lies on the offeror. It should therefore be in the offeror's interests to avoid the application of the postal rule and it would be preferable to do this expressly.

❗ *Don't fall into the trap*

The postal rule applies only to acceptances. It has no application to offers, or to revocations of offers, to which the actual communication requirement applies. It is a serious error to apply the postal rule to, for example, a revocation of an offer. This demonstrates how important it can be to correctly identify the particular communication.

Examiners' favourites

❗ *Don't fall into the trap*

Don't assume that the postal rule will apply to every acceptance that has been posted.

In practice it is relatively easy to draft an offer in order to avoid the application of the postal rule and ensure that the offeror controls the point at which the agreement (and therefore the contract) takes effect. All the offeror needs to do is use words requiring **actual communication of the acceptance** (*Holwell Securities Ltd v Hughes* (1974): 'notice in writing to [the offeror]').

What other forms of wording do you think will suffice? Examples: 'Let me know your answer', 'I must know by . . .'. Compare this form of wording with 'send your response to . . .'.

Examiners are extremely fond of setting this particular trap so you need to be aware of it.

In addition, the postal rule of acceptance may also be inapplicable on the facts either because:

(a) a postal response is out of line with the general context for contracting, e.g. all previous communications have been by instantaneous means and it is known that a quick response is required, or

(b) having regard to all the circumstances the parties cannot have intended to be bound until receipt of any acceptance (Lawton LJ in *Holwell Securities v Hughes*: application of the postal rule would produce 'manifest inconvenience and absurdity'. Lawton LJ gives examples in his judgment).

Scenario 1: Bilateral agreement

✳✳✳✳✳✳✳✳✳✳

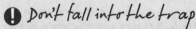

❗ Don't fall into the trap

Another examiner's favourite is to include *a communication* which attempts to undo (or **overtake) an acceptance sent by post**. Let us assume that the postal rule applies in principle (although examiners like to inject some complexity and will often draft so that there is the possibility of ousting the postal rule) and the particular postal communication is overtaken by another communication indicating that there is no wish to accept.

Is it possible to overtake a postal acceptance?

Practical example

What if Becky posts her acceptance on Monday morning but later that afternoon she telephones Alex in order to withdraw it. The postal acceptance does not reach Alex (the offeror) until Tuesday. Is there a valid acceptance on Monday morning or has it be validly withdrawn so that there is no agreement between the parties?

This question tends to puzzle students because the natural reaction is to treat the postal rule as a 'rule' so that once an acceptance has been posted it is binding and cannot be undone. It is argued that any other position would give the offeree the best of all worlds, i.e. protection against revocation on posting but the ability to revoke if market conditions made acceptance less palatable.

However, there is an opposing argument (see e.g. Hudson, 'Retraction of Letters of Acceptance' (1966) 82 LQR 169) which places emphasis on what is known by the parties and the avoidance of disadvantage.

When Becky telephones Alex on Monday afternoon she may simply tell him that she does not want the bicycle. He would therefore know nothing about the acceptance posted earlier that day. It would be quite reasonable for Alex to act on Becky's telephone call and sell the bicycle to Charlie. Should he be in **breach** of contract by doing so?

Therefore, we could argue that Alex has not been disadvantaged if we allow the telephone call to overtake the postal acceptance; indeed, on these facts, he will be disadvantaged if the postal acceptance prevails.

The case law on this question is equivocal (which may explain why examiners are so fond of this particular moot point). *Countess of Dunmore v Alexander* (1830), a Scottish case, may suggest that it is possible to overtake a postal acceptance, but it is far more likely that the case is actually allowing an overtaking revocation of an offer, which is possible at any time before acceptance. Whilst *dicta* in the New Zealand decision of *Wenkheim v Arndt* (1873) suggest that overtaking a postal acceptance is not possible, the other case frequently cited in support of this position, the South African decision in *A to Z Bazaars (Pty) Ltd v Minister of Agriculture* (1974), only provides this support at first instance. By comparison, in the Appellate Division there are *obiter* remarks suggesting that it did not necessarily follow that a postal acceptance could not be overturned.

Telephone and fax communications

The actual communication (receipt rule) applies to communications by telephone and other instantaneous methods of communication such as telex and fax, which are treated as if they were made face-to-face (*Entores Ltd v Miles Far East Corporation* (1955)). It follows that a contract will be made in the jurisdiction in which the acceptance is received, i.e. the offeror's jurisdiction.

> ✔️ *Looking for extra marks?*
>
> Understand the meaning of actual communication for instantaneous and non-instantaneous communications, e.g. machine failures or out-of-hours communications. This law can be complex so that if you can explain and apply the correct principles and understand the rationale, you will convince the examiner that there is depth to your knowledge.

Problems that can occur in communicating using instantaneous means

Denning LJ in *Entores* resolved these problems by stating that the onus was on the communicator to get his message through and by focusing on 'fault' in the communication process.

(i) *Communicator fault*: if the telephone line goes dead, the communicator will know that the message must be repeated if he is to ensure that it is received. Lord Denning used the analogy of shouting an acceptance across a river to the offeror just at the moment when an aircraft flies overhead and drowns out the acceptance. The offeree would know that the message must be repeated. This position will clearly apply to fax acceptances where the communicator is informed if the message has been successfully communicated.

(ii) *Recipient fault*: where the recipient is aware that a message is being sent to him but has not received it, and the communicator wrongly believes the message has been communicated, it is the recipient who must ask for the message to be repeated. If she fails to do so, she will be estopped (i.e. prevented) from denying that the communication was effectively received. If a fax communication is complete (in terms of the number of pages) but illegible, the onus would be on the recipient to request that it be resent since the communicator will act reasonably in acting on the notification of successful transmission.

(iii) *No fault*: acceptance does not reach recipient but the communicator reasonably believes the message was communicated. The recipient was unaware that any message had been sent. There had been no effective communication of the acceptance and therefore there is no contract.

Scenario 1: Bilateral agreement

✱✱✱✱✱✱✱✱✱✱✱

Taking these principles further:

> Is there actual communication when the acceptance appears on the offeror's telex or fax machine or when he actually reads it? Does 'actual communication' of an acceptance mean communication to the machine or to the offeror?

The key statement is an *obiter* comment of Lord Wilberforce in *Brinkibon Ltd v Stahag Stahl GmbH* (1983) concerning such non-instantaneous telex (and presumably fax) messages: **'No universal rule can cover all such cases; they must be resolved by reference to the intentions of the parties, by sound business practice and in some cases by a judgment where the risks should lie.'**

This provides general guidance but more specific guidance is given in the case law in the context of communications to businesses.

Guidance: The distinction based on office hours in the business context

In this context a distinction, based on the onus on the communicator, what the communicator could reasonably expect, and the fault principles in *Entores*, can be seen to exist between messages sent within ordinary office hours and messages sent outside those hours.

- Communications to a business sent **within office hours** when it might reasonably be expected that the messages will be read: **communication to the machine is actual communication because the communicator has done all that he might reasonably be expected to do** (*The Brimnes, Tenax Steamship Co. Ltd v The Brimnes (Owners)* (1975), and see also Lord Fraser in *Brinkibon Ltd v Stahag Stahl GmbH* who stated that it was the recipient's fault if he did not man his telex machine during office hours, i.e. messages would be at the recipient's risk in this period).

- Communications to business addresses sent **outside office hours** when it must be clear that the message will not be read until the next working day: communication to the machine is not sufficient to constitute actual communication. This will not occur until the message might reasonably be expected to be seen, normally on the next working day (*Mondial Shipping and Chartering BV v Astarte Shipping Ltd* (1995)—reflecting what Gatehouse J referred to as a solution based on commercial common sense).

The **key issue** here will be the uncertainty over the meaning of 'ordinary office hours' and examiners are likely to exploit this. You should note the following:

(i) The message in *The Brimnes* was sent and received between 17.30 and 18.00 hrs. This was considered to be within 'office hours', whereas the message in *Mondial Shipping* was very clearly sent and received outside office hours (23.41 hrs on a Friday). It did not take effect until the following Monday. *Obiter* in *Thomas v BPE Solicitors (a firm)* (2010), Blair J considered that the receipt rule applied to email acceptances. However, he did not consider 18.00 hrs to be outside working hours. The email was available to be read within working hours despite the fact that the recipient had in fact gone home at 17.45 hrs.

(ii) Friday afternoons are likely to feature in questions as many businesses finish work earlier than normal. Equally, messages may be sent and received during holidays and Bank Holidays. The communicator should reasonably assume that a Bank Holiday is taken as holiday but arguably should be entitled to believe that a machine is manned unless the recipient communicates the fact that the business is shut, e.g. holiday shutdown. Thus, objective knowledge will be assumed but matters which depend on subjective knowledge of business practices of the particular firm may not be. In the case of the latter, the onus would be on the business recipient to make its practices clear.

Telephone answering machines

Is communication of the message to the telephone answering machine sufficient as actual communication or must the message be listened to?

There is no case law on telephone answering machines but the very fact that an answering machine is operational should indicate that communication is not instantaneous so that the principles discussed above should apply, i.e. *Entores* principles with the onus on the communicator to keep repeating the communication until it is listened to. However, Professor Brian Coote ('The Instantaneous Transmission of Acceptances' (1971) 4 New Zealand UL Rev 331–42) argued that the postal rule should apply so that communication to the machine would be sufficient. This conclusion can be reached if it is possible to argue that in leaving the message (equivalent to dispatch), the communicator has effectively put the message out of his control. However, this is difficult to sustain since the mere fact that the machine is operational would indicate that the recipient is not receiving communications on an instantaneous basis and therefore, if a business, not accepting the risk usually associated with not manning machines during normal office hours (*The Brimnes*).

Electronic contracting

A distinction exists between website trading and contracting via email since the **Electronic Commerce (EC Directive) Regulations 2002** apply only to website trading.

Website trading (i.e. placing order on a retailer's website)

The Regulations apply and indicate that the receipt rule is applicable to such communications.

By **Reg. 12** it is likely that the website will be the invitation to treat since the order *may be* the offer. Receipt of orders must be acknowledged electronically and without undue delay (**Reg. 11**) and, although this acknowledgement may serve only to warn customers of orders placed unintentionally, if it acts as the acceptance it is clear that both this and the order are *deemed to be received* when the parties to whom they are addressed are able to access them (**Reg. 11**). It follows that once the message is received by the recipient's machine (which could be in the middle of the night) it is available to be accessed and therefore such a message would not need to be read in order to be actually communicated.

Scenario 1: Bilateral agreement

✱✱✱✱✱✱✱✱✱✱

Contracts by exchange of emails

Such contracts are explicitly excluded from the operation of the Regulations (**Regs. 9(4) and 11(3)**) but it would seem that, by analogy, the same principles should apply as for websites. On the other hand, it can be argued that the postal rule should apply to electronic 'mail' so that an acceptance email would be effective on dispatch. However, this assumes that on sending an email the communicator has put the message outside her control whereas emails can, in some circumstances, be recalled.

Obiter in *Thomas v BPE Solicitors (a firm)* Blair J considered that the receipt rule applied to email acceptances.

Step 6: Was there a communication which purported to revoke the offer and was it capable in law of acting as a revocation?

Once acceptance has occurred a purported revocation of the offer will be too late (*Payne v Cave* (1789)). It follows that **revocation is possible at any time before acceptance**.

Can revocation occur before any acceptance if the offer period has not yet elapsed?

Practical example

On Thursday Alex offers (or promises) to sell his bicycle to Becky for £150 and states that the offer is open for acceptance until 4 p.m. on Friday. Can Alex change his mind and revoke his offer at 9 a.m. on Friday?

This is a **firm offer**, i.e. the offeror has stated that he will keep the offer open for a certain period. It is clear that after 4 p.m. on Friday the offer will lapse, but would an earlier revocation be effective to terminate the offer? Yes, **in English law the offeror is free to revoke as long as the offeree has given or promised nothing in exchange for the promise to keep the offer open until 4 p.m. on Friday** (*Routledge v Grant* (1828)).

Step 7: Has the revocation been effectively communicated before any acceptance takes effect or is it too late?

Revision tip

In a bilateral context this is likely to involve questions about the point at which the acceptance and the revocation take effect and, in particular, the operation of the postal rule to acceptance, whereas revocations must be actually communicated.

Byrne & Co. v Van Tienhoven & Co. (1880)

FACTS: On 8 October the defendants in Cardiff posted a revocation of their offer to the plaintiffs in New York. The revocation arrived on 20 October. On 11 October the plaintiffs telegraphed their acceptance of the defendants' offer (postal rule applies to telegrams).

HELD: The acceptance took effect on 11 October (when the telegram was sent). The revocation needed to be actually communicated to take effect. It therefore did not take effect when it was sent (8 October) but when it arrived (20 October) and accordingly the revocation was too late.

However, revocation need not be communicated by the offeror himself (*Dickinson v Dodds* (1876): The plaintiff knew from a third party that the defendant no longer intended to sell the property to him).

This places a burden on the offeree to decide whether the third party can be relied upon.

Scenario 2: Unilateral agreement

Unilateral agreements consist of a promise in exchange for an act, i.e. they exist in reward situations.

Examination tip

There are a number of special principles which apply to unilateral offers and agreements, or principles that are more likely to arise in this context. You should therefore look for these once you have identified the problem context as unilateral.

- Unilateral advertisements are offers rather than invitations to treat.
- Acceptance must be in response to the offer—and with knowledge of it. This is particularly likely to arise as an issue in the unilateral context of rewards, although the principle also applies in the bilateral context.
- There is an implied waiver of the need to communicate acceptance of a unilateral offer.
- There are special principles applicable to attempts to revoke unilateral offers in terms of both (i) whether it is possible to revoke at all and (ii) the meaning of actual communication in the context of a revocation of a unilateral offer to the whole world.

Unilateral contracts may also be employed as a means of imposing liability in respect of a particular pre-contractual promise ('the two-contract analysis').

Unilateral advertisements

A **unilateral advertisement (a promise in exchange for an act) is an offer** (*Carlill v Carbolic Smoke Ball Company* (1893) and *Bowerman v Association of British Travel Agents Ltd* (1996)).

Scenario 2: Unilateral agreement
✱✱✱✱✱✱✱✱✱✱

This ensures that the promise is enforceable if performance of the requested act has occurred.

Practical example of unilateral advertisement (offer)

If Daniel advertises a free watch to anyone who returns three tokens from the packets of cereal he manufactures together with a cheque for £5, this advertisement will constitute an offer rather than an invitation to treat, so that Emily will accept when she performs the requested act, namely returning the three tokens with her cheque for this amount.

A unilateral offer of reward cannot be accepted if there is no knowledge of the offer (*R v Clarke* (1927))

It may be necessary to look at the precise terms of the offer to determine whether there is knowledge at the crucial time (*Gibbons v Proctor* (1891): terms of the offer required the information to be given to a particular person and at the time the information was received by that person the offeree had the required knowledge). However, as long as the offeree has knowledge of the offer, his motive in responding is irrelevant (*Williams v Carwardine* (1833)).

Implied waiver of the need to communicate acceptance of unilateral offer (*Carlill v Carbolic Smoke Ball Company*)

In a unilateral contract it is the performance of the requested act which constitutes the acceptance. There is therefore no need to communicate the fact that the offeree is attempting to perform that act, e.g. attempting to find the lost dog or attempting to collect the three tokens from the cereal packets.

> **Revision tip**
> It follows that the principles determining the communication of acceptances, e.g. instantaneous and non-instantaneous communications, are likely to be encountered in the bilateral context only.

Of course, if the unilateral offer is a reward for the supply of information, the communication of that information is necessarily part of the requested act.

Special principles applicable to revocations of unilateral offer

Is it possible to revoke a unilateral offer once the offeree has started to perform the requested act?

If we applied the general rules on acceptance and revocation to unilateral contracts, it would be very harsh on the offeree because acceptance is the performance of the requested act and revocation at any time before complete performance of that act should therefore be possible.

Practical example

Daniel could cancel his offer at any time before Emily had finished collecting the cereal tokens and returned them with her cheque. Although this may appear harsh to Emily, it would be equally unfair to Daniel to expect him to keep his offer open indefinitely in order to allow anyone to finish collecting the tokens. Daniel, the manufacturer will, at some stage, stop issuing packets containing the qualifying tokens.

English law has now accepted that:

- **The terms of the offer may contemplate that it is not possible to revoke once the offeree has 'started to perform the act', although the exact theoretical basis for this is unclear.**

- **Equally, the terms of the offer may contemplate that revocation should be possible despite commencement of the performance of the act.** *Luxor (Eastbourne) Ltd v Cooper* (1941): commission payable on completion of sale so that the offer contemplated that the offeror was reserving the right to revoke at any time before completion occurred.

Errington v Errington & Woods (1952) **(CA)**

FACTS: There was a promise by the father (to transfer the house in exchange for the act of paying all the mortgage instalments).

HELD: This unilateral promise could not be revoked once the couple had started to perform this act.

However, this could be because:

(i) A unilateral offer involves two promises

  – an express promise to pay on performance of the requested act; and

  – an implied promise (or offer) not to revoke once performance of the act has been commenced.

Unfortunately this analysis (see McGovney (1914) 27 Harv L Rev 644, 659) does not prevent revocation. It merely provides a remedy in **damages** (for breach of the implied promise) if revocation occurs once performance has commenced. This is clearly the analysis relied upon by Goff LJ in *obiter* comments in *Daulia v Four Mill Bank Nominees Ltd* (1978) and is also the analysis considered by the House of Lords (HL) in *Luxor v Cooper*, although on the facts their Lordships refused to imply any term that the vendors had undertaken not to prevent the sale.

(ii) Alternatively, revocation could be prevented if acceptance of the unilateral offer occurs once the offeree commences performance of the act, although the reward would not be payable until it has been completely performed. This analysis was adopted by the Law Revision Committee in its 6th Interim Report, 1937.

The problem with this analysis is that it appears contrary to the one-sided nature of the unilateral contract since it would compel the offeree to perform. Normally only the offeror is bound to perform at the outset whereas the offeree should be free to change his mind and discontinue the performance. This point was made clear by Goff LJ in comments in *Daulia v Four Mill Bank Nominees Ltd*.

Practical example

Unless the terms of the offer contemplate otherwise, either Emily will accept by starting to collect the tokens or there may be an implied offer not to revoke. It would seem, however, that breach of the implied offer would entitle Emily to damages but Daniel could prevent her from being in a position to claim her watch.

Communication of revocation of unilateral offers made to the whole world where the offerees are necessarily not identified

In this situation it is impossible for the offeror to comply with the normal rule requiring actual communication of revocation to the offeree. In the American case of *Shuey v US* (1875), it was held that it was sufficient if 'the same notoriety' is given to the revocation as the original offer. Thus, if the same channel is used for the revocation, the fact that an individual offeree does not see it will be irrelevant.

The two-contract analysis—bilateral and unilateral contract

This analysis is employed in order to impose liability in respect of a particular pre-contractual promise.

Tenders or bids

Express promise to award the work to the lowest tender or to sell goods to the highest bidder

Normally, a requestor of tenders is free to accept or reject any tender to do the work, even if it is the lowest. This is because the tender is an offer and the bilateral contract is controlled by the requestor's decision as to which bid to accept (*Spencer v Harding*).

However, if the requestor has expressly undertaken to award the work to the lowest tender, it would be wrong not to recognize that promise. In *Harvela Investments Ltd v Royal Trust Co. of Canada (CI) Ltd* (1986), Lord Diplock considered this promise to amount to a unilateral offer and therefore adopted a two-contract analysis of the tender situation (explained in Table 1.1 and illustrated with a practical example at Figure 1.1).

Table 1.1 Request for tenders and express promise to consider highest or lowest

	Main bilateral contract *(awarding goods/ services)*	Unilateral contract *(promise: accept most competitive tender)*
Invitation to tender	Invitation to treat.	Offer: express promise to accept most competitive tender (e.g. lowest tender).
Tenders	Each tender: offer.	Acceptance: submitting lowest tender (act).
Request or decision (freedom to determine which tender (if any) will be accepted)	Acceptance of tender = contract awarding work.	If bilateral contract is not awarded to lowest tenderer = breach of unilateral contract (damages).

Practical example

Figure 1.1 Practical example: tenders

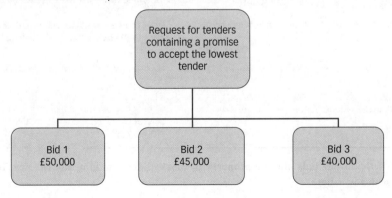

The two-contract analysis—bilateral and unilateral contract
****

The contract is awarded to Bid 1 but Bid 1 is not the lowest bid. Bid 3 is the lowest bid. The offer in Bid 1 has been accepted under the bilateral contract and Bid 1 has been awarded the work. However, this necessarily involves a breach of the unilateral contract based on the promise to award the contract to the lowest bid. All bidders accept this unilateral contract by making their bids but it is Bidder 3 that suffers loss. Bidder 3 is entitled to damages to compensate for the loss it suffers as a result of the breach of this unilateral contract.

In some circumstances there may be a binding contractual obligation to consider conforming tenders (Blackpool & Fylde Aero Club Ltd v Blackpool Borough Council (1990))

Analysis

- The request to submit tenders in this instance **also** amounts to a unilateral offer to consider conforming tenders.

This unilateral offer is accepted by submitting a conforming tender. If the conforming tender is then not considered, there will be a breach of this binding unilateral contractual promise to consider such tenders and the requestor of the tenders will be liable in damages for this breach.

- There is a bilateral contract with the tenderer whose bid is actually accepted, i.e. this contract determines the person who gets the work.

Auctions 'without reserve'

If an auction is advertised as being held 'without reserve' the auctioneer is promising that no reserve price will be applied and that the owner will not bid in an attempt to raise the bidding price. There is a unilateral promise to sell to the highest genuine bidder (see Table 1.2).

Table 1.2 Auctions without reserve

	Main bilateral contract (awarding goods/services)	Unilateral contract *(promise: auction without reserve)*
Advertised auction	Invitation to treat.	Offer promise to sell to highest bidder, without reserve (vendor will not bid).
Bids	Each bid: offer.	Acceptance: highest genuine bid (act).
Auctioneer decision (on successful bidder)	Acceptance of auctioneer = the fall of the hammer.	If bilateral contract is not awarded to highest bidder = breach of unilateral contract (damages, but not entitled to property sold).

What if the owner bids and the property is knocked down to him, can the next-highest bidder seek any relief?

Yes, *Warlow v Harrison* (1859) (*obiter*). As a result of the two-contract analysis, there is a unilateral offer to hold the auction without reserve. However, the next-highest bidder will only be entitled to damages for breach of this unilateral contract. The bilateral contract determines who gets the goods under the bidding process.

What if the auctioneer refuses to accept the highest (and only) bid at such an auction and withdraws the goods? Does the bidder have a remedy?

Yes, *Barry v Davies (t/a Heathcote Ball & Co.)* (2000). The result of the two-contract analysis is that there is a binding unilateral contract not to apply any reserve price and therefore to sell if there is one bona fide bidder at such an auction. That person is entitled to damages to compensate in the event that the goods are withdrawn from the sale, i.e. damages amounting to the cost of purchasing replacements minus the amount of the auction bid.

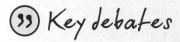 **Key debates**

Typical essay question issues on agreement might include:

1. **How the existence of agreement is determined**. This involves examining the meaning of objectivity in this context (see Poole, *Textbook on Contract Law*, 12th edn (Oxford University Press, 2014), 2.1) and the external evidence used to determine the existence of agreement, i.e. offer and acceptance (traditional and technical approach) and the non-traditional methods such as that employed by Lord Denning in **Butler Machine Tool Co. Ltd v Ex-Cell-O Corporation (England) Ltd**, in **GHSP Inc. v AB Electronic Ltd** (2010), and by the majority of the CA in **Gibson v Manchester City Council** (1978). It also appears that the courts will find it much easier to find the existence of agreement where there has been performance **Trentham Ltd v Archital Luxfer** (1993), per Steyn LJ (see Poole *Textbook* 2.1.3).

2. **The use of the two-contract analysis in order to create a unilateral contract based on a particular promise and thereby impose pre-contractual liability** (discussed p. 22, 'The two-contract analysis').

3. **Difficulties inherent in the analysis of the silence principle in** *Felthouse v Bindley* (see Miller (1972) 35 MLR 489 and discussion in Poole *Textbook* 2.4.5.1) **and exceptions where silence can constitute acceptance**. Exceptions where silence can constitute acceptance in bilateral context:

   • course of dealing between the parties and the offeree has taken the benefit of services, e.g. window cleaning, insurance policy renewals

   • where the offeree is seeking to hold the offeror to a silence stipulation made by the offeror, e.g. if the nephew in **Felthouse v Bindley** had acted on the uncle's statement, delivered the horse but the uncle had refused to take delivery of it

   • where the offeree was responsible for the silence stipulation in the contract, i.e. for the statement that the offeree's silence would constitute acceptance.

Key cases

✱✱✱✱✱✱✱✱

4. **Critique of the communication principles, especially in the e-commerce age**. This may involve issues such as the relevance and scope of application of the postal rule of acceptance, non-instantaneous communications etc.

Final point to note: you should be guided by the emphasis placed in your particular module on the issues within this topic but bear in mind the practical fact that we noted at the outset: **agreement lends itself to the setting and answering of problem-style questions**.

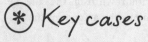 **✱ Key cases**

Case	Facts	Principle
Gibson v Manchester City Council (HL)	Council had written 'may be prepared to sell' council house. HL held that language used indicated this was invitation to treat, inviting tenant to make offer to purchase, rather than an offer to sell which the tenant had accepted.	Distinction between invitation to treat and offer. Response to invitation to treat does not result in a contract at that point.
Hyde v Wrench	Offer to sell for £1,000. Response offering £950 was counter-offer which destroyed original offer. Original offer was thus no longer available to be accepted.	Effect of counter-offer—not acceptance and destroys the original offer.
Butler Machine Tool Co. Ltd v Ex-Cell-O Corporation (England) Ltd (CA)	Seller offered to sell machine tool on terms including price-variation clause. Buyers placed order on their own terms (no price variation) and sellers completed tear-off slip at bottom of this order stating that they accepted the order on terms in the order. Each considered the contract had been made on its terms. CA held there was a contract on buyers' terms since (majority applying **Hyde v Wrench**) the buyers' order was a counter-offer which had been expressly accepted by sellers when they returned the tear-off slip.	Battle of forms—counter-offer analysis is applied. The battle was won by last shot since this had been expressly accepted. The last shot often wins through acceptance by conduct of the last form, e.g. taking delivery of the goods.

Case	Facts	Principle
Household Fire Insurance Co. v Grant (CA)	D applied for shares in P company which allotted the shares and sent a postal acceptance but it never arrived. Held: D had become a shareholder. The letter was effective on posting (postal rule of acceptance) and it was irrelevant that the letter of acceptance did not arrive.	Postal rule: where the acceptance is posted but is never received. Remember that the postal rule can be ousted by requiring actual communication of the acceptance (*Holwell Securities Ltd v Hughes*).
Entores v Miles Far East Corporation Ltd (CA)	English company received telex offer from Dutch company. English company sent a response (a counter-offer) and this counter-offer was accepted by the Dutch company. Where was the contract made? CA held it was where the acceptance was received and that was in England because the acceptance had been sent by the Dutch to the English company.	Actual communication (receipt) principle applied to telex communications so that the communication took effect when received. Denning LJ analysed position if problems in the communication process, e.g. telephone line goes dead or message is drowned out by aircraft overhead.
Byrne & Co. v Van Tienhoven & Co.	1 October Ds in Cardiff made offer in letter to Ps in New York. Ps received this on 11 October and immediately sent telegram accepting (postal rule applies). However, on 8 October Ds had sent a revocation of their offer and this arrived 20 October. Held: there was a binding contract on 11 October when acceptance was dispatched since the revocation needed to be communicated to be effective.	Postal rule does **not** apply to the revocation of offer so that a revocation is not effective until received, whereas a postal acceptance sent after dispatch of revocation but before its arrival would result in immediately binding contract.
Carlill v Carbolic Smoke Ball Company (CA)	Ds advertised that they would pay £100 to any person contracting influenza after using their smoke ball three times daily for two weeks. CA held that the advertisement was a unilateral offer of reward which was intended to be legally binding. This offer was accepted by anyone who performed the requested act. Since P had used the smoke ball as directed and had caught influenza, she was entitled to £100.	Most famous example of a unilateral contract (act in exchange for a promise). Unilateral advertisement is an offer. Acceptance was the performance of the requested act so that there was no requirement to communicate the fact that an offeree is attempting to perform.

Key cases

✳✳✳✳✳✳✳✳✳

Case	Facts	Principle
Errington v Errington (CA)	Father promised son and daughter-in-law that if they paid all of the mortgage instalments on the house where they lived, he would transfer the house to them. CA held that the father's promise was unilateral (act in exchange for promise) and once they had started to pay the instalments they had a contractual right to remain in possession and seek to complete the act.	It is not possible to revoke a unilateral offer once the offeree has commenced performed of the requested act.
Luxor v Cooper (HL)	Commission was payable to an agent on completion of the sale of cinemas and there was no implied promise by the vendors not to revoke that promise before completion occurred.	The terms of a unilateral offer may contemplate that the offeror is to remain free to revoke the offer at any time before complete performance of the requested act.

#2

Agreement problems

Key facts

- The terms of an agreement must be sufficiently certain or the agreement will be **void** for uncertainty. Agreements for the parties to agree a matter, such as the price, will generally lack the necessary certainty. However, if nothing is said about the price, in some circumstances statute may imply a reasonable price.

- If there is uncertainty so that no contract results, in some circumstances there may nevertheless be an obligation to pay the reasonable value for requested performance (a **quantum meruit**).

- An agreement mistake will occur where one or both of the parties allege that they made a *fundamental* **mistake as to a term** which prevents agreement. Such a mistake means that the contract is void. Alternatively a contract may be **voidable for a mistake as to attributes** and this protects innocent third parties who have acquired the contract goods.

- It may be possible to **rectify** a written record of an agreement where there is a transcription mistake in recording that agreement accurately. The plea of *non est factum* ('this is not my deed') may very rarely be available where it is claimed that a signed document has been signed by mistake because the document is fundamentally different in nature to the document believed to have been signed.

Introduction

This chapter is concerned with issues which may prevent the parties from reaching agreement (the terms are not sufficiently certain or there is no agreement because of a mistake). Agreement problems generally impact the agreement by rendering it void. It is necessary, however, to be able to distinguish a void contract from one which is merely voidable.

Key terminology

Void: where a contract is void **it is automatically of no effect from the very beginning.** There is no, and never was, agreement (and hence there is no contract). The important word is 'automatically'. This effect has nothing to do with action being taken by either of the parties. A contract may be **void** because the terms of the agreement are too uncertain or because a fundamental mistake as to a term has occurred, e.g. the parties are not agreed on the subject matter as they are at cross-purposes and neither party's interpretation is the more reasonable, or one party has misled the other as to a crucial contractual term (such as the other's identity or the contract price).

Voidable: where a contract is voidable it is liable to be set aside by one party using the remedy of **rescission**. Once it is set aside the contract is treated as never having existed. However, there are bars to rescission so, for example, it is not possible to rescind once a third party has acquired rights in the property which is the subject matter of the contract. In such instances the voidable contract remains valid and binding.

A contract may be voidable for duress (see Chapter 3), for undue influence (Chapter 10), or for misrepresentation (Chapter 9), including misrepresentation as to identity (so-called attributes mistake) which is discussed below.

There are two core topics examined in this chapter: (i) **Certainty of terms and (ii) Agreement mistakes—mutual mistake and unilateral mistake.**

Think like an examiner

Much depends on the individual syllabus but certainty of terms is rarely set as a full question. It can appear (see the practical example, p. 31, 'Vague terms') as part of an agreement problem question, or possibly as a problem or essay concerning agreements to agree and negotiating in good faith—and it may be necessary to consider the consequences of uncertainty and claiming a *quantum meruit* based on performance. In practical terms it is an important subject as it can determine whether or not there is a contract (compare *British Steel Corporation v Cleveland Bridge & Engineering Co. Ltd* (1984) and the Supreme Court decision in *RTS Flexible Systems Ltd v Molkerei Alois Müller GmbH & Co. (UK Production)* (2010)).

Following the decision of the House of Lords (HL) in *Shogun Finance v Hudson* (2003) it is difficult to set a full problem question on mistake as to identity, although it may appear as a part, possibly with the other part tackling the issues of cross-purpose and/or unilateral mistake as to terms. The *Shogun* decision is sufficiently controversial to be capable of generating an essay title all of its own, e.g. the debate about identifying a written contract.

Certainty of terms

If an apparent agreement is too uncertain in its terms, then the courts will not enforce it because they will not construct a binding contract for the parties.

A contract may be too uncertain because:

(a) it is vague or

(b) essential terms are missing and the contract is therefore incomplete.

(There is often some overlap between the two.)

Vague terms

Practical example

Alex agrees to sell his bicycle to Becky, price to be determined by independent valuers, one to be appointed by each of the parties. The terms are agreed as 'those usually operating in the sale of bicycles'.

If an essential term is vague, the apparent agreement is **VOID (automatically of no effect from the very beginning)** and the courts will not supply the details UNLESS:

- it is possible to do so based on clear commercial practice, **AND**
- the 'agreement' has been executed (already acted upon).

Scammell & Nephew Ltd v Ouston (1941) **(HL)**

FACTS: Agreement to purchase a van on hire purchase terms but the details of these hire purchase terms had not been agreed.

HELD: There were so many possible interpretations of hire purchase terms that the courts could not imply terms based on commercial practice and the contract was therefore void for uncertainty of terms.

Compare with *Hillas & Co. Ltd v Arcos Ltd* (1932) **(HL)**

FACTS: The Ps agreed to buy '22,000 standards of softwood goods of fair specification' for 1930 and there was a further option for 100,000 'standards' for 1931.

Certainty of terms

****

> **HELD:** The agreement was binding as it had been performed in 1930 and there was an accepted understanding of the meaning of these words in commercial practice.

Severing a meaningless clause

It is only possible to sever a clause if it is meaningless (as opposed to a clause that has still to be agreed). The policy objective underlying this principle is the need to prevent a party from escaping from a contract by inserting a meaningless clause.

> **Nicolene Ltd v Simmonds** (1953) **(CA)**
>
> **FACTS:** The agreement referred to acceptance as being on 'the usual conditions of acceptance'. In fact there were no such usual conditions and, when the D failed to deliver, the Ps brought an action for **breach** of contract.
>
> **HELD:** The clause in question was severed so that the rest of the agreement was enforceable.

Practical example

It would appear that there are no specific standard terms usually governing the sale of bicycles so that this clause ought to render the contract void for uncertainty. However, it is meaningless and a court might therefore sever this clause in order to leave the agreement enforceable.

However, what about the price term in the practical example? Is this sufficiently certain?

Incomplete terms

The agreement may leave an essential matter (such as price) either undecided or impossible to calculate so that the courts will not enforce that agreement.

Agreements to negotiate

Agreements to negotiate on a particular term are incomplete and so too uncertain to be a contract.

> **Walford v Miles** (1992) **(HL)**
>
> **FACTS:** The Ds were negotiating for the sale of a company to the Ps. They had entered into an agreement whereby, in return for the provision of a comfort letter from the Ps' bank (indicating that loan facilities had been granted to cover the price of £2m), the Ds agreed to terminate any negotiations with third parties, agreed not to entertain **offers** from any other prospective purchasers, and agreed to deal exclusively with the plaintiffs (a lock out). Although the Ps complied with their side of the agreement, the Ds withdrew from the negotiations and decided to sell to a third party. The Ps claimed **damages** for breach of this lock out agreement.

HELD: It was only an agreement to negotiate and was therefore unenforceable for uncertainty. Although there was **consideration** for the lock out, it extended for an indefinite period.

The HL rejected the argument that there was an implied duty placed on the party who had agreed to the lock out to negotiate in good faith with the party to that lock out for a reasonable period of time. Their Lordships considered that such an implied duty could not be reconciled with the adversarial nature of contractual negotiations.

When the price is missing

If there is no mechanism in the contract for fixing the price (i.e. nothing is said about the price), then statute may provide for a 'reasonable price'.

Section 8 Sale of Goods Act (SGA) 1979 provides that the contract may fix the price for goods or provide a mechanism for fixing the price. Where there is no such mechanism the buyer must pay a reasonable price. See also **s. 15 Supply of Goods & Services Act (SGSA) 1982**: where no mechanism for fixing price for a service a reasonable charge is payable (B2B contract) and **s. 51 Consumer Rights Act (CRA) 2015**: B2C contract from effective date of the CRA.

However, if there is a mechanism for fixing the price but it has not been implemented, s. 8 SGA, s. 15 SGSA and s. 51 CRA cannot apply to allow the implication of a reasonable price.

May & Butcher Ltd v R (1934) **(HL)**

FACTS: The contract provided for the price to be agreed upon by the parties from time to time. There was no party agreement.

HELD: The contract contained a mechanism for fixing the price but this had failed. Therefore the argument that the agreement should be construed as an agreement to sell at a fair or reasonable price was rejected.

Practical example

The agreement between Alex and Becky provides a mechanism for fixing the price. If that has worked and there is an agreed price then the terms are certain.

But what if Alex has appointed a valuer but Becky has not and is instead claiming that a 'reasonable price' should apply? Technically the mechanism has failed, **May & Butcher** ought to apply and the contract would be void.

However, the courts have devised ways around *May & Butcher* and we need to determine whether either of these 'exceptions' applies on these facts.

Certainty of terms

✳✳✳✳✳✳✳✳✳✳

Exception 1: If the agreement has already been executed and the price is to be agreed by the parties but has not been, the courts may not be prepared to declare the contract void

> **Foley v Classique Coaches Ltd (1934) (CA)**
>
> **FACTS:** There was an agreement to purchase petrol at a price to be agreed by the parties from time to time. The Ds had purchased their petrol from the P for three years when they sought to avoid the contract by arguing that it was invalid because there was no agreement as to price.
>
> **HELD:** The agreement was binding and, if any dispute arose as to a reasonable price, it could be resolved under the terms of the arbitration clause in the contract that covered this type of dispute.

In the practical example there is a specific price mechanism which has not been fully activated in order to fix the price.

Exception 2: Does the principle in *Sudbrook Trading Estate Ltd v Eggleton* apply?

> **Sudbrook Trading Estate Ltd v Eggleton (1983) (HL)**
>
> **FACTS:** The agreement provided that a tenant was permitted to purchase the premises at a price to be agreed upon by two valuers nominated by the lessor and tenant. The lessor had refused to appoint a valuer and claimed that the agreement was void for uncertainty.
>
> **HELD:** Where machinery existed solely for the purpose of fixing a fair price (as opposed to an essential factor in determining the price) and it had broken down, then the court could substitute its own machinery to calculate a fair price.

However *Sudbrook* was distinguished by the CA in *Gillatt v Sky Television Ltd* (2000): the machinery was integral and essential. In addition, it had failed because the claimant had not acted in accordance with its terms and so could not turn round and claim that the machinery meant nothing and should be replaced by a determination of the court.

The practical example is also similar to *Gillatt* in that the mechanism is the essential factor in fixing the price and Becky is claiming that there should be a 'reasonable price' rather than the one fixed by the valuers (the mechanism she had agreed to for fixing the price). It follows that in this situation *May & Butcher* (and not *Sudbrook*) will apply and the contract will be void.

The significance of performance

As a general factor, where the agreement has in fact been executed (performed) by the parties, it is most unlikely that the courts would refuse to enforce it on the basis that it is too uncertain (*Trentham Ltd v Archital Luxfer* (1993)).

However, much depends on the facts and whether there is agreement on the essential terms, e.g. in *British Steel Corporation v Cleveland Bridge & Engineering Co. Ltd* (1984): the parties were still in the process of negotiating in the expectation that a contract would follow. There was no agreement on essential terms such as the price despite the fact that performance had been requested and goods manufactured. In *Baird Textiles Holdings Ltd v Marks & Spencer plc* (2001), there was no evidence on which to determine the essential terms of the alleged contract, although plenty of evidence of past dealings.

RTS Flexible Systems Ltd v Molkerei Alois Müller GmbH & Co. (UK Production) (2010)

The Supreme Court considered that a contract had come into existence between the parties although they had been negotiating subject to contract and although the initial understanding was that they would not be bound unless a contract was signed and executed.

FACTS: The work was completed and 70 per cent of the agreed price paid when a dispute arose as to whether the equipment which had been supplied complied with the specifications.

HELD: The parties had reached agreement on all terms of 'economic significance' and had not intended agreement on the terms outstanding to preclude agreement. Since there had been performance on both sides, it was possible to conclude that the parties were proceeding with a contract on the basis of all the essential terms they had agreed.

Consequences of uncertainty

Although uncertainty of terms means that the agreement will be void and so automatically of no effect from the very beginning, a party **may** still be required to pay for performance under an uncertain contract on the basis of a *quantum meruit* (reasonable value of services). *This is a restitutionary remedy based on the desire to prevent unjust enrichment* (see Chapter 7).

In *British Steel Corporation v Cleveland Bridge & Engineering Co. Ltd* (1984) although the parties were still in the process of negotiating in the expectation that a contract would follow, the Ps had been requested to commence work immediately, which they had done. No formal contract was concluded but delivery had occurred. The Ps sought payment for the goods manufactured on the basis of a *quantum meruit*. The judge held that, since the Ds had requested the performance and had received a benefit at the expense of the Ps, it would be unjust for them to retain that benefit without recompensing the Ps on a *quantum meruit* for the reasonable value of the goods supplied.

This case was distinguished in *Regalian Properties plc v London Dockland Development Corporation* (1995) and it is only possible to recover performance expenses where the performance was specifically requested by the other party.

Basis on which expenditure in anticipation of a contract can be recovered on a quantum meruit

Countrywide Communications Ltd v ICL Pathway Ltd (2000): There could be recovery only in 'exceptional cases' and, in particular, there had to be a benefit to the D in performance of the services which the D had requested.

The other factors to be considered were:

- the terms in which the request to perform was made and whether it was reasonable to assume the claimant would be compensated
- whether they were services of a kind which would normally be given free of charge
- the circumstances in which the anticipated contract had failed to materialize and whether the D was at fault.

Agreement mistakes

An apparent agreement may be void where the parties entered into the agreement under a 'fundamental' mistake which the law recognizes as preventing the parties from ever reaching agreement. In other words, there is an appearance of agreement but there is no sufficient matching offer and acceptance in relation to the contract terms (objectively judged).

There are two types of agreement mistake (which prevent agreement being reached): mutual (or cross-purposes) mistake and unilateral mistake.

Table 2.1 Types of agreement mistakes

Mutual mistake	Both parties are mistaken as to term.	Each party makes a different mistake in their reasonable interpretation of a term—*Raffles v Wichelhaus* (cross-purposes mistakes).
Unilateral mistake	**One** party is mistaken as to a term, e.g. identity.	The other party knows of that mistake—*Shogun Finance v Hudson*.

(There is a third type of mistake—**Common Mistake**—see Chapter 8. However, common mistake does not prevent agreement and is therefore not an agreement mistake.)

Mutual mistakes (where the parties are at cross-purposes)

Both parties are mistaken but they each make different mistakes.

Practical example

Freddie offers to sell Georgina his 'car' for £7,000. Georgina accepts believing that Freddie has only one car and that it is a Volkswagen Golf. She has failed to notice that there are two cars parked on Freddie's driveway. The other car is a Vauxhall Astra and it is the Astra which Freddie is offering to sell and which he believes is the subject matter of their agreement. Georgina is refusing to accept and pay for the Astra.

There will be no agreement as a result of mutual mistake where it is not possible for the reasonable man to say which party's interpretation is the more reasonable (using the objective test for contract formation) because of the ambiguity in the offer terms. Such a 'contract' is void, i.e. of no effect from the very beginning.

Raffles v Wichelhaus (1864)

FACTS: The P agreed to sell the Ds cotton that was to arrive ex 'Peerless' from Bombay. There were two ships of this name sailing from Bombay and the P intended to sell goods on the December ship whereas the Ds considered that they were buying goods on the October ship.

HELD: The P could not succeed in an action against the Ds for refusing to take delivery of the goods on the December 'Peerless'. Objectively it was not possible to say which 'Peerless' was intended and which party's interpretation was the more reasonable. Such an agreement will be void.

Scriven Brothers & Co. v Hindley (1913)

FACTS: The Ds mistakenly bid for bales of tow believing they were hemp. At the auction the Ds had examined a sample, which happened to be hemp, and thought that all the bales were hemp because they all had the same shipping mark. This was accepted as a reasonable interpretation but so too was the auctioneer's belief that the bales being sold were tow.

HELD: There was no contract and the Ds did not have to pay for the tow.

However, in **Tamplin v James** (1880) the purchaser mistakenly believed the lot of property being sold included some garden but had failed to check the plan which indicated that no garden was included. The purchaser was at fault and could not avoid the contract by citing his mistake.

Unilateral mistakes

A unilateral mistake occurs where one party is mistaken as to a term of the contract and the other knows or ought to know of this mistake and cannot be allowed to take advantage of it.

Practical example

Haroon sends a letter to Jessica as an email attachment in which he offers to sell his Volkswagen Golf car. Haroon intended to type the price as £11,000 but his finger slips and he types the price as £1,000. Jessica immediately sends back an email stating that she accepts on the terms of Haroon's letter. Haroon later discovers his mistake and claims that he is not bound as the agreement is void for mistake.

Agreement mistakes
✱✱✱✱✱✱✱✱✱✱✱

To avoid the agreement there must be a mistake as to a term.

This occurs where A makes an offer to B and B is aware or ought to be aware that A is making a fundamental mistake relating to a term in that offer and seeks to 'snap it up'.

Hartog v Colin & Shields (1939)

FACTS: The D mistakenly offered to sell hare skins at a price per pound instead of per piece and the Ps accepted this.

HELD: The Ps could not enforce the contract on the basis of these alleged terms. The negotiations had been conducted on the basis of a price per piece and this was the normal trade practice. The Ps must have known about the D's mistake as to this term when they accepted (price per pound would have been much cheaper) and therefore the contract was void.

Practical example

Clearly it would not be difficult to establish that Jessica knew that Haroon had made a mistake concerning the price term at which he intended to sell the car and that she had attempted to 'snap it up'. This is a fundamental unilateral mistake as to a term and such a contract is void.

However, if the mistake does not relate to a term of the contract but to a collateral matter or matter relating to the quality of the subject matter, then it will not be fundamental and will not prevent agreement.

Smith v Hughes (1871)

FACTS: The D alleged that the P knew that the D required old oats (and not new oats which had been purchased) and that therefore the contract was void for mistake.

HELD: There was a valid contract. There was no misrepresentation or term that the oats sold had to be old and therefore this was a collateral matter (relating to the quality of the subject matter) which did not affect the agreement reached between the parties.

Mistakes as to identity

This occurs where one party is mistaken as to the identity of the other contracting party (a term of the contract) and that other knows of the mistake (usually because he will have fraudulently misrepresented his identity).

Practical example

Alex sells his bicycle to Becky because she represents that she is Victoria Pendleton (the Olympic cyclist). He allows her to take the bicycle on credit in return for a promise of the cash the following day. In the meantime Becky sells the bicycle to Charlie for cash and disappears. Charlie knows nothing about how Becky acquired the bicycle but pays a discounted price as Becky tells him she needs a quick sale since she is emigrating to Australia the following day.

Alex wants the return of his bicycle from Charlie. Charlie claims he paid for the bicycle and it is now his.

- **This type of mistake will only render the contract VOID if it is** *fundamental*.
- **If it is not a fundamental mistake, then the contract will only be voidable (capable of being set aside) for fraudulent misrepresentation.**

This distinction between void and voidable is particularly important where the goods have been sold by the rogue to an innocent third party.

- The goods can only be recovered from that third party if the contract was void, so that the rogue had no title (ownership) to pass on.
- If the contract with the rogue was merely voidable for fraudulent misrepresentation, the right to set aside the contract will have been lost when an innocent third party acquires rights in the goods. In such circumstances the innocent third party can keep the goods.

Example

Alex is the mistaken party.
Becky is the rogue.
Charlie is the innocent third party purchaser.

Figure 2.1 Mistaken identity

Alex ————————————▶ Becky ————————————▶ Charlie

The parties' position is determined by whether the contract between Alex and Becky is void or voidable.

If it is void for fundamental mistake as to identity then Alex can recover the bicycle (and Charlie will have 'converted' the bicycle since he has possession of property which is not his).

If it is voidable (and has not been avoided before Charlie acquires the goods) Charlie, as innocent third party purchaser, can keep the bicycle.

Until fairly recently the policy of the courts had been seen as protecting the innocent third party by holding that the contract is only voidable for this type of mistake. The courts had achieved this objective by drawing a distinction (artificial and much criticized) between true mistakes as to identity (void) and mistakes as to attributes, such as credit-worthiness (which only rendered a contract voidable). They applied a presumption in face-to-face cases that

Agreement mistakes

✳✳✳✳✳✳✳✳✳✳✳✳

there was an intention to deal with the person physically present so that any mistake was as to attributes, and the contract was merely voidable.

The important distinction since the decision of the HL in *Shogun Finance Ltd v Hudson* (2003) is between written contracts and these face-to-face contracts without writing.

Written contracts

The HL in *Cundy v Lindsay* (1878) had held that a contract made by written correspondence was void for mistake as to identity since identity would be of fundamental importance to the formation of a written contract by post. The offer to contract would be made only to the person named in the written contract so that only that person could accept it.

Cundy v Lindsay (1878) **(HL)**

FACTS: Rogue (Blenkarn) of 37 Wood Street, Cheapside had sent a written order for handkerchiefs and had made it appear that the order had come from a respectable firm, 'Blenkiron & Co.' of 123 Wood Street. The Ps had heard of Blenkiron and accordingly sent the goods on credit to Blenkiron at 37 Wood Street. The Ps were never paid. Blenkarn sold the goods to the Ds (innocent third party) and the Ps brought a conversion action against the Ds.

HELD: The contract was void since identity was crucially important and the sellers had intended to deal with Blenkiron and not Blenkarn. It followed that the Ds were liable in conversion.

Shogun Finance Ltd v Hudson (2003) **(HL)**

FACTS: Rogue expressed an interest in purchasing a Mitsubishi Shogun at a car dealership. He then identified himself as Mr Dulabh Patel and produced a stolen driving licence as proof of identity and address. The dealer faxed a copy of the finance agreement in this name to the claimant finance company with a copy of the driving licence. The rogue signed the agreement as Mr Patel. The finance company carried out the usual credit checks before approving the finance. The dealer therefore allowed rogue to take the vehicle. The rogue sold the car (dealership price of £22,500) to the D for £17,000. The finance company brought a claim against the D for damages in tort of conversion.

HELD: (3:2) that the finance contract was void because Mr Patel was the customer named in the written agreement and his signature had been forged. (This was not a face-to-face contract because the identity term was contained in writing, i.e. the offer to purchase in the finance agreement.)

Examination tip

To adequately answer an essay question concerning mistake as to identity and the policy questions it is necessary to be familiar with the different approaches taken by the members of the HL in this case. You also need to be aware that the policy objective of the majority was to protect lenders against the consequences of identity theft.

Boulton v Jones (1857)

FACTS: The D sent a written order to Brocklehurst's (B's) shop but B had already sold the business.

HELD: P (the new purchaser of the business) could not fulfil the order. Identity was crucial in this case because the D wished to use a set-off (type of credit note) that he had against Brocklehurst (a fact known to the P). It followed that it was clear that the offer was intended for Brocklehurst and therefore the P could not accept it.

However, there must be **two existing entities** for identity to be crucial and for the contract to be void for mistake as to identity. An offer can only be made to, and accepted by, an existing entity. It is not enough that there is only one entity with two names, one of which is false.

King's Norton Metal Co. Ltd v Edridge, Merrett & Co. Ltd (1897) **(CA)**

FACTS: A written order was sent by 'Hallam & Co.' on notepaper which indicated that the company was large and successful. There was no such company. It was merely an alias for a rogue. The rogue acquired the goods on credit and sold them to the Ds (innocent third party). The Ps (mistaken party) sought damages for conversion from the Ds alleging that they (the Ps) had only intended to deal with Hallam & Co.

HELD: The Ps intended to deal with the writer of the letter, whoever that was, and had not mistaken one person for another because there was only one existing person. Therefore there was a contract between the Ps and the rogue, which was not void for mistake.

Face-to-face contracts

There is a series of cases applying a presumption in face-to-face contracting whereby the mistaken party is presumed to intend to deal with the person who is physically present, i.e. the rogue (*Phillips v Brooks Ltd* (1919) and *Lewis v Averay* (1972)). These mistakes are therefore treated as attribute mistakes relating to the decision to allow the rogue to have possession of the goods on credit. The contract is voidable and this protects the innocent third party purchaser who acquires the goods from the rogue.

Practical example

Alex is the mistaken party and Becky was pretending to be Victoria Pendleton to persuade him to contract with her. The crucial question is whether this contract is void for fundamental mistake as to identity or merely voidable for misrepresentation. If void then Alex can recover the bicycle from Charlie or seek damages in conversion. If voidable then Charlie can keep the bicycle as an innocent third party purchaser for value.

Agreement mistakes
****

Following **Shogun Finance v Hudson** the crucial distinguishing factor is whether the contract is written or an oral face-to-face contract. It is made face-to-face so that there is a presumption that Alex intends to contract with whoever is physically present—Becky (**Lewis v Averay**). The mistake Alex makes is a mistake as to attributes and credit-worthiness. The contract between Alex and Becky is merely voidable and not void. Since Becky has already sold the bicycle to Charlie, Alex cannot avoid the voidable contract. Charlie would keep the bicycle.

Would it make any difference to your answer if Becky had written to Alex and he had agreed to sell in a written response? This would be a **Shogun** situation and identity would now be crucially important. Alex would make an offer to sell the bicycle to Victoria Pendleton and only she could accept that offer. The contract A/B would therefore be void for fundamental mistake as to identity and Alex could recover the bicycle.

Document mistakes

The court may be asked to **rectify a written document** to reflect accurately what the parties in fact agreed, i.e. to reflect their common continuing intentions (*Joscelyne v Nissen* (1970): the parties had agreed that the daughter was to pay certain household expenses but this had not been spelt out in specifics in the contract. Rectification was ordered to reflect the parties' continued common intention).

Chartbrook v Persimmon Homes Ltd (2009) **(HL)**

To secure rectification it had to be shown that the parties were in complete agreement on the terms of their contract but by an error wrote them down wrongly. This could be demonstrated here by reliance on pre-contractual letters as an outward expression of the continuing common intention.

In *Daventry District Council v Daventry and District Housing Ltd* (2011), the CA adopted an objective approach to the determination of whether there was a continuing common intention, i.e. 'by reference to what a hypothetical reasonable observer, aware of all the relevant facts known to both parties, would conclude'. This has been criticized since rectification ought to be based on subjective intentions.

Rectification has not been allowed where the parties were agreed as to the terms of their agreement but made a mistake as to the meaning of those terms.

Frederick E. Rose (London) Ltd v William H. Pim Junior & Co. Ltd (1953) **(CA)**

FACTS: The Ps were asked to supply 'feveroles' and thought 'feveroles' was another word for 'horsebean'. Accordingly they entered a contract with the Ds for supply of 'horsebeans' but feveroles were a superior type.

HELD: The contract between the Ps and the Ds would not be rectified to read 'feveroles' because the parties were agreed that the Ds were to supply only 'horsebeans'. There was no error in terms of expression of the contract which would permit rectification.

The plea of *non est factum*

A successful plea of *non est factum* ('this is not my deed') means that the person signing a document is fundamentally mistaken as to the nature of the document signed. If the plea succeeds the written contract is void and a third party cannot acquire a good title under it. However, as innocent third parties may have relied to their detriment upon this signature as being binding, the plea has been very narrowly construed.

- **The transaction must be fundamentally different in nature from the one signed.**
- **The mistake regarding the nature of the document signed must not be a mistake which is the result of carelessness on the part of the person signing.**

Saunders v Anglia Building Society (1971) **(HL)**

FACTS: An elderly widow of 78 signed a written document relating to her interest in a house. She had broken her spectacles and could not read it. She asked the third party requiring her signature about the nature of the document and signed it when told that it was a deed of gift of the house to her nephew. In fact it was a transfer of the house to that third party who mortgaged it to a building society and then defaulted. The widow pleaded *non est factum* and asked for a declaration against the building society that the transfer was void.

HELD: Her plea failed because she had intended the document to enable her nephew to raise money on the security of the house and the document she had signed was not fundamentally different. In addition, she had been careless in signing the document.

---

⑨ *Key debates*

1. Broad questions about the nature of mistake in English law and its history. See Macmillan, *Mistakes in Contract Law* (Hart Publishing, 2010) and the excellent summary in Morgan, *Great Debates: Contract Law*, 2nd edn (Palgrave Macmillan, 2015), pp. 172–6.

2. *Shogun Finance v Hudson* and policy considerations affecting the law's development. See Macmillan, 'Rogues, Swindlers and Cheats: The Development of Mistake of Identity in English Contract Law' [2005] CLJ 711.

Key cases

****

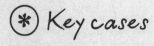 Key cases

Case	Facts	Principle
Walford v Miles (HL)	Enforceability of agreement not to negotiate with any other prospective purchasers. HL held it was only agreement to negotiate and unenforceable for uncertainty as it extended for indefinite period.	Agreements to agree are uncertain. No implied duty to negotiate in good faith.
British Steel Corporation v Cleveland Bridge & Engineering Co. Ltd	Parties negotiating and had not reached agreement on essential terms. However, performance had been requested and goods had been delivered. The judge allowed recovery on a *quantum meruit* (reasonable value) on a restitutionary basis.	No contract due to uncertainty of terms but there can be recovery of reasonable value (not any contract price) in some circumstances for performance requested and received.
Raffles v Wichelhaus	Two ships named 'Peerless' sailing from Bombay. Each party thought contract was for different 'Peerless'. Objectively it was not possible to say which was intended. No contract.	Mutual (cross-purposes) mistake and not possible to say which party's interpretation is the more reasonable, then there is no contract.
Smith v Hughes	Purchase of 'oats'. D wanted 'old' oats and P was selling 'new' oats. Held: the contract was valid as there was no misrepresentation or term describing the oats.	The mistake must relate to a term of the contract and not to a collateral matter (quality of the goods). The parties were agreed on sale and purchase of 'oats'.
Cundy v Lindsay (HL)	Rogue ordered goods by post pretending to be another respectable firm so that the goods were obtained on credit. Rogue sold the goods to innocent third party purchaser. HL held contract was void for mistake as to identity.	Identity was of crucial importance to making this contract by post. The offer to contract would be made only to the person named in the written contract so that only that person could accept it.
Shogun Finance Ltd v Hudson (HL)	At car dealership the rogue pretended to be someone else (having stolen their identity documents). The name of the real person was used on copy of finance agreement. HL held the finance contract was void. It was a written contract rather than face-to-face.	Most important decision on applicable principles governing identity mistakes. Considered to be written contract so that only the person named could accept the offer of credit. The innocent third party purchaser lost out.

Case	Facts	Principle
Lewis v Averay (CA)	The rogue went to see P's car advertised for sale. He then made P believe that he was famous film actor (Richard Greene of *Robin Hood* fame). He produced a film pass and wrote a cheque in the name 'R. A. Green'. P allowed him to take the car away. The cheque was dishonoured but meanwhile the rogue had sold the car to innocent purchaser. CA held the contract was not void since this was a mistake as to credit-worthiness. The third party was 'more innocent'.	Example of face-to-face-contract where the mistaken party intends to contract with the person physically present and mistake is one of credit-worthiness in allowing the goods to be taken on credit. Innocent third party is protected.

#3
Enforceability criteria

Key facts

- Only **enforceable promises** in an agreement can be relied upon before the courts.

- To be enforceable **a formation promise** (promise made as part of an agreement where there is no existing agreement between these parties covering this subject matter), there must be (a) an intention to be legally bound by the promise (known as intention to create legal relations), and (b) either the promise must be expressed in the form of a **deed** (indicating that any promise is taken seriously), *or* the party who is seeking to enforce the promise of the other must show that he has given something in exchange for that promise (i.e. it is a **bargain**, as opposed to a gratuitous promise or gift).

- Intention to be **legally bound** is judged objectively through the use of two presumptions. These may be rebutted by clear evidence to the contrary. Domestic or social agreements are presumed not to be intended to have legally enforceable consequences and to rebut this presumption there needs to be reliance, certainty of terms, and evidence of the seriousness of the promise. By comparison, parties to commercial agreements are presumed to intend to be legally bound unless there are clear words indicating the absence of a promise or that the parties have agreed to be bound in honour only.

- **Consideration** means **an act or a promise given in exchange for the promise (i.e. the price for which the other's promise was bought).** Consideration need not be adequate but must be sufficient. This means that the courts will not examine whether what has been given in exchange is of equivalent value but some acts or promises are not recognized by the law as being good consideration, e.g. past consideration, performance of an existing legal duty.

- In order to enforce **an alteration promise** the enforcing party must also show that **it has provided consideration for, or purchased, that promise**. Performing an existing contractual formation obligation was not recognized as sufficient consideration since there was no new exchange. But where the alteration promise is a promise to pay more, which has been freely made (see the doctrine of **duress**), the decision of the Court of Appeal (CA) in *Williams v Roffey Bros.* means that where there are **factual benefits** to the **promisor** from making the alteration promise, that promise is treated as supported by consideration and will be enforceable.

- By contrast, if the promise is an alteration promise to pay less there must be fresh 'exchange' consideration for the promise to be enforceable despite the fact that there may be factual benefits to the creditor in accepting less from the debtor and agreeing not to sue for the balance.

- Where an alteration promise is not supported by consideration, that promise may have *some binding effect* (although not the same binding effect as where consideration is present) on the basis of **the doctrine of promissory estoppel**. Promissory estoppel prevents a promisor going back on his promise where that would be inequitable because the promisee has relied upon that promise and the promise was freely given (again the doctrine of duress may be relevant).

- There are some difficulties with the scope of operation of the doctrine of promissory estoppel in English law.

- As noted, in practice the enforceability of a promise may be determined by whether that promise was freely given since the doctrine of **duress** (coercion or threat to the person or his property, or illegitimate pressure or threats to his financial interests) renders any such promise **voidable** (and so liable to be treated as having no effect).

Introduction

This chapter examines the question of whether the promises contained in the agreement are enforceable so that there is a legally binding contract in place (formation). The same question of enforceability applies to promises which vary or alter the terms of an existing contract (alterations).

The chapter therefore considers the parties' intention to be legally bound (formation) and the need to establish that the promises are part of a bargain (as opposed to gratuitous promises which need to be contained in a special legal document—a deed). The same bargain requirement applies to alteration promises, although in practice the treatment of alteration promises is not as strict and it is possible for freely made alteration promises to be enforceable when not strictly bargained for (i.e. paid for with another promise or action). Promises obtained as a result of threats or extortion are not freely made and are voidable for duress (and hence unenforceable on that basis).

Think like an examiner

The decision in **Williams v Roffey Bros.** (1991) is likely to feature somewhere in questions on enforceability.

Problem questions tend to include a number of very predictable components relevant to consideration and whether the defence of promissory estoppel can operate, often with the odd issue of whether a promise was freely given (duress) and, less often, a small issue relating to a domestic or social agreement (usually the enforceability of a promise made by a relative) and whether the presumption against intention to be legally bound can be rebutted on the facts. Most of the issues concerning consideration will arise in the context of alteration promises but past consideration issues can arise for formation promises or possibly whether performance of existing duties can constitute formation consideration.

The problem/essay split is about equal and you need to be alert to your tutor's emphasis when delivering the topic. Bear in mind that there needs to be sufficient to occupy you for the 45 minutes or hour allocated for any examination answer so that the most likely focus would be on the scope of **Williams v Roffey Bros.**, whether the difference in treatment between alteration promises to pay more or accept less can be justified, and whether the **Roffey** approach to finding consideration is less preferable than the Australian approach of recognizing greater flexibility for the doctrine of estoppel—or even whether reliance ought to be the sole criterion for the enforceability of promises. How would you set about reforming the law in this area?

Revision tip

Given the importance of the decision in **Williams v Roffey Bros.**, it is advisable to be familiar with the facts, the fact that the promise was found to be supported by consideration (and hence the need to establish consideration to support alteration promises), and the nature of the **Roffey** consideration (students often get this last part wrong and this tends to undermine the effectiveness of the law stated correctly elsewhere; see discussion of this p. 61, 'Alteration promises', scenario 1—promises to pay more).

Is the agreement promise enforceable?
Is it legally binding?

Practical example

Alex has made an **offer** to Becky to sell her his bicycle for £150. Becky has accepted by promising to pay £150 for it.

If Alex delivers the bicycle but Becky refuses to pay, can Alex enforce the promise of payment? Is Becky bound to pay that price?

The terminology for enforceability questions

We are seeking to establish **whether a promise made by the promisor** (Becky in this example) **can be enforced against her by the promisee** (Alex). Has the **promisee** (Alex) supplied consideration to support the promise made by the **promisor** (Becky)? If so, then refer to the promisor's promise as being **'supported by consideration'**, and at this stage we can start talking about a **'contract'** between the parties as opposed to merely **'agreement'**.

In addition, an act or promise which the law would recognize as a **sufficient** consideration is referred to as **'good consideration'**.

The promise may nevertheless be **unenforceable** if it is **voidable** and the contract has been **set aside for duress** (promise obtained as a result of illegitimate pressure or threats).

Although a promise freely given may not be supported by consideration, in the context of some alteration promises the promisee may be able to **prevent the promisor from going back on that promise** where this would be **inequitable** (or unfair). This is the doctrine of promissory estoppel and usually operates to delay enforcement of the promise (the estoppel therefore has a **'suspensory effect'**), rather than preventing it forever (referred to as **'extinguishing liability'**, which would be the case where the alteration promise was supported by consideration).

Structure for answering all problem questions on enforceability

- Identify the promise or promises that are to be tested for enforceability.
- Consider whether there is any real issue in relation to intention to create legal relations by identifying the type of agreement and its context; e.g. if there is a straightforward commercial agreement with no attempt to avoid legal liability attaching to the promises, it would be superfluous to discuss the question since there is no doubt that intention to be legally bound will be presumed.
- Consider whether the promisor's promise was freely given or was it extracted by illegitimate pressure or threats from the promisee.

Step 1: Identify the promise
****

- Was the promise contained in a deed? Bear in mind that it is unlikely that any examiner would set something this straightforward and you need only state that, 'since this promise is not contained in a deed it can be enforceable only if it is shown to be supported by consideration'.

- Assess whether there is any consideration supplied by the promisee to support the promise made by the promisor. Can this constitute a good consideration?

- If not, in the context of an alteration promise, assess whether promissory estoppel can operate as a defence to an attempt to enforce a promise. If so, assess the extent of operation of the estoppel, as compared to full enforceability of the promise, and the practical consequences of this for the parties' positions.

The key distinction: Formation and alteration promises

In broad terms promises will be one of two types:

- **A promise on the formation of a contract** where there is no existing contract in place between these parties covering this subject matter, e.g. the promises relating to the bicycle in the Alex and Becky example. These promises are **formation promises**. Consideration is vital to establish such a contract in English law and requirements are strict.

- **A promise which alters a term of an existing contract between the parties (an alteration promise).** Consideration is also a requirement to enforce such a promise but the approach to identifying consideration is not as strict and, even if consideration is not present, the promisor may find himself bound in practical terms by the alteration promise because he is prevented from going back on it.

It is helpful therefore to make this distinction before proceeding to consider whether a promise is supported by consideration. However, we must first consider the earlier steps in the structure to apply when answering problem questions.

Step 1: Identify the promise that one party is seeking to enforce against the other

You may be fortunate and the instruction may be explicit, asking you to advise whether a promise may be enforced. It is perhaps more likely that you will be asked simply to 'advise' one of the parties. If so, look at what has gone wrong. Who hasn't done what they 'promised' they would do? Or who has made a promise and is now seeking to avoid being bound by it? The question may tell you that the party in **breach** is denying any obligation to pay a sum of money they promised to pay, or is trying to recover a sum of money they had earlier promised to forego. Can they be held to the promise?

Step 2: Did the promisor intend to be legally bound by the promise?

✳ ✳ ✳ ✳ ✳ ✳ ✳ ✳ ✳

Alex has made an offer to Becky to sell her his bicycle for £150. Becky has accepted by promising to pay £150 for it. Alex delivers the bicycle but Becky refuses to pay. Advise Alex.

It is Becky's payment obligation that Alex wishes to enforce. Alex therefore needs to establish that the promise is legally binding and enforceable against Becky.

❗ Don't fall into the trap

There are follow-up issues, namely whether the promise has in fact been broken—and the remedies available to the promisee if it has. Therefore, where there are no real issues associated with enforceability since the parties accept that they are bound, the question may be about breach and remedies rather than enforceability. Familiarity with the enforceability issues in this chapter will enable you to identify questions where enforceability is the issue.

Step 2: Did the promisor intend to be legally bound by the promise?

Is there an intention to create legal relations?

This may not be a controversial question on the facts and rarely will more than a paragraph of an answer be devoted to it, e.g. in the case of **commercial agreements** intention to be legally bound is presumed once a **promise** has been made and is only likely to be rebutted where clear words to opposite effect are used, e.g. honour clauses whereby the parties agree to exclude the courts and to rely only on each other's honour (*Rose & Frank Co. v J. R. Crompton & Brothers Ltd* (1925) and *Jones v Vernon's Pools Ltd* (1938)), or where there is extreme uncertainty of terms so that there is no clear contract (*Baird Textiles Holdings Ltd v Marks & Spencer plc* (2001): lack of certainty as to terms of alleged 'implied' contract confirmed the absence of intention to create legal relations despite the existence of a commercial relationship).

In the context of commercial agreements it may be necessary to distinguish an advertising gimmick (having no legal consequences) from a promise intended to be legally binding (e.g. *Carlill v Carbolic Smoke Ball Co.* (1893): commercial agreement and not a mere advertising gimmick because the company had deposited £1,000 with its bank to show its sincerity).

The key question is: would the promise be understood by the reasonable person as constituting a binding offer? See *Bowerman v ABTA Ltd* (1996): if ABTA wished to avoid the reasonable conclusion that its scheme of protection was intended to be legally binding it could have made this clear by the use of express words but it had failed to do so.

It is more likely that your examiner will slip in a promise made by a relative (often an uncle or aunt) to the promisee to see whether you spot this as relevant to intention to be legally bound (a **domestic or social agreement**), and can address whether the usual presumption of no intention to be legally bound (*Balfour v Balfour* (1919)) can be rebutted on the particular facts.

Step 3: Consider the possibility of duress
****

It seems that there must be both reliance on and evidence of certainty of the terms of the parties' agreement in order to rebut the presumption in the case of promises by relatives. (Compare *Parker v Clark* (1960): agreement between relatives with strong reliance on the promises coupled with detailed terms, with *Jones v Padavatton* (1969): mother and daughter's agreement for funding to study for the bar exams evidenced reliance but lacked certainty of terms, and there were problems with the duration of the promise.)

If the parties to the promise are husband and wife then it is likely that the presumption will only be rebutted if (i) the promises in the agreement are made when the parties have decided to separate (*Merritt v Merritt* (1970), compare *Balfour v Balfour*); and (ii) the promise is sufficiently certain in its terms (*Gould v Gould* (1970): for 'as long as I can manage it' is not sufficiently certain).

Tip

You need to be aware of the reasons why promises made in the domestic context are not generally legally enforceable. Why do we not want to see such promises being litigated before the courts? See *Balfour v Balfour*, and the speech of Atkin LJ, for a discussion of the public policy rationale.

Balfour v Balfour (CA): husband's promise to wife whilst living together (although they later separated) was not intended to be legally binding. Atkin LJ explained the policy reason for the unenforceability of promises in the domestic or social context as the avoidance of the opening of the floodgates and nature of such agreements as informal.

! Don't fall into the trap

The nature of the agreement is more significant than the identities of its parties.

You should not think that all agreements between relatives would be categorized as domestic or social. If the nature of the agreement is commercial, e.g. concerning a family business, then the fact that the parties are brothers would not bring this agreement within the presumption of no intention to be legally bound. The presumption would be that applicable to a commercial agreement (*Snelling v John G. Snelling Ltd* (1973)).

Step 3: Consider the possibility of duress

Was the promise freely given or was it extorted by illegitimate pressure or threats from the promisee?

Threats will usually be threats affecting a person's business interests or financial well-being, e.g. a threat to breach an existing commercial contract, such as a threat to cancel supplies of goods unless a new, higher, price is paid. (This explains the relevance of duress in the context of alteration promises.)

Practical example

The terms of an existing contract provide that Axel Ltd is to supply Brandon Ltd with supplies of light bulbs according to an agreed schedule for delivery and payment. Axel Ltd then threatens to stop these supplies unless Brandon Ltd pays double the agreed price, knowing that Brandon Ltd will be unable to secure an alternative supply at short notice to fulfil its own contract with a retailer, Cutprice plc.

Brandon Ltd reluctantly agrees to pay the extra price to secure its supply. The contract term has now ended and Brandon Ltd is seeking the return of all monies paid in excess of the original contract price. Is Brandon Ltd's promise to pay more enforceable?

Was the alteration promise to pay more obtained as a result of duress? If it was then the promise is voidable and, assuming that Brandon Ltd does not affirm the alteration promise, it will not be enforceable against Brandon Ltd (or to put it another way, Brandon Ltd is not bound by it). Any question of whether the alteration promise is supported by consideration (the next step) is then of academic interest only.

Do these circumstances constitute economic duress?

In *Pao On v Lau Yiu Long* (1980) it was held that for a contract to be voidable for economic duress:

- there must be a threat or pressure which is illegitimate and
- that pressure or threat must amount to a 'coercion of will that vitiates consent'.

Is there evidence of pressure or a threat?

In the Axel Ltd/Brandon Ltd (A Ltd/B Ltd) example this is easily established since there is a clear threat. Identifying where the line is crossed in cases of pressure is more difficult. As we will see, in *Williams v Roffey Bros.* the CA had no difficulty in concluding that there was no duress since the initiative for the promised extra payment came from the main contractor. There was no evidence of any pressure or threat from the subcontractor. But what do you think the position would have been if the subcontractor had made a factual statement as to his financial position? Would this be pressure?

Is the pressure or threat illegitimate?

The difficulty is to know what constitutes an illegitimate threat. Clearly the threat in the A Ltd/B Ltd example is illegitimate since A Ltd cannot be acting lawfully where there is no default by B Ltd and terms were agreed.

However, if, e.g. a commercial lender threatens to call in a loan repayable on demand from a commercial customer then, because the lender is exercising its legitimate rights, reasonable pressure will not be 'illegitimate' and hence not constitute duress. A distinction appears to exist between commercial and consumer contracts. In *CTN Cash and Carry Ltd v Gallaher Ltd* (1994) (a commercial contract) the threat was to withdraw credit facilities

Step 3: Consider the possibility of duress

✳✳✳✳✳✳✳✳✳✳✳✳

unless payment was made for a consignment of cigarettes which the supplier thought had been delivered but had in fact been stolen. The supplier had a legitimate right to demand payment for goods delivered. The CA rejected an argument to recognize 'lawful act duress' in **an arm's length dealing between two trading companies,** on the basis that this would create uncertainty in commercial dealings. This leaves open the position in consumer contracts.

In *Progress Bulk Carriers Ltd v Tube City IMS LLC* (2012), the judge held that 'illegitimate pressure' could be constituted by conduct which was not in itself unlawful, although it would be an unusual case where that was so, particularly in the commercial context. On the facts the ship-owner had refused to supply an alternative vessel unless the charterer waived its right to full compensation for the ship-owner's breach. This amounted to illegitimate pressure.

According to Lord Scarman in *The Universe Sentinel* (1983), there will be duress if a lawful threat is being used to achieve a goal which is unlawful (such as blackmail). The majority of the House of Lords (HL) considered that it was unlawful/an illegitimate threat for a trade union to refuse to allow tugs to assist vessels to leave harbour unless the owners of the vessels made a payment to the trade union's welfare fund. If they could not leave and had to lie idle, the losses would have been catastrophic. The majority concluded that legislation, which might have protected the trade union's action as lawful action 'in furtherance of a trade dispute', did not cover this situation.

Coercion of will that vitiates consent (compulsion)

It is clear that a party in the position of B Ltd in the example knows full well that it is agreeing to pay double the agreed price for the light bulbs. Rather, B Ltd has agreed because it feels that it has no realistic commercial choice other than to agree given that alternative supplies are unavailable at short notice and it will otherwise find itself in breach of its contract with C plc.

B & S Contracts & Design Ltd v Victor Green Publications Ltd (1984) **(CA)**

FACTS: There was an agreement to erect exhibition stands for the Ds. Workers threatened not to complete unless the Ds paid £4,500. The Ds paid, since although they could have brought a claim for breach, the failure to erect the stands on time would have exposed the Ds to claims from those to whom they had let the exhibition stands.

HELD: The extra payment was voidable for duress.

See also *Adam Opel GmbH v Mitras Automotive (UK) Ltd* (2008) and *Atlas Express Ltd v Kafco* (1989).

Causation: in a claim for economic duress it must be this illegitimate threat or pressure that is the reason why the promisor agreed to make the promise, e.g. why B Ltd agreed to pay A Ltd double the originally agreed price (*Huyton SA v Peter Cremer GmbH & Co.* (1999)). This can be compared with the position in *Pao On v Lau Yiu Long* where the majority shareholders made the indemnity promise as a commercial decision and did not think that the share price would fall, so triggering the indemnity promise.

The need to protest and avoid affirmation

Duress renders the promise **voidable** and the **bars to rescission** apply (see Chapter 9, p. 197, 'Step 1: Always start by considering whether rescission is possible'). The victim of duress must therefore be careful to avoid **affirmation** as he will then lose the ability to **rescind** or avoid the promise. In *The Siboen and the Sibotre* (1976), Kerr J said that it would be central to ask: *did the victim protest at the time or shortly thereafter and seek to reopen the issue?*

In *North Ocean Shipping Co. Ltd v Hyundai Construction Co. Ltd, The Atlantic Baron* (1979), there was clear evidence of duress in relation to a promise to pay more for the construction of an oil tanker which had already been chartered by the owner. Nevertheless the owners had left it until nine months after the ship had been delivered before seeking to reclaim the monies paid under duress. It followed that the owners had affirmed and so lost the right to avoid liability on this promise.

Step 4: Was the promise contained in a deed?

Do not delay here unless you have a deed. This is most unlikely since it would mean that the examiner would not be asking you to demonstrate the existence of consideration to support such a promise.

Definition

A **deed** is a legally binding document which is expressed as a deed, is validly executed as a deed (i.e. it is signed in the presence of witnesses who attest to the signature) and is delivered as a deed (**s. 1(2) and (3), Law of Property (Miscellaneous Provisions) Act 1989**).

Step 5: Was any consideration supplied by the promisee to support the promise made by the promisor?

Identifying consideration

Was the promise broken a formation or an alteration promise?

Formation promises

Consideration is whatever is asked for and given in exchange for the promise (Lord Dunedin in *Dunlop Pneumatic Tyre Co. Ltd v Selfridge & Co. Ltd* (1915): the price for which the other's promise is bought).

- **In the case of a bilateral contract, each party's promise is the consideration to support the promise given by the other.** Therefore parties to a bilateral contract are bound on the exchange of promises although neither has yet undertaken any performance of those promises.

Axel Ltd promises to deliver a consignment of light bulbs to Brandon Ltd by 1 October. Brandon Ltd promises to pay for them on delivery. Axel Ltd is late in delivering the light bulbs. Brandon Ltd wishes to sue the seller for **damages** for breach of the delivery promise.

Brandon Ltd is seeking to enforce Axel Ltd's delivery promise so that Brandon Ltd must establish that it gave consideration in exchange for this promise by Axel Ltd.

Brandon Ltd's consideration is its own promise to pay for the goods on delivery.

- **In the case of a unilateral contract, consideration is the performance of the act which was requested in order to earn the reward in the promise.** The promise is not capable of being enforced until the act is completed.

Consideration need not be adequate

It need not match the value of the promise sought to be enforced.

Chappell & Co. Ltd v Nestlé Co. Ltd (1960)

Trivial acts (three chocolate wrappers) as part payment for the supply of a record were regarded as part of the consideration because they had been requested. The fact that the wrappers were of trivial economic value and were thrown away was irrelevant as consideration need not be adequate.

Alex has made an offer to Becky to sell her his bicycle for £150.

Becky has accepted by promising to pay £150 for it. It is irrelevant to the enforceability of the promise to sell if the bicycle is in fact worth £100.

Consideration must be sufficient

The consideration merely needs to be requested by the other party and be something which the law will recognize as consideration.

The following will *not* be a sufficient (good) consideration:

- sentimental motives (*Thomas v Thomas* (1842): testator's desire could not act as consideration)
- anything that is not capable of expression in economic terms, e.g. promising to refrain from doing something that you have no right to do anyway (*White v Bluett* (1853))
- past consideration, although see the previous request device
- performance of a duty imposed by law

* performance of an existing contractual duty owed to the other party (compare performance of an existing contractual duty owed to a third party which is a good consideration).

Revision tip

Questions involving formation promises are likely to involve one or more of the following principles:

(i) the past consideration rule and its avoidance

(ii) performance of a duty imposed by law.

If there is already an existing contractual duty owed by the promisor to the promisee, any further promise will involve an alteration of an existing contract.

Past consideration is not a good consideration

Any act carried out before a promise is given is not given in exchange for the promise and therefore cannot be consideration to support that promise (*Re McArdle* (1951): improvements carried out before the promise to pay for them).

Tip

This is linked to the agreement principle of accepting in response to the offer and the typical problem scenarios tend to involve a unilateral context of a promise of reward. However, past consideration involves an act followed by a promise whereas a unilateral contract requires a promise followed by the requested act.

There is a device which allows the past consideration rule to be side-stepped and the key question is whether it applies to the facts in any case.

Practical example: previous request device

1. Junaid **requests** that Kate perform a particular act such as finding customers for a product.
2. This request carries with it an **implied promise to pay** for these services.
3. Kate finds the customers (**performs the requested act**).
4. There is a **later promise** which fixes the amount of her reward.

There is now a promise that predates the performance of the act and in exchange for which the promise is performed. The later express promise merely fixes the amount of the payment already impliedly promised by Junaid. (*Pao On v Lau Yiu Long* (1980) and *Re Casey's Patents* (1892)).

The crucial question therefore is whether this is an appropriate context for the request to give rise to the implied promise to pay for the services, e.g. this would be unlikely if I am drowning in a lake and ask you to rescue me (domestic or social context), but quite likely in the context of professional services (commercial context) as in the Junaid and Kate example above.

Step 5: Was any consideration supplied?
✱✱✱✱✱✱✱✱✱✱✱

Performance of a duty imposed by law is not a good consideration

---

Practical example

James promises Kelly that he will do something which he is already bound by the general law to do. This promise or performance cannot be a good consideration because James is promising to do no more than he is already legally bound to do (*Collins v Godefroy* (1831): promise of payment for giving evidence in court when the promisee had been subpoenaed to attend and give that evidence and was thereby under a legal duty to do so).

Going beyond that duty imposed by law will be consideration

Going beyond the duty is seen as incurring additional detriment and/or giving additional benefit and therefore supplying fresh consideration. See *Glasbrook Bros. v Glamorgan CC* (1925) (police services over and above services required by law could amount to consideration to support a promise of specific payment for those services) and *Ward v Byham* (1956) (majority of the CA considered that although the mother of an illegitimate child owed a statutory duty to maintain her child, this mother had provided consideration for a payment of support by promising that the child would be 'well looked after and happy').

Note that in *Ward v Byham* and *Williams v Williams* (1957) Lord Denning had considered that unless it would be contrary to public policy to enforce such a promise, consideration *should be* provided by performing a legal duty as this was a **factual benefit** to the promisor.

You should compare performance of legal duty with performance of an existing contractual duty owed to a third party.

Performance of an existing contractual duty owed to a third party

Performance of an existing contractual duty owed to a third party is a good consideration (see the illustration in Figure 3.1).

Figure 3.1 Performance of an existing contractual duty owed to a third party

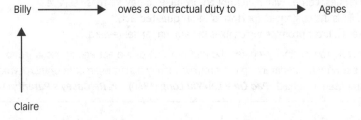

Billy owes a contractual duty to Agnes.

Claire promises Billy that Claire will pay Billy a sum of money if Billy does what Billy is already bound to do under Billy's contract with Agnes.

Billy can use the promise or performance owed to Agnes as consideration to support Claire's promise. (In relation to this promise given by Claire to Billy, Agnes is a third party.)

New Zealand Shipping Co. Ltd v A. M. Satterthwaite & Co. Ltd, The Eurymedon (1975) **(PC)**

Figure 3.2 *The Eurymedon*

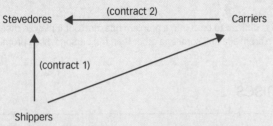

- The first contract was made between the shippers and the carriers for carriage of machinery. This contract contained a Himalaya clause (exemption from liability for servants, agents, and independent contractors).
- The carriers then made the second contract with the stevedores whereby the carriers employed the stevedores to unload goods at port of destination.
- The Privy Council recognized a third contract between the shippers and the stevedores based on the shippers' unilateral promise of exemption made to the stevedores. **The stevedores could enforce this promise of exemption because they had provided consideration by unloading the goods.** This was the performance of an existing contractual duty owed to a third party to this contract, namely to the carrier under the second contract.

Pao On v Lau Yiu Long (1980) **(PC)**

Figure 3.3 *Pao On v Lau Yiu Long*

FACTS: The plaintiffs acquired shares in the Fu Chip Company. The defendants were majority shareholders who were concerned about a fall in the value of their holding if the plaintiffs decided to sell these shares. The plaintiffs were persuaded to make a promise to the Fu Chip Company that they would not sell 60 per cent of their shares for one year. They made this promise at the request of the defendants and on the basis that they would be protected if the share price fell and they were unable

Step 5: Was any consideration supplied?

✱✱✱✱✱✱✱✱✱✱✱

> to sell this 60 per cent in that period. The defendants later made a promise to indemnify the plaintiffs against such a loss. Was this promise enforceable by the plaintiffs?
>
> **HELD:** The plaintiffs had provided consideration for the indemnity promise by promising the Fu Chip Co. that they would retain the shares. This amounted to promising to perform an existing duty owed to a third party to the indemnity contract, namely to Fu Chip.

Tip

This type of consideration is difficult to draft into a problem question but it may be there. Look out for a contract between the promisee and someone other than the person whose promise they are seeking to enforce.

Alteration promises

Practical example

Peter promises Rachel that he will do something that he is already bound by a contract with Rachel to do (**promises to pay or do more**); or

Peter promises Rachel that he will accept a smaller sum than Rachel owes in full payment of her debt (**promises to accept less**, which impliedly involves promising not to sue for the balance on the debt).

Can Rachel enforce these alteration promises?

The key difficulty Rachel faces is that such alteration promises, not contained in a deed, must be supported by consideration and performance of an existing duty owed to the promisor (Peter) is not a good consideration because Rachel has supplied no additional legal benefit to Peter and has incurred no additional detriment. Rachel, as promisee, will have done no more than she was already legally bound to do.

Key Point

There must be some independent consideration to support alteration promises: *Stilk v Myrick* (1809) (promises to pay more) and *Foakes v Beer* (1884) (promises to accept less).

However, the approach to enforceability of alteration promises has long been more generous than in the case of formation promises, and the 1940s saw recognition of the **doctrine of promissory estoppel** which gave limited enforceability to alteration promises that had been acted upon. In the late 1980s the CA in *Williams v Roffey Bros.* made it much easier to establish the consideration necessary to support certain alteration promises.

Since a distinction has been drawn between the legal treatment of alteration promises to pay more and alteration promises to accept less, examiners also emphasize (and query) this distinction. As a result, problem questions involving alteration promises and their enforceability will often involve both types of promise in different factual situations. The Peter and Rachel example above is a good (simple) illustration.

Scenario 1: Alteration promises to pay more than the promisor is contractually obliged to pay

There is a strong link with the possibility of duress in this scenario. If the promise was obtained as a result of duress it will be voidable and the presence or absence of consideration will be irrelevant in practice, although an examiner would expect you to assess whether there is consideration.

Practical example

There is an existing contract whereby Ampere Ltd (A Ltd) is employed as the electrical services subcontractor by Builder Ltd (B Ltd), the main building contractor. B Ltd has itself been engaged by Creative plc (C plc), the landowner and developer. A Ltd has agreed to perform the work for a fixed price and to a fixed deadline. You are also told that this fixed deadline is designed to ensure that B Ltd is able to meet the hand-over date and that if B Ltd is late it will become liable to pay 'a penalty' according to the terms of its contract with C plc. B Ltd discovers that A Ltd is struggling to meet the deadline and voluntarily offers (so no duress) to pay A Ltd an extra £7,000 to ensure that the original deadline is met. A Ltd promises to meet the deadline, and does so, but B Ltd now refuses to pay the extra claiming that A Ltd has not supplied any consideration to support the promise to pay more.

Is B Ltd's promise supported by consideration?

A Ltd does have a potential problem here since simply promising to meet the deadline involves A Ltd promising no more than it was already bound to do under the terms of its contract with B Ltd. There is no additional benefit or detriment.

> ### *Stilk v Myrick* (1809)
>
> **FACTS:** On a voyage where two of the sailors deserted, the ship's captain had promised the remaining crew extra wages to sail the ship to the home port. However, the contract terms required this to happen anyway in the event of such minor desertions.
>
> **HELD:** this promise of extra wages was unenforceable because (i) the sailors had done no more than they were contractually bound to do in any event and/or (ii) the promise was obtained as a result of extortion so that policy dictated that it should not be enforceable.

However, A Ltd does have two possible arguments that it can put:

(i) Going beyond the scope of the contract terms

If A Ltd (as promisee) can demonstrate additional performance beyond the scope of the terms of the contractual duty this will constitute fresh consideration to support the promise to pay more.

Step 5: Was any consideration supplied?

✱✱✱✱✱✱✱✱✱✱

The first task therefore is to examine the scope of the contract terms to see whether the promisee has exceeded the existing contractual duty (compare *Stilk v Myrick* and *Hartley v Ponsonby* (1857)).

If in the example A Ltd had agreed to improve the quality of the electrical specification for some fittings as part of the alteration promise to pay more, A Ltd would have agreed to suffer an additional detriment and to provide B Ltd with an additional benefit. (It would be irrelevant that the improved fittings cost significantly less than the £7,000 extra being promised since consideration need not be adequate.)

Since, there is no evidence of A Ltd agreeing to do anything extra in exchange for the £7,000, A Ltd will need to focus on the second argument.

(ii) Argue that there is consideration for the promise to pay more in the form of factual benefit (or practical benefit) arising to B Ltd from making the promise to pay more (*Williams v Roffey Bros. & Nicholls (Contractors) Ltd*)

Williams v Roffey Bros. (1991) **(CA)**

FACTS: A promise was given by the main contractor to pay more money to the subcontractor in order to get the subcontract work completed by the original deadline in the contract with the building owner and thereby avoid payment of a penalty.

HELD: The promise was enforceable as supported by consideration since there were factual benefits to the promisor in making such a promise.

The decision is based on the argument that since the doctrine of duress exists to prevent the enforcement of alteration promises extracted under threats, there is no longer a need for such a strict approach to consideration in the alteration context as was evidenced in *Stilk v Myrick* (although that decision was not overruled in *Roffey*).

The factual benefit is the consideration.

❶ Don't fall into the trap

Roffey **consideration:** Be careful not to state that factual benefits are provided by the promisee. They are not. The factual benefit arises from the making of the promise and not from anything done by the promisee (i.e. it is about benefit rather than detriment—and clearly does not move from the promisee: see Colman J in *South Caribbean Trading v Trafalgar Beheer BV* (2004)). This is controversial (and you can comment on this for extra marks since *Roffey* consideration does not move from the promisee). Equally you will lose a significant number of marks if you cannot state the consideration accurately since this will be indicative of confusion and a lack of precision.

The worst error of all is to state that *Roffey* does away with the need to show consideration in the case of alteration promises to pay more. The CA's decision indicates quite the opposite.

Step 5: Was any consideration supplied?

Thus, the next question is to ask whether in making the promise to pay more the promisor (B Ltd in our example) derives any factual benefit. If so, the promise will be enforceable as it will be supported by consideration.

What constitutes a factual benefit?

In *Williams v Roffey* the factual benefit was identified as:

- the fact that the promisor intended to avoid having to make payment for late performance under a penalty clause in its contract with the building owner
- the fact that the promisor was seeking to avoid the hassle of finding another subcontractor to complete the work.

Revision tip

The practical example is based on **Roffey**, as, it seems, are so many problem question scenarios. They are not difficult to spot, i.e. often a construction contract and evidence of difficulties in meeting a contractual deadline with consequences for the promisor.

If, as seems to be the case, factual benefits are judged subjectively by the promisor, any promise to pay more will be supported by consideration as the promisor would not agree to pay more unless he subjectively considered this to be of benefit to him. It is only if factual benefit is to be viewed objectively that any difficulty is likely to arise in establishing the existence of a binding promise to pay more.

It follows that consideration means something more than the price for which the promise of the other was bought in this context of alteration promises to pay more.

Scenario 2: Alteration promises to accept less than the promisee is legally bound to pay (or perform) under an existing contract

Practical example

Simple debt

Tareq (debtor) owes Usman (creditor) £1,000 due on Friday 1 October.

On 1 October Usman agrees to accept £750 in full payment and agrees (i.e. promises) not to sue for the £250 balance.

Is Usman's promise enforceable or can Usman go back on his promise and sue Tareq for the balance of £250?

As is the case with all promises not in deeds, any promise to alter the terms of that debt contract must be supported by consideration if it is to be enforceable. Since promising to perform an existing duty (paying the debt) is not a good consideration because there is no

Step 5: Was any consideration supplied?

✱✱✱✱✱✱✱✱✱✱

additional benefit or detriment in law, promising to perform only part of that duty cannot be consideration (*Pinnel's Case* (1602) and *Foakes v Beer*).

Foakes v Beer (1884) **(HL)**

FACTS: Existing judgment debt was to be paid by instalments and the creditor therefore promised not to take any enforcement proceedings in relation to the debt. However, the instalments did not cover the interest on the judgment debt and the creditor sought to go back on this promise to recover that sum.

HELD: The creditor could do this because the debtor had not provided any consideration for the promise not to sue on the debt. Part payment of an existing debt was no more than the debtor was already contractually bound to pay.

Does *Williams v Roffey* affect this position? Can factual benefit to the promisor constitute the consideration?

No, *Roffey* does not apply to alteration promises to accept less (only to alteration promises to pay more) (*obiter* in *Re Selectmove Ltd* (1995)).

Factual benefit to the promisor (Usman) in accepting £750 in full satisfaction of Tareq's debt, on the basis that some of the debt is preferable to securing none at all, cannot be a good consideration for Usman's promise.

In *Foakes v Beer* the 'factual benefit as consideration' argument had been rejected by the HL (although see the comments of Lord Blackburn on this point). The CA in *Selectmove* considered that it was bound by the decision of the HL in *Foakes v Beer*, which had not been raised in argument before the CA in *Roffey*. It was a simple matter of following precedent.

The result is a distinction between alteration promises to pay more (*Roffey* can apply) and alteration promises to accept less. The anomalies produced by this distinction can be the subject of an essay question.

Is there consideration to support Usman's promise?

There are nevertheless some recognized ways to provide the necessary independent consideration, so that Usman would be bound by his promise and unable to sue for the £250 balance of the debt:

- paying a smaller sum **in advance** at the creditor (Usman's) request (additional benefit/ detriment; this is in fact the *ratio* in *Pinnel's Case*).

Step 5: Was any consideration supplied?

✳✳✳✳✳✳✳✳✳✳

If Usman had asked Tareq to pay £750 in full satisfaction on 15 September when the full debt was repayable on 1 October then Tareq would provide consideration for Usman's promise to forgo the balance.

- payment of a smaller sum **at a different place** at creditor's (Usman's) request (additional benefit/detriment).

If Usman has asked Tareq to pay £750 in full satisfaction on 1 October but in Birmingham when the full debt was repayable in London on that date, this would be a detriment to Tareq; and because Usman requested it, it would be a benefit to Usman.

- **payment in kind** (a chattel) which is **accepted by** Usman (**the creditor**) (no enquiry into adequacy of the consideration; it is consideration because the creditor accepts it).

If Usman agrees to accept Tareq's watch (worth £750) in full satisfaction of the £1,000 debt.

Usman would also be bound (but not on the basis of consideration):

- where his promise is part of a **composition agreement** with Tareq's other creditors, e.g. each agrees to take 75p in the £, OR
- where the **part payment of £750 is made by Vankeet (a third party)** since this prevents Usman from suing Tareq for the balance (*Hirachand Punamchand v Temple* (1911)).

This seems to be because it would be a fraud on the third party to accept the *smaller sum in full satisfaction* and then promptly sue the debtor for the balance. Examiners like to slip in a part payment by a third party, e.g. usually a parent or other relative.

❶ *Don't fall into the trap*

Failing to address the consideration question and rushing into promissory estoppel: if the alteration promise to accept less is not supported by consideration, or otherwise enforceable, on the basis of any of these facts, we then need to consider whether it is possible for an alteration promise to be enforceable despite the absence of consideration. However, always try to establish the existence of consideration first since its existence will mean that the promise is fully and completely enforceable. The temptation may be to rush into promissory estoppel, particularly if the question involves a landlord agreeing to accept less rent than the tenant owes, but this presents a lower form of enforceability in English law and provides the promisee with limited protection.

Step 6: Promissory estoppel

Is it possible to enforce an alteration promise, such as Usman's when Tareq has provided no consideration to support it?

There may be limited enforceability using **the equitable doctrine of promissory estoppel**.

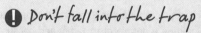

❶ Don't fall into the trap

Some issues of scope and practicality: if the promise is made on the formation of a new contract, it must be supported by consideration (unless contained in a deed). **We are only concerned here with alteration promises to existing contracts.**

Roffey means that consideration is likely to be present to support alteration promises to pay more and the relevance of promissory estoppel tends to be confined to alteration promises to accept less or forgo existing rights where the promisor goes back on these promises.

Definition

Promissory estoppel is an equitable doctrine designed to prevent the promisor going back on their promise where this would be inequitable (unfair) because the promisee has relied on it.

Where the parties have an existing legal relationship and party A promises party B that a right which party A has under the contract will not be fully enforced, intending party B to rely upon that promise and party B does rely on the promise, the promisor (party A) cannot go back on that promise where it would be inequitable to do so.

To this extent promissory estoppel gives limited enforceability to (alteration) promises.

Central London Property Trust Ltd v High Trees House Ltd *(High Trees House)* (1947) **(Denning J)**

FACTS: The landlords of a block of flats promised to reduce the rent charged to tenants during the bombing in the Second World War when the tenants were unable to sublet. The reduced rent was paid until September 1945 when the landlords claimed to receive the full rent.

HELD: Despite the fact that the tenants had provided no consideration to support the promise to accept less rent, the landlord could not go back on that promise, because of the tenant's reliance on it, until it was no longer inequitable to do so. *Obiter*: the landlord was unable to recover the balance on the rental payments while this estoppel operated.

Defence only

In English law promissory estoppel operates purely as a defence by the promisee to an action by the promisor where the promisor seeks to go back on this promise, e.g. Usman

purports to go back on his promise to Tareq that he will accept the £750 as discharging the debt and will not sue him for the £250 balance.

In English law, as it currently stands, promissory estoppel cannot be used as a cause of action in itself (*Combe v Combe*; this also explains why there was no promissory estoppel argument in *Williams v Roffey* since the subcontractor needed to sue on the promise to pay more money).

Combe v Combe (1951) **(CA)**

Husband's promise to pay ex-wife was not supported by consideration and promissory estoppel could not apply on the facts because (i) this was a formation issue rather than an alteration to an existing contract and (ii) in any event, promissory estoppel operates as a defence where a promisor goes back on a promise not to sue. It could not be used as a cause of action ('shield not a sword').

Examination tip

Examiners can be generous and have been known to formulate questions involving consideration, promissory estoppel, and alteration promises around the *Roffey* factual scenario of construction (promise to pay more) and *High Trees* factual scenario of a landlord and tenant relationship (promise to accept less). You are advised to be familiar with these facts and decisions.

When will the promissory estoppel doctrine operate?

This depends on **identifying the conditions for its operation.**

1. **There must be a clear promise that *existing* legal rights will not be fully enforced.** The context is alteration promises since the doctrine applies to promises which forgo or amend existing legal rights.

2. **The promise must be intended to be binding and to be acted upon and it must in fact be acted upon.** The essential element is reliance but it need not be detrimental reliance. *W. J. Alan & Co. Ltd v El Nasr Export and Import Co.* (1972): need to have been led to act differently.

3. **It must be inequitable to allow the promisor to go back on his promise.** This is easier to establish where there has been detrimental reliance: *The Post Chaser* (1982).

D & C Builders Ltd v Rees (1966): it will not be inequitable to go back on a promise where that promise was not freely given (i.e. if it was extracted by duress, see p. 52, 'Step 3: Consider the possibility of duress').

Step 6: Promissory estoppel

✳✳✳✳✳✳✳✳✳✳✳

> ### D & C Builders Ltd v Rees (CA)
>
> **FACTS:** The defendant owed plaintiff builders £482. The defendant was taken to know that the plaintiff was in financial difficulties when the defendant offered £300 in full settlement. The plaintiff accepted the smaller sum and then sought to recover the balance.
>
> **HELD:** There was no consideration to support the plaintiff's promise to accept the smaller sum. Lord Denning considered that promissory estoppel could not operate on these facts since it was not inequitable for the plaintiff to go back on a promise that was not freely given.

What is the effect of promissory estoppel? Does it have the same effect as the presence of consideration?

The next question to consider is the scope of the estoppel and its duration. **Promissory estoppel suspends legal rights and, unlike consideration, it does not generally extinguish them**. This means that where a promise to accept less is supported by consideration, the entire debt will be discharged. However, promissory estoppel merely suspends the legal right to full payment while the estoppel conditions operate (or until the estoppel comes to an end), i.e. when it is no longer inequitable to go back on the promise.

It follows that, in the absence of consideration, Usman could go back on his promise to accept the £750 in full satisfaction if, two days later, he learnt that Tareq had just inherited a significant sum of money.

However, the result of *obiter* comments in *High Trees* is that periodic payments (as part of a continuing obligation to pay, e.g. rental) which were made while an estoppel operated, will be extinguished so that it is not possible to sue for the balance on the individual rent payments. However, once the promissory estoppel ends the general right to full payment will revive, i.e. for the future the full rent will be payable each month or quarter.

How is the promissory estoppel brought to an end? Reasonable notice given and notice period has expired

This issue is complicated by the facts of *High Trees* since the estoppel in that case was considered to turn on the bombing in the Second World War and so came to an end automatically when the conditions under which the estoppel operated ceased to exist. However, the HL in *Tool Metal Manufacturing Co. Ltd v Tungsten Electric Co. Ltd* (1955) revived the strict legal rights only after the promisor had given reasonable notice of an intention to do so and that notice had elapsed.

It seems safest to demonstrate the giving of reasonable notice as a means of showing fairness and that it is no longer inequitable to go back to the strict contractual rights rather than assuming that the estoppel conditions have come to an end. In any event, court action would probably be required to enforce the strict legal position so that it would be necessary to initiate proceedings. This is exactly what happened in *High Trees*.

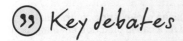

Key debates

1. Consideration requirement and alteration promises

Should it be necessary to establish consideration to support alteration promises? Compare the different approaches to avoid it and their legal credentials—**Roffey** pragmatism and Denning's promissory estoppel.

Chen-Wishart, 'Consideration, Practical Benefit and the Emperor's New Clothes' in Beatson and Friedmann (eds.), *Good Faith and Fault in Contract Law* (Oxford University Press, 1995).

Chen-Wishart, 'A Bird in the Hand: Consideration and Contract Modification' in Burrows and Peel (eds.), *Contract Formation and Parties* (Oxford University Press, 2010).

Should consideration be replaced by 'reliance' in this context? Reliance-focused remedial approaches include:

- Atiyah's arguments on reliance (Atiyah v Treitel). Atiyah, 'Consideration in Contracts: A Fundamental Restatement' in *Essays in Contract Law* (Oxford University Press, 1990); Treitel, 'Consideration: A Critical Analysis of Professor Atiyah's Fundamental Restatement' (1976) 50 Australian LJ 439.

- § 90 of the American Restatement of Contract (2d):

  (1) A promise which the promisor should *reasonably expect to induce action or forbearance on the part of the promisee or a third person and which does induce such action or forbearance* is binding if injustice can be avoided only by enforcement of the promise. *The remedy granted for breach may be limited as justice requires.*

Although this is based on reliance the remedy may not equate to full enforcement of the promise.

- *Antons Trawling Co. Ltd v Smith* (2003) (Court of Appeal of New Zealand): alteration promise had been acted upon (reliance) and was enforceable on that basis.

2. The limitations and future of promissory estoppel in English law—and the link to perceived deficiencies with *Roffey*

Limitations of promissory estoppel in English law

- It operates only in the context of alteration promises (however this is not as controversial as the other two limitations).
- **It operates only as a defence and not as a cause of action** (compare proprietary estoppel and estoppel by convention).
- **The exact meaning of its suspensory effect is unclear.**

Waltons Stores (Interstate) Ltd v Maher (1988) **(High Court of Australia)**

The Australian approach: unconscionability.

FACTS: The plaintiff sought **specific performance** of a lease on the basis that had been encouraged by the defendant to believe that the lease would be executed and so had acted to its detriment in demolishing existing structure on the land.

HELD: It was unconscionable to have adopted a course of action encouraging this detrimental conduct and therefore the defendant was estopped from denying that it was bound.

Key cases

****

> This estoppel therefore operated although there was no pre-existing contractual relationship between the parties and it also operated as a cause of action enabling the plaintiff to enforce the representation.

This principle has far greater flexibility than the English doctrine of promissory estoppel since:

- It uses a general category of estoppel.
- It enables the courts to take 'sufficient action' to prevent the detriment resulting from the unconscionable conduct. (Compare with consideration, the existence of which allows for full and direct enforcement of a promise.)
- It was applied in *Walton Stores* to enable direct enforcement of a promise rather than as a defence but also to create liability where there was no existing relationship between the parties (i.e. formation issue). The latter point would be particularly controversial if imported here.

On the other hand, as currently expressed, there is a clear link with detrimental action in reliance which rarely features in English case law applying promissory estoppel.

The *Walton Stores* argument—i.e. general category of estoppel and no limitation that estoppel cannot operate as cause of action—was attempted (unsuccessfully) before the CA in *Baird Textiles v Marks & Spencer*. However, the CA left open the question for consideration by the HL in a future case.

Arguments based on extending estoppel appear to be favoured due to the questions which arise when *Roffey* is subjected to scrutiny. Whilst that decision was initially greeted favourably as a pragmatic solution to the enforceability of alteration promises freely made, it can be criticized as 'invented consideration' (i.e. the consideration does not move from the promisee; there is no real explanation of why *Stilk v Myrick* was not overruled) and since *Selectmove* there is the arbitrary distinction affecting its application, i.e. it does not apply to alteration promises to accept less.

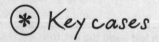 Key cases

Case	Facts	Principle
Pao On v Lau Yiu Long (PC)	When Ps acquired shares in a company its majority shareholders wanted to protect themselves against a fall in value of shareholding if shares all sold at once. At request of Ds and on basis of some form of protection being provided by Ds, Ps promised the company that they would not sell 60 per cent of their shares for one year. Ds later made a promise to indemnify Ps against a loss in not being able to sell. Ps wanted to enforce this promise. Held it was not a promise extracted as a result of duress and Ps had provided consideration for it through their promise to the company (promising to perform an existing duty owed to a third party—the company). Consideration was not past consideration since the promise had been made following a request by Ds which carried with it a promise of protection. The later promise of indemnity merely fixed the method of protection.	This is an important case discussing: • ingredients for a claim in duress • previous request device as a means of avoiding past consideration • consideration in the form of promising to perform an existing contractual duty owed to a third party.

Case	Facts	Principle
Stilk v Myrick	On a voyage where two of the sailors deserted, the ship's captain had promised the remaining crew extra wages to sail the ship to the home port. But the contract terms required the sailors to sail the ship anyway if there were such minor desertions. The promise was unenforceable since (i) the sailors had done no more than they were contractually bound to do in any event and/or (ii) the promise was obtained as a result of extortion so that policy dictated that it should not be enforceable.	Alteration promise to pay more: need to show consideration to support that promise and the general rule is that the consideration cannot be performing a contractual duty already owed to the same promisor.
Williams v Roffey Bros. (CA)	Promise by main contractor to pay more money to the subcontractor in order to get the subcontract work completed by the original deadline in the contract with the building owner and thereby avoid payment of a penalty. The promise was enforceable as supported by consideration since there were factual benefits to the promisor in making such a promise.	Alteration promise to pay more—avoiding the *Stilk v Myrick* restriction where the promisor's promise gives rise to factual benefits to the promisor (and so provides consideration to enforce the promise). Note that this consideration is not provided by anything done by the promisee.
Foakes v Beer (HL)	Existing judgment debt was to be paid by instalments and creditor therefore promised not to take any enforcement proceedings in relation to the debt. However, the instalments did not cover the interest on the judgment debt and the creditor went back on this promise to recover that sum. The creditor could do this because the debtor had not provided any consideration for the promise not to sue on the debt. Part payment of an existing debt was no more than the debtor was already contractually bound to pay.	Alteration promise to accept less than the debt owed: needs to be supported by consideration and this consideration is not provided by performance of existing contract, i.e. by making a part payment of the existing debt. More is required, e.g. payment earlier at creditor's request.
Central London Property Trust Ltd v High Trees House Ltd (High Trees House) Denning J	Landlords of block of flats promised to reduce the rent charged to tenants during the bombing in the Second World War when the tenants were unable to sublet. The reduced rent was paid until September 1945 when the landlords claimed to receive the full rent. Despite the fact that the tenants had provided no consideration to support the promise to accept less rent, the landlord could not go back on that promise because of the tenant's reliance on it until it was no longer inequitable to do so. *Obiter*: the landlord was unable to recover the balance on the rental payments while this estoppel operated.	Promissory estoppel as a defence to prevent a promisor from going back on his promise to forgo legal rights (accept less than he is owed) where the debtor has acted on that promise and it would be unfair to do so.

Key cases

****

Case	Facts	Principle
D & C Builders Ltd v Rees (CA)	D owed P builders £482 and was taken to know that P was in financial difficulties when D offered £300 in full settlement. P accepted the smaller sum and then sought to recover the balance. CA held that there was no consideration to support P's promise. Lord Denning considered that promissory estoppel could not operate on these facts since it was not inequitable for P to go back on a promise that was not freely given.	It is not unfair to go back on a promise to forgo legal rights and accept less than is owed where that promise was obtained by duress. Duress will prevent the promissory estoppel defence from operating as the promise must be freely given.

#4

Privity and third party rights

Key facts

- The doctrine of **privity of contract**, which remains the general rule in England, provides that a person who is not a party to a contract (called a 'third party'), cannot acquire rights under or enforce the provisions of that contract or rely on its protections even if the provisions were intended to benefit that third party. In addition, **consideration** must move from the promisee—and a third party is not the promisee.

- At common law there are complex, and sometimes artificial, ways to avoid this conclusion such as the use of agency to allow a third party to enforce an **exemption clause** in a contract to which the third party is not a party.

- More significant nowadays is the attempt to reform this principle by legislation in **the Contracts (Rights of Third Parties) Act 1999**, allowing third party beneficiaries who satisfy the **s. 1** test of enforceability to enforce the provisions of contracts. Where the **s. 1** test is satisfied, it will not matter that the third party may not have provided consideration for the promise it is seeking to enforce, as long as the promise is supported by consideration supplied by another.

- If the third party has not been given an enforceable right under the 1999 Act, it is still possible for the promisee to enforce the promise for the third party's benefit. However, there is a need to avoid the usual principle preventing the recovery of substantial **damages** if the promisee's loss is nominal. The courts have devised methods to avoid the 'black hole' problem (the party who suffers loss cannot sue due to privity and the contracting party is unable to recover more than nominal loss) since this would permit the party in **breach** to avoid having to pay substantial damages for that breach.

Introduction

In this topic the key question is **who may enforce the contract?** i.e. who may rely on **terms** in the contract (such as exemption clauses) and who may obtain remedies in the event of a breach?

Key things that you need to know and need to be able to explain

1. The doctrine of privity and its relationship with the doctrine of consideration (use correct terminology and understand the difference between contracting parties and a third party).

2. Reasons for reform in the context of intended third party beneficiaries.

3. The test of enforceability (**s. 1 Contracts (Rights of Third Parties) Act 1999**—accurately and in detail) and the scope and limitations of the Act.

4. Devices developed at common law to avoid the operation of privity in the context of an intended third party beneficiary—in particular the agency/*Eurymedon* device and the position in a similar scenario under the 1999 Act.

5. The ability of the promisee to secure **specific performance** in favour of the third party or to recover substantial damages to cover the third party's loss.

Think like an examiner

This topic tends to be set as an essay question; typically examining the scope of the **Contracts (Rights of Third Parties) Act 1999**, e.g.:

'The Contracts (Rights of Third Parties) Act 1999 does not abolish privity and fails to achieve its objective of enabling intended third party beneficiaries to enforce contractual provisions in their favour. This has meant that the courts have needed to be ever more ingenious in finding ways to allow a promisee to recover substantial damages to compensate for that third party's loss.' Discuss.

The particular question may be so broad (like this one) that it can encompass consideration of most of the issues covered in this chapter.

Problem questions are not easy to draft—and tend to be predictable by focusing on whether a third party can rely on an exemption clause in a contract to which it is not a party where the clause purports to provide protection. There are some template scenarios throughout this chapter which examiners tend to use as the basis for a more complex question. A fuller example problem-style question appears towards the end of the chapter.

It would be folly to revise this topic without having a detailed knowledge and understanding of the provisions of the 1999 Act and some case law explaining its scope.

Who may enforce the contract?

Who may rely on terms in the contract (such as exemption clauses) and who may obtain remedies in the event of a breach?

Practical example

Alex makes a contract with Becky where, in exchange for Becky's promise to pay £150, Alex promises to deliver his bicycle to Charlie.

In relation to this contract, Alex and Becky are the contractual parties. Charlie is a beneficiary of the contract but he is not a party to it. He is a 'third party'. The terminology is admittedly quite confusing!

Traditionally, the doctrine of privity of contract provides a restrictive answer to the question of WHO may enforce a contract.

Key point

The **doctrine of privity of contract** provides that only the parties to a contract may enjoy the benefits of that contract: only the parties can enforce the contractual obligations or rely on its protections.

A related rule is that **consideration** must move from the promisee.

Practical example

Alex promises Becky to deliver his bicycle if she pays the price of £150. On exchange of these promises the parties are bound.

Who is the promisor and who is the promisee turns on which promise is being enforced. Students often find it difficult to grasp the concept that the same parties can have differing roles:

(1) Alex fails to deliver the bicycle and Becky wishes to sue him for this non-delivery. She is therefore enforcing the promise to deliver. In relation to this promise Alex is promisor and Becky is promisee. To enforce the delivery promise Becky needs to have provided consideration to support Alex's promise. She has promised to pay £150 on delivery. As this is executory consideration it need not have taken place. A promise to pay is sufficient.

(2) Becky fails to pay the price and Alex wishes to sue her for non-payment. Alex is therefore enforcing the promise to pay. In relation to this promise Becky is the promisor and Alex is the promisee. To enforce the payment promise Alex needs to have provided consideration to support Becky's promise. He has promised to deliver the bicycle.

The rule that consideration must move from the promisee was interpreted to mean that a plaintiff (claimant or person seeking to enforce the promise) had to have supplied the consideration to support it. Inevitably this excluded the vast majority of third parties, even where

Who may enforce the contract?

✱✱✱✱✱✱✱✱✱✱✱

the contract was made for their benefit, since they have rarely provided any obvious consideration, e.g. in the practical example above: Becky provides the consideration (promising to pay £150) but it is Charlie who would wish to sue Alex in the event that Alex did not deliver the bicycle.

Tweddle v Atkinson (1861)

Figure 4.1 _Tweddle v Atkinson_

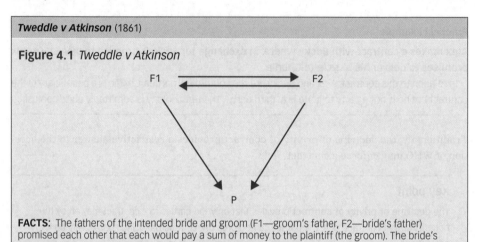

FACTS: The fathers of the intended bride and groom (F1—groom's father, F2—bride's father) promised each other that each would pay a sum of money to the plaintiff (the groom). The bride's father (F2) failed to pay. Could the groom enforce it?

HELD: Although the promise was for the plaintiff groom's benefit, he was unable to enforce it because (i) he was not a party to the contract containing the promise, and (ii) he had not provided any consideration to enable him to enforce it. (The consideration for F2's promise was provided by F1.)

These principles were applied to the same effect by the House of Lords (HL) in **_Dunlop Pneumatic Tyre Co. Ltd v Selfridge & Co. Ltd_**.

Dunlop Pneumatic Tyre Co. Ltd v Selfridge & Co. Ltd (1915) **(HL)**

Figure 4.2 _Dunlop Pneumatic Tyre Co. Ltd v Selfridge & Co. Ltd_

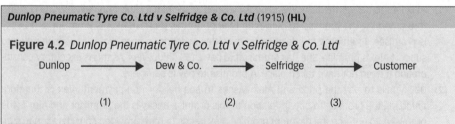

FACTS: Dunlop sold tyres to Dew & Co. Under the terms of this contract (contract 1) Dew & Co. promised not to sell the tyres at less than list price and to obtain a similar undertaking from trade buyers. In return Dew & Co. received a discount from Dunlop. Dew & Co. sold some tyres to Selfridge (contract 2) and Selfridge promised Dew & Co. to abide by the list price. In breach of this undertaking in contract 2, Selfridge sold tyres to customers (e.g. contract 3). Dunlop sued Selfridge for breach of its undertaking not to sell at below list price.

HELD: Dunlop could not succeed because:

(i) It was not a party to the contract containing that promise made by Selfridge (i.e. contract 2).

(ii) Dunlop had also not provided any consideration to support Selfridge's promise. The discount applied only between Dunlop and Dew & Co. with no obligation to pass it on.

Tip

It is clear that any reform of privity would also need to explain the relationship with the consideration requirement. (This is discussed below in the context of reform.)

The difficulty of refusing enforcement to third party intended beneficiaries

Whereas it has generally been accepted that a third party who is a total stranger should not be able to enforce a contract or contractual provision, it has been more difficult to justify why a third party intended beneficiary should not be able to enforce the contract, e.g. like the groom in *Tweddle v Atkinson* or Charlie in the practical example.

- **Intentions of the original contracting parties are thwarted:** it is clear in the practical example that both Alex and Becky's original intentions are that the bicycle is to be transferred to Charlie.

- **Injustice to the third party:** Charlie (the third party) appears unable to secure the promised bicycle but may well have acted in reliance on the promise that the bicycle would be his.

- **The person who has suffered loss cannot sue, whereas the person who has suffered no loss can sue (the 'black hole' problem):** Becky is the promisee and has provided consideration. She could sue Alex on the basis of his breach of their contract but her loss would be nominal if the breach is non-delivery and she has yet to pay Alex. The person suffering loss is Charlie—but Charlie cannot sue.

These inconsistencies led to:

- **case law-based devices to avoid the privity doctrine** (These devices retain some relevance due to the limited scope of the legislative reform. They are however, acknowledged to have introduced 'complexity, artificiality and uncertainty' into the law.)

- **eventually recommendations for statutory reform of the third party rule in order to allow a third party beneficiary, in certain circumstances, to enforce a contractual provision.** (See Law Commission Report: *Privity of Contract: Contracts for the Benefit of Third Parties*, Law Com. No. 242, Cm. 3329, 1996, and especially pp. 39–50 for the arguments in favour of reform.)

This statutory reform is contained in the **Contracts (Rights of Third Parties) Act 1999**.

The Contracts (Rights of Third Parties) Act 1999

Tip

The Act, and its scope of application, is extremely popular with examiners and you must ensure that you are familiar with its provisions, particularly the 'test of enforceability'.

Third party enforcement

In principle

In its report the Law Commission recommended that the privity rule be reformed by legislation in order to 'enable contracting parties to confer a right to enforce the contract on a third party', i.e.:

(a) the right to enforce remedies for breach of contract that would have been available had the third party been a contracting party (**s. 1(5)**)

(b) the right to enforce an exemption clause as if the third party was a party to the contract (**s. 1(6)**).

Contracts (Rights of Third Parties) Act 1999

Section 1(5): For the purpose of exercising his right to enforce a term of the contract, there shall be available to the third party any remedy that would have been available to him in an action for breach of contract if he had been a party to the contract (and the rules relating to damages, injunctions, specific performance and other relief shall apply accordingly).

Section 1(6): Where a term of a contract excludes or limits liability in relation to any matters references in this Act to the third party enforcing the term shall be construed as references to his availing himself of the exclusion or limitation.

When might a third party be able to enforce a contract? The test of enforceability

---

Section 1(1):

Subject to the provisions of this Act, a person who is not a party to a contract (a 'third party') may in his own right enforce a term of the contract **if –**

(a) **the contract expressly provides that he may, or**

(b) subject to subsection (2), **the term purports to confer a benefit on him.**

Section 1(2):

Subsection (1)(b) does not apply if on a proper construction of the contract it appears that the parties did not intend the term to be enforceable by the third party.

Summary of the test of enforceability

A third party will be able to enforce a contractual provision in its favour if:

either s. 1(1)(a)

- there is an express term in the contract stating that the third party may enforce the contractual term

or s. 1(1)(b) and s. 1(2)

- the contract must purport to confer a benefit on the third party AND there must be nothing in the contract which indicates that the parties did NOT intend that the term should be enforceable by the third party.

❗ *Don't fall into the trap*

It is not the case, despite what you may have read, that the **s. 1(2)** proviso applies to both parts of **s. 1(1)**. It applies only to **s. 1(1)(b)** as can be clearly seen by examining the wording of that subsection.

The first alternative: s. 1(1)(a). Is this part of the test satisfied?

If this part of the test is satisfied the contract between Alex and Becky would include a term which provided: 'and Charlie shall have the right to enforce the terms of this contract for his benefit as against the contractual parties' (or words to similar effect). This is the clearest way to ensure that the third party has direct enforcement rights and/or could rely on the protection of an exemption clause which sought to protect him.

The second alternative: s. 1(1)(b) and s. 1(2) proviso. Is this part of the test satisfied?

Step 1: Determining if the contract 'purports to confer a benefit' on the third party

In *Dolphin & Maritime & Aviation Services Ltd v Sveriges Angfartygs Assurans Forening, The Swedish Club* this argument failed.

Dolphin & Maritime & Aviation Services Ltd v Sveriges Angfartygs Assurans Forening, The Swedish Club (2009)

FACTS: A contract between U (underwriters of vessel involved in collision) and the Club (C), with which that vessel was registered, provided for C to pay sums recovered to Dolphin (D), a recovery agent for those underwriters, who would pass these sums on to U. When C paid the sums direct to

---

Who may enforce the contract?

✳✳✳✳✳✳✳✳✳✳✳

U, U had refused to pay D any commission. D had therefore sought to enforce the provision in the contract with C, arguing that the contract 'purported to confer a benefit' on D.

HELD: The contract was concerned with how payment was to be made to U and D was not a beneficiary of the agreement, albeit it was more convenient for D to receive the sums so that it could deduct its commission before passing on the balance.

Christopher Clarke J referring to **s. 1(1)(b)** stated:

74. A contract does not purport to confer a benefit on a third party simply because the position of that third party will be improved if the contract is performed. The reference in the section to the term purporting to 'confer' a benefit seems to me to connote that the language used by the parties shows that one of the purposes of their bargain (rather than one of its incidental effects if performed) was to benefit the third party.

This can be contrasted with the Alex, Becky, and Charlie scenario where it is clear that the contract purports to confer a benefit, namely delivery of the bicycle, on Charlie. Equally, a Himalaya clause which purports to confer the protection of an exemption clause on 'servants, agents or independent contractors' is clearly intended to confer this protection on these named third parties.

Step 2: Consider the effect of s. 1(2)

There must be nothing in the contract which denies the third party a right to enforce the term or rely on it for protection. This proviso has caused some difficulties because it appears to suggest having to prove a negative. This is not necessary.

Nisshin Shipping Co. Ltd v Cleaves & Co. Ltd (2003)

FACTS: C had negotiated charter contracts on behalf of the owners of the vessels (N) and each contract had provided for the payment of commission to C, although the contracts were made between N and the individual charterers. C sought the commission and argued that the 1999 Act applied. Clearly the commission clauses purported to confer a benefit on C (**s. 1(1)(b)**), but N argued that C could not show that the parties intended that the benefit of this term should be directly enforceable by C, which N argued was a requirement due to the **s. 1(2)** proviso.

HELD: This was not necessary. The test of enforceability was satisfied and C could enforce the commission clause directly.

Tip

Thus the **s. 1(2)** proviso will only operate to deny enforceability by a third party if the contracting party denying this is able to satisfy the court that the parties' contract indicates that the parties were denying any right of enforcement or protection to the third party (i.e. this burden fell on N in **Nisshin Shipping**). Where the contract says nothing at all about this (as is usual) then **s. 1(1)(b)** applies.

The primary limitation in the test of enforceability is the first part of s. 1(3)

Section 1(3) The third party must be expressly identified in the contract by name, as a member of a class or as answering a particular description but need not be in existence when the contract is entered into.

Avraamides v Colwill (2006) (CA)

FACTS: A had employed C to refurbish A's bathroom. C's performance was defective and C was therefore liable to A. However, before enforcement, C sold its business to B on terms whereby B assumed C's liabilities 'to pay in the normal course of time **any liabilities properly incurred by C as at 31 March 2003'.**

Did this mean that A, as a third party beneficiary to the contract C/B, had the ability to enforce this agreement against B?

HELD: A did not have rights of direct enforcement. Since A, as third party, was not expressly identified in the contract C/B by name, it could not be said that the effect of the agreement was to give those with rights against C the ability to enforce those rights directly against B.

Tip

This is a major limitation on the ability of the Act to give third parties enforceable rights.

✅ *Looking for extra marks?*

It is vital to stress the importance of the test of enforceability to the scope of the Act—and hence to the scope of reform. The privity doctrine remains intact unless the test of enforceability is given a liberal interpretation. The reality is that although the proviso in **s. 1(2)** has been interpreted in a way which is helpful to intended third party beneficiaries, **s. 1(3)** may not be helpful. In addition, the fact that the Act is often excluded by party agreement is telling.

It is also helpful to be able to demonstrate to the examiner that you appreciate the scope of the test of enforceability by considering whether cases involving claims to third party enforceability before the 1999 Act would be covered by this test, e.g. ***New Zealand Shipping v Satterthwaite*** (see p. 83, 'Agency').

If the third party has a direct right of enforcement, could the promisor argue against enforcement on the basis that the third party has not supplied any consideration for the promise?

Can Alex argue that even if Charlie can satisfy s. 1 of the 1999 Act and enforce the promise to deliver the bicycle, Charlie has not provided any consideration—only Becky has?

Clearly the entire reform would fail in its purpose if the third party could be prevented from enforcing the contract on the basis that he had not provided consideration. Although there is no provision in the 1999 Act relating to consideration, it must be clear from s. 1(1) that the right of a third party to enforce a contractual term cannot be defeated by an argument that the third party (Charlie) did not provide consideration to support that promise (although there must be consideration provided by the promisee (Becky) in order to make the promise enforceable).

In other words, **consideration to support Alex's promise would have to be provided (by the promisee, Becky) but need not be provided by Charlie, the third party**.

Variation and cancellation of the third party's rights

Can the original contracting parties (Alex and Becky) maintain their right to vary or cancel the contract so as to deprive the third party (Charlie) of his benefit at a later stage? Could they, for example, decide that the bicycle should instead be delivered to Becky? This would seem onerous if Charlie (the third party) has relied on the fact that he will receive this bicycle on the delivery date.

Section 2(1) of the 1999 Act provides:

Subject to the provisions of this section, where a third party has a right under section 1 to enforce a term of the contract, the parties to the contract may not, by agreement, rescind the contract, or vary it in such a way as to extinguish or alter his entitlement under that right, without his consent if –

- (a) the third party has communicated his assent to the term to the promisor (s. 2(2) explains this assent and ousts the postal rule in the case of assent by post),

- (b) the promisor is aware that the third party has relied on the term, or

- (c) the promisor can reasonably be expected to have foreseen that the third party would rely on the term and the third party has in fact relied on it.

Therefore the usual right of contracting parties to vary contract terms is maintained unless:

- (a) either the third party has communicated his assent to the term to the promisor (Charlie has informed Alex that he agrees to accept the bicycle, which is somewhat artificial) OR

- (b) the third party has relied on his rights and the promisor knows this (or ought reasonably to have foreseen it). (It might be questioned whether a promisor should always assume some form of reliance as long as there is knowledge that the third party knows it is to benefit under the terms of the promise.)

The overall effect of s. 2(1) in practical terms is to protect the third party. However, the balance is re-struck by the remainder of this section. Contracting parties are permitted to expressly opt out of this by stipulating for a different crystallization test (not reliance or acceptance) or by reserving the right to vary or cancel the third party's right irrespective of reliance or acceptance by the third party (s. 2(3) of the Act). Of course, in order to opt out the parties would need to be aware of their ability to do so (which may translate as having legal advice when drafting a contract).

Even if they were unaware of the right to opt out, there is a specific judicial discretion to vary or cancel irrespective of reliance or acceptance by the third party in certain circumstances (**s. 2(4)–(7)** of the Act).

Tip
The examiner will wish to know whether you appreciate the overall balance in terms of the parties' position and that of the third party which is achieved by **s. 2**. In practice, contracting parties are likely to have expressly reserved their cancellation rights.

Overlapping claims and the question of priority of action

Can the promisee (Becky in the scenario) sue Alex on the promise to deliver in addition to Charlie seeking to enforce this promise by means of s. 1 of the 1999 Act?

Section 4 'Section 1 does not affect any right of the promisee to enforce any term of the contract'. (Preserves the promisee's right to sue.)

Section 5 This expressly seeks to avoid double liability by explaining that where the promisee has recovered substantial damages (or agreed sum) for the third party's loss, the third party will not be entitled to a duplicate damages sum because 'the court . . . shall reduce any award to the third party to such extent as it thinks appropriate to take account of the sum recovered by the promisee'. (However, there is no provision to assist a third party in recovery of these sums from the promisee who had recovered damages on his behalf.)

Common law devices to avoid privity in the context of an intended third party beneficiary

The Act preserves the existing devices used to avoid privity in this context.

Section 7(1) Section 1 does not affect any right or remedy of a third party that exists or is available apart from this Act.

Tip
It is sufficient to focus attention on a few key examples or any answer to a question is likely to resemble a 'shopping list' of examples and this would favour description at the cost of analysis. Strong analysis is essential for a 2:1 (or 60% plus) mark.

Agency

Establishing an agency relationship is a possible means of avoiding the doctrine of privity since the true contracting party is revealed.

Who may enforce the contract?

✳✳✳✳✳✳✳✳✳✳

Practical example

If it could be shown that Becky was acting as Charlie's agent (i.e. on his behalf, and not on her own behalf) for the purposes of securing Alex's promise, then Charlie, as principal, would have a direct contract with Alex encompassing the promise to deliver (see Figure 4.3).

There are 2 contracts here:

1. the contract between Becky (agent) and Charlie (principal) which establishes Becky's authority to contract on behalf of Charlie
2. the contract for the sale of the bicycle which may appear to present privity problems—Charlie as third party. However, due to the agency Charlie is actually the other contracting party because Becky contracted for him. Becky steps out of the picture.

Figure 4.3 Agency

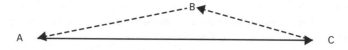

But the real difficulty in establishing the direct contract between Alex and Charlie, so that Charlie can enforce the delivery promise directly as a result of Becky's agency, will be to show that Charlie provided consideration for Alex's promise. On the facts in our practical example Charlie has provided no consideration.

✅ Looking for extra marks?

It helps to show your understanding of case law, e.g. in *Dunlop v Selfridge* (Figure 4.2) the agency argument was attempted by Dunlop, i.e. they argued that Dew & Co. was acting as agent for Dunlop (as principal) in order to obtain the contractual undertaking from Selfridge. However, Dunlop could not establish that it had provided any consideration for Selfridge's promise made to Dew & Co. in contract 2.

The agency argument has been used to enable a third party to rely on an exemption clause in a contract to which it was not a party (on the basis that its agent contracted that it should have this protection).

Practical example

Adjusting our fact scenario, Alex is to sell a bicycle to Becky (contract 1: A/B). Alex employs Charlie as carrier to deliver it (contract 2: A/C). Contract 1 contains a clause which states that neither Alex, nor any carrier he employs, will be liable beyond £100 in the event that the bicycle is damaged by Alex or the carrier and Alex is contracting as agent on behalf of any such carrier for the purposes of securing the benefit of that clause. (This is a simple 'Himalaya clause'.)

Can Charlie rely on that clause, which is clearly intended to benefit Charlie (as a carrier employed by Alex) although Charlie is not a party to the contract A/B containing it?

The courts have employed the agency argument to achieve this. Lord Reid set out the applicable criteria in *Scruttons Ltd v Midland Silicones Ltd* (1962).

(1) The main contract (contract 1 in our scenario) **must make it clear that the third party is intended to be protected by the clause in the contract between the shipper and the carrier.**

(2) The main contract must make it clear that the carrier is also acting as **agent** for the third party in contracting for the benefit of the clause.

(3) The carrier must have authority from the third party to so contract.

(4) The third party must have provided consideration for the main contract promise of protection.

The first requirement makes it clear that only a third party who was expressed to be an intended beneficiary of the clause can use this agency argument.

New Zealand Shipping Co. Ltd v A. M. Satterthwaite & Co. Ltd, The Eurymedon (1975)

(See earlier discussion in Chapter 3, p. 59, 'Consideration' for the full facts and note the use of the ship's name to abbreviate this case name.)

Figure 4.4 *The Eurymedon*

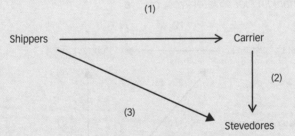

The Privy Council recognized contract 3 between the shippers and the stevedores based on the shippers' promise of exemption made to the stevedores, via the carriers as agents for the stevedores. (The carriers and stevedores were companies in the same group so that the agency contract was established.) The stevedores could enforce this promise of exemption because they had provided consideration by unloading the goods.

Who may enforce the contract?
✱✱✱✱✱✱✱✱✱✱✱

Would the s. 1 test of enforceability under the 1999 Act now enable the stevedores in *The Eurymedon* to rely directly on the Himalaya clause?

The stevedores are expressly mentioned in the contract as the intended beneficiaries of the clause (i.e. they fall within a class which is expressly mentioned—namely 'independent contractors' of the carrier). The clause purports to confer a benefit on the stevedores (s. 1(1)(b)) and there is nothing in the contract to indicate that the parties did not intend the stevedores to be able to enforce the benefit of that protection (s. 1(2) proviso).

Exactly the same analysis can be applied to the Alex/Becky/Charlie scenario in order to enable Charlie to rely on the protection in the limitation clause.

By comparison, the protection clause in the Canadian case of ***London Drugs Ltd v Kuehne and Nagel International Ltd*** (1993) was expressly stated to apply to the 'warehouseman' and was only impliedly extended to other employees. This would be insufficient in English law since it fails to satisfy Lord Reid's first requirement in *Scruttons*, **that the main contract must expressly extend the protection of the clause to the third party beneficiary and also fails to satisfy s. 1(3).**

Collateral contracts

The collateral contract **avoids privity** by finding a separate collateral contract between the third party and the promisor relating to the contractual obligation. This is also the effect of the unilateral contract analysis in *The Eurymedon*, i.e.:

- contract between shipper and carrier containing the exemption clause
- collateral contract (shipper and stevedores—offer by shipper as to the benefit of the exemption. This offer is accepted by stevedore's act of unloading).

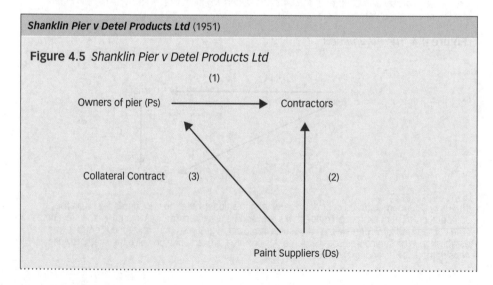

Shanklin Pier v Detel Products Ltd (1951)

Figure 4.5 *Shanklin Pier v Detel Products Ltd*

---

(1) Contract whereby the Ps (owners of pier) employ the contractors to paint the pier and have the right to specify the paint to be used.

(2) Contract between contractors and the Ds (paint suppliers) for the purchase of the paint (sale of goods contract).

(3) Collateral contract between the Ds and the Ps based on the statement made by the Ds to the Ps that the Ds' paint was suitable for painting the pier and that two coats would last seven years. The consideration for this contract was the instruction leading to the making of contract (2).

Trust of contractual obligations

It may be possible to argue that a contracting party holds the benefit of a contractual promise on trust for a third party (*Les Affréteurs Réunis SA v Leopold Walford (London) Ltd* (1919)). This would, for example, involve arguing that Becky held the benefit of the delivery promise on trust for Charlie. If a trust existed then Becky may sue Alex as trustee for Charlie. However, there is no evidence to support the creation of such a trust since there must be an express intention to create a trust of the promise (*Re Schebsman* (1944): a trust will not be implied simply because there is a contract to benefit a third party). The promisor would need to be aware of the trust at the time of contracting.

The court recognized such an express trust of a promise in *Nisshin Shipping Co. Ltd v Cleaves & Co. Ltd* (2003), i.e. the ship-owners promised the charter that they would pay the broker a commission but then refused to pay this. The broker's action was treated as if the charterers (as trustees for the brokers) had been added as claimants and so could enforce the clause against the ship-owners. The judge also confirmed that it did not follow from the recognition of a trust that there could therefore be no reliance on the direct enforceability rights contained in the 1999 Act.

Remedies available to the contracting party in respect of wrongs done to a third party (promisee remedies)

Tip

The Law Commission's Report recommended that the question of reform of the remedies available to a promisee (e.g. damages recovered by the promisee for the loss suffered by a third party) should be left to the courts. It follows that this is an area of interest and can feature in essay, and even in problem, questions.

Practical example

Alex has promised Becky that he will deliver the bicycle to Charlie. Could Becky bring an action against Alex in the event of non-delivery? Could she enforce the delivery obligation or recover damages for its breach on Charlie's behalf?

Who may enforce the contract?

✱✱✱✱✱✱✱✱✱✱

Of course, the real issue here is why she would wish to do this. She would have more incentive if she also benefitted from the promise which Alex has failed to perform, e.g. if Becky was to receive Alex's bicycle helmet and Charlie was to receive the bicycle.

Specific performance may be available in limited circumstances

An award of **specific performance** is an order of the court which compels the promisor to carry out their promise and the third party therefore gets the intended benefit under the contract resulting from this ordered performance. However, as we can see in Chapter 7, specific performance is a discretionary remedy and will only be awarded where damages would not be an adequate remedy. It also has no application to instances of defective performance, as opposed to the Alex example where there is a failure to perform the contractual obligation.

> ### *Beswick v Beswick* (1968) **(HL)**
>
> **FACTS:** A nephew had acquired his uncle's coal business and in exchange had promised his uncle that he would pay a £5 a week annuity to the uncle's widow on the uncle's death.
>   The nephew failed to pay the widow and she brought an action seeking enforcement in two capacities: (i) in her personal capacity and (ii) as administratrix of her late husband's estate. She faced the privity problem when suing in her personal capacity since she was not a party to the contract containing the nephew's promise, although she was the intended beneficiary of that promise.
>
> **HELD:** The HL allowed specific performance in the widow's capacity of administratrix of her husband's estate—so ordering the nephew to perform his promise. This did not present a privity issue since the husband was a party to the agreement with his nephew and the HL held that it was an appropriate remedy because damages would be an inadequate remedy for her husband's estate. The estate had suffered no substantive loss due to the breach of this promise. On the facts, the only way to ensure that there would be an effective remedy for the nephew's breach was to order specific performance.

Promisee may be able to recover substantial damages in respect of loss suffered by the third party

Generally it will not be possible for the promisee to recover substantial damages for the loss suffered by a third party because a party is limited to recovering for losses it has suffered and the promisee's loss may be purely nominal, e.g. Becky's loss if Alex's only promise relates to delivering the bicycle to Charlie will be purely nominal.

There are, however, two clearly recognized exceptions where substantial damages for a third party's loss can be recovered:

Exception 1

Where, for reasons of convenience, a contract is made by one person (party) for the benefit of a group of people, that person can recover substantial damages for the losses suffered by members of that group (e.g. holidays, meals in restaurants—see Lord Wilberforce in *Woodar v Wimpey*).

Lord Denning had attempted a broader recovery in *Jackson v Horizon Holidays Ltd* (1975). The case concerned a family holiday booked by a husband on behalf of his wife and children where the holiday failed to meet contractual promises. The husband was able to recover for his own loss and that of his wife and family, although they were not parties to the contract, simply on the basis that the contract was made for their benefit. The HL in *Woodar Investment Development Ltd v Wimpey Construction UK Ltd* considered that such a broad principle was unsupported by authority and limited recovery to **'party convenience'** contracts.

Woodar Investment Development Ltd v Wimpey Construction UK Ltd (1980) **(HL)**

FACTS: Wimpey had contracted to purchase development land from Woodar. The purchase price was £850,000, and £150,000 of this was payable to a third party. The property market fell and it was argued that Wimpey had wrongfully repudiated the contract.

HELD: There had been no breach of contract (so there was no need to decide whether Woodar could recover for the third party's loss in addition to its own). Nevertheless, the HL held that there was no general principle permitting substantial recovery in such circumstances. Lord Wilberforce recognized the contracts 'calling for special treatment', i.e. 'party convenience' contracts, where substantial damages could be recovered.

Tip
Even in 'party convenience' cases it may be necessary for the contracting party (promisee) to have suffered loss before he can also recover for third party loss. Both Mr Jackson and Woodar had also suffered loss as a result of the breach.

Exception 2

The *St Martins Property* exception ('black hole' problems): the narrow-ground principle in *Linden Gardens Trust Ltd v Lenesta Sludge Disposals Ltd* (1994) (the St Martin's appeal—*St Martins Property Corp. Ltd v Sir Robert McAlpine & Sons Ltd*) allows for recovery of substantial damages suffered by another by a party who has not suffered any loss.

The factual scenario is not uncommon in the context of property development and the solution avoids the 'black hole' problem.

A is a land-owning developer who has contracted with B (building contractor) for B to carry out work on the property. A sells the building (so transfers property rights) to C so that C is the person suffering loss in the event that B defectively performs the building contract (see Figure 4.6). However, A is not successful in its attempt to transfer the benefit of the building contract to C (or there is a prohibition on assignment/transfer) which would have transferred the contractual rights enabling C to sue B in his own right.

Who may enforce the contract?

✳✳✳✳✳✳✳✳✳✳

Figure 4.6 'Black hole' problems

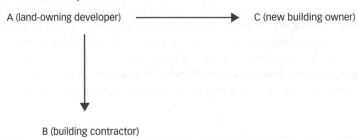

C, as the new building owner, is the person who suffers the loss resulting from defective performance of the building contract by B.

The *St Martin's Property* exception means that A nevertheless retains its right to sue B in respect of the defective performance of the building contract and can recover substantial damages despite not having personally suffered a financial loss as a result of the breach. (Originally this exception was considered to rest on the fact that B would contemplate that A might transfer the property to another so that the other, and not A, would suffer loss in the event of B's breach of that contract. However, it has subsequently been held to arise by operation of law rather than party contemplation.)

Limitation

It follows that where **the new building owner or person suffering loss has a direct right of action against the contractor**, the original developer/contracting party cannot rely on the narrow ground to argue that it can also recover substantial damages. It is instead limited to recovering nominal loss.

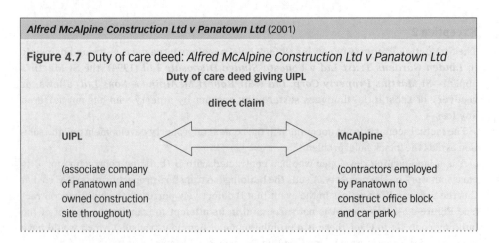

Alfred McAlpine Construction Ltd v Panatown Ltd (2001)

Figure 4.7 Duty of care deed: *Alfred McAlpine Construction Ltd v Panatown Ltd*

Duty of care deed giving UIPL

direct claim

UIPL

(associate company of Panatown and owned construction site throughout)

McAlpine

(contractors employed by Panatown to construct office block and car park)

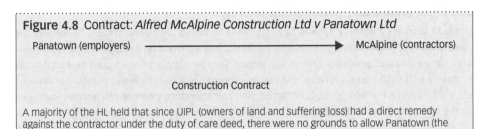

Figure 4.8 Contract: *Alfred McAlpine Construction Ltd v Panatown Ltd*

Panatown (employers) ⟶ McAlpine (contractors)

Construction Contract

A majority of the HL held that since UIPL (owners of land and suffering loss) had a direct remedy against the contractor under the duty of care deed, there were no grounds to allow Panatown (the employer) anything more than nominal damages.

The narrow ground (the *St Martin's Property* exception) was applied by the CA in *Darlington Borough Council v Wiltshier Northern Ltd* to a situation where the contractual rights had been assigned. However, an assignee (the person to whom the contractual rights have been transferred) cannot acquire greater rights than those possessed by the transferor. It was therefore essential to establish that the transferor building owner could recover substantial damages in the event of the contractor's breach.

Darlington Borough Council v Wiltshier Northern Ltd (1995) **(CA)**

Figure 4.9 *Darlington Borough Council v Wiltshier Northern Ltd*

Morgan Grenfell ⟶ Council

⟱

Wiltshier (contractor)

FACTS: The Council owned land on which it wished to construct a leisure centre. However, the Council was unable to enter into a construction contract at this time due to restrictions on such local authority expenditure. MG was engaged to enter into the construction contract. The contractor was fully aware that the centre was for the Council and was being built on Council land and the contractual rights were assigned (transferred) from MG to the Council. The Council sought to bring a claim against the contractor for defective work but needed to establish that MG could have recovered substantial losses despite not owning the land and therefore could transfer that right to the Council via assignment.

HELD: applying the **St Martin's Property** exception and concluding that the assignor (MG) had the right to recover substantial damages (which it had validly assigned). It was clearly contemplated by the contractor that the centre was being constructed for the Council on Council land.

Who may enforce the contract?

✱✱✱✱✱✱✱✱✱✱✱

The broad ground and 'performance interest'

In the *St Martin's Property Appeal* Lord Griffiths had used the 'broad ground' to support his conclusion that the landowner/developer could recover substantial damages in this scenario. The 'broad ground' provides that in a contract for the supply of work and materials, the promisee will suffer a loss (even if she has no property interest) because she did not receive the performance for which she contracted. She can therefore recover substantial damages on the basis of her own loss of bargain.

Example

Suppose I contract with a kitchen company to supply and install a kitchen in my daughter's home as a special gift. My daughter is not a party to that contract but she owns the property in which the kitchen is being fitted and, in the event that either the installation or the kitchen is defective, my daughter will suffer loss. I can sue for breach of contract but my loss seems purely nominal. The broad ground, on the other hand, recognizes that if the kitchen or workmanship is defective then I have not received what I bargained for and should be able to recover for the loss incurred (irrespective of ownership rights) simply on the basis of failure to fulfil my interest in performance.

There is some support for this ground from the dissenting members of the HL (Lords Goff and Millett) in *Alfred McAlpine Construction Ltd v Panatown Ltd*. However, this ground has such far-reaching implications for contractual damages that the academic debate is continuing (see p. 94, 'Key debates').

Template problem question

In April 2013 Carlton International plc, a property developer, entered into a contract with Ace Construction Ltd for the construction of an office complex on a site owned by Carlton International. The contractual completion date was 1 September 2014 and the contract also contained a clause prohibiting assignment without the express approval of Ace Construction Ltd.

In addition, clause 4.1 of the contract stated that the liability of Ace Construction Ltd, as main contractor, for loss or damage attributable to defects or delay was limited to £300,000 and the clause also stated that this protection extended to 'servants or agents of Ace Construction Ltd and every independent contractor from time to time employed by Ace Construction Ltd acting in the course of, or in connection with, his employment or contractual obligations'.

Clause 4.2 stated that, for the purposes of clause 4.1, Ace Construction was deemed to be acting as agent on behalf of and for the benefit of all such persons mentioned in clause 4.1 as being entitled to the protection of the limitation of liability.

In October 2013 Ace Construction Ltd employed Blitz Plumbing to undertake all plumbing work for the main construction contract. This work was to be completed by August 2014.

Blitz Plumbing had arranged for their plumbing materials for performance of this contract to be stored in a warehouse owned and operated by Easi-Store Ltd. The contract for storage contained a limitation clause limiting the liability of the company's 'warehouse staff' to £150. Fred, a clerical assistant, damaged sensitive plumbing valves whilst he was completing an inventory of the storage warehouse. Fred claims that he is protected by the limitation clause in the contract between Blitz Plumbing and Easi-Store.

Blitz Plumbing was unable to acquire replacement valves of the same quality and therefore used another type of valve in the plumbing for the office complex. The valve was defective and caused a flood.

Blitz Plumbing also delayed completion of the plumbing works, which had knock-on effects for other subcontractors and meant that Ace Construction Ltd was unable to formally complete the works until March 2015.

Carlton International Ltd wishes to claim £2m from Ace Construction Ltd in respect of the delay and £800,000 from Blitz Plumbing in respect of the defective plumbing.

Advise all of the parties.

Some general pointers: this part of the question concerns the limitation of liability clause, its enforceability (see Chapter 6) and whether the plumbing subcontractor (B), which is not a party to the contract (C/A) containing the limitation, can rely on the clause.

- First, it is necessary to consider the enforceability of the clause in general terms. Consider incorporation, construction (especially construction of limitation clauses as opposed to total exclusion clauses), and the application of the **Unfair Contract Terms Act (UCTA)** (breaches of delay and defective goods in a work and materials contract— **ss. 3 and s.7(3) UCTA 1977**) to a limitation clause in a commercial contract. **(Note that this contract predates the CRA 2015 but see s.7(1A) UCTA 1977 for contracts after the CRA 2015 is in force.)

- In relation to whether the plumbing subcontractor (B) can rely on the clause, the question is whether the **s. 1** test of enforceability in the **Contracts (Rights of Third Parties) Act 1999** is satisfied. B is identified as a member of the named class of independent contractors who are intended to be protected by the clause.

- Easi-Store and Fred—can Fred rely on clause in contract to which not a party? He is outside the **s. 1** test of enforceability as not covered by wording of protection (similarities with *London Drugs* and also same problem as in *Scruttons*).

Could Carlton International plc succeed in its claim if, in July 2013, Carlton International plc had sold the office complex and site to Devenport Developments plc, without obtaining the necessary approval from Ace Construction Ltd for the assignment of the contractual rights under the construction contract?

Carlton International plc appears to suffer no loss because it does not own the property at relevant time.

- Loss is suffered by Devenport Developments plc but, because of the prohibition on assignment, Devenport Developments is not a party to the contract and cannot sue to enforce that contract.

- It is also outside **s. 1** test of enforceability in 1999 Act as not in existence at time of construction contract C/A.

- Can Carlton International obtain remedy for Devenport Developments? Discussion of *St Martin's Property* exception (*Darlington, McAlpine v Panatown*)—narrow ground—but also mention possibilities if the broad ground of Lord Griffiths in *St Martin's Appeal* is accepted and applied.

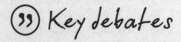 **Key debates**

Since this topic is more likely to feature as an essay than as a problem, these debates have already been touched upon but further reading is suggested below.

1. The need for reform

The arguments are rehearsed in the Law Commission's 1996 Report and the judicial dissatisfaction can be seen in the speeches of members of the HL in e.g. *Beswick v Beswick* and *Woodar v Wimpey*, and Steyn LJ in *Darlington BC v Wiltshier Northern*. However, in defence of privity see Kincaid, 'Third Parties: Rationalising a Right to Sue' [1989] CLJ 243 and Smith 'Contracts for the Benefit of Third Parties: In Defence of the Third Party Rule' (1997) 17 OJLS 643.

2. Detailed critique of the Act, its provisions and scope, and the fact that it does not 'abolish' privity

Burrows, 'The Contracts (Rights of Third Parties') Act 1999 and its Implications for Commercial Contracts' [2000] LMCLQ 540.

Andrews, 'Strangers to Justice No Longer: The Reversal of the Privity Rule under the Contracts (Rights of Third Parties) Act 1999' [2001] CLJ 353.

Beale, 'A Review of the [1999 Act]' in Burrows and Peel (eds.), *Contract Formation and Parties* (Oxford University Press, 2010).

3. The broad ground/performance-interest debate

Coote, 'The Performance Interest: *Panatown* and the Problem of Loss' (2001) 117 LQR 81.

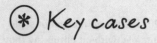 **Key cases**

Case	Facts	Principle
Tweddle v Atkinson	Groom was named intended beneficiary of promise made in contract between groom's father and bride's father. Held the groom could not enforce the bride's father's promise.	Privity meant that the groom was not party to that contract and he had not provided any consideration to support the promise.

Case	Facts	Principle
***Dunlop Pneumatic Tyre Co. Ltd v Selfridge & Co. Ltd* (HL)**	Dunlop sold tyres to Dew & Co. and Dew & Co. promised (in return for a discount) not to sell the tyres at less than list price and to obtain a similar undertaking from trade buyers. Dew & Co. sold some tyres to Selfridge (contract 2) and Selfridge promised Dew & Co. to abide by the list price but broke it. Dunlop sued Selfridge for breach of its undertaking but failed because it was not a party to contract 2 containing Selfridge's promise.	Privity means that only a party to a contract can enforce its promises. Dunlop had also not provided any consideration to support Selfridge's promise (so an argument that Dew & Co. were acting as its agents also failed).
Nisshin Shipping Co. Ltd v Cleaves & Co. Ltd	Contracts between owners and charterers contained commission clause providing for payment to named broker. 1999 Act applied and clause purported to confer a benefit on broker so the broker could enforce it directly.	**s. 1(2)** proviso to **s. 1(1)(b)** of 1999 Act will only operate to deny enforceability by a third party if the contracting party denying this is able to satisfy the court that the parties' contract indicates that the parties were denying any right of enforcement or protection to the third party. The third party does not need to prove a negative.
***New Zealand Shipping Co. Ltd v A. M. Satterthwaite & Co. Ltd, The Eurymedon* (PC)**	Stevedores could rely on exemption clause in contract between ship-owners and carriers since carriers contracted as their agents for that clause and contract was clear that they were intended to be protected and they had provided consideration for the ship-owners exemption promise by unloading the goods (performance of contractual duty owed to third party).	Agency device to establish a binding promise of exemption between a contracting party and third party to the clause.
***Beswick v Beswick* (HL)**	Nephew had promised uncle that he would pay weekly sum to uncle's widow on uncle's death. The widow could not enforce this because of privity but acting as her late husband's representative she could. Since the estate had not suffered loss and could not recover substantial damages, specific performance was awarded.	Promisee remedies and the difficulties of the promisee seeking to enforce a promise in favour of a third party beneficiary. Specific performance was available because the promisee could not recover substantial damages if it had no loss.

Key cases

✳✳✳✳✳✳✳✳✳✳✳ ✳

Case	Facts	Principle
Alfred McAlpine Construction Ltd v Panatown Ltd (HL)	McAlpine had been employed by Panatown to construct an office building on land belonging to UIPL, an associate company of Panatown. Defects arose with the building and Panatown sought damages. McAlpine claimed that Panatown had suffered no loss as a result of its breaches of contract because Panatown neither owned the land nor occupied the building. HL refused the recovery but the decision was based on the fact that McAlpine had entered into a separate duty of care deed directly with UIPL, giving UIPL remedies for defective work and that deed had to prevail.	HL held that normally (absent the duty of care deed) the narrow ground in the **St Martin's Property Appeal** would have enabled a party in the position of Panatown to recover substantial damages. Where a contract between a builder and an employer was for the construction of a building on the land of a third party who would own that building, the employer could seek substantial damages from the builder for defects where the third party had no direct remedy against that builder.

#5
Terms and breach of contract

- A **term** is a statement, pre-contractual and/or included in a written contract, constituting a contractual promise. If the term/promise is broken it amounts to a **breach** of contract, giving rise to remedies for breach of contract (Chapter 7). Terms need to be incorporated as such into the contract (e.g. written terms on a coach ticket purchased from the booking office; see discussion in Chapter 6).

- On the other hand, some pre-contractual statements are not terms but are merely **representations**. Representations are statements which induce the contract but do not involve any binding promise. If a representation turns out to be false, there will be legal remedies in misrepresentation (Chapter 9) which are not the same as remedies for breach of contract. In the consumer context, consumers are given certain 'rights to redress' for misleading actions under the **Consumer Protection from Unfair Trading Regulations 2008 (CPRs 2008)** and these may replace the remedies otherwise available such as the ability to recover damages for misrepresentation under other legislation.

- The terms of the contract, whether the contract is written, oral, or both oral and written, will consist of those promises expressly undertaken or agreed to by the parties. However, the terms may also consist of implied terms which the parties do not mention expressly but which are nevertheless implied into the contract. These terms are implied (i) by statute (e.g. in contracts for the sale of goods or supply of goods and services, including those with digital content in the consumer context), (ii) because the courts consider the term should be implied, or (iii) as a result of custom or trade usage. (The statutory implied terms are referred to as 'statutory rights' in the consumer context because they cannot be excluded or restricted (**Consumer Rights Act 2015 (CRA 2015)**; see also Chapter 6).)

Key facts
****

- A breach of contract will occur where, without lawful excuse (e.g. **frustration**; see Chapter 8), a party either fails or refuses to perform a performance obligation imposed upon it under the terms of the contract or performs that obligation defectively, in the sense of failing to meet the required standard of performance.

- Every breach of contract will give rise to a right to claim **damages**. However, unless the breach constitutes a **repudiatory breach**, the contract will remain in force. If the breach is repudiatory the non-breaching party will have the option either to accept the breach as terminating the contract (in which case both parties' future obligations will be discharged) or to affirm the contract (in which event the contract remains in force for both parties).

- Breaches of certain statutory rights (relating to goods and services) in the consumer context under the **CRA 2015** give rise to a special extended range of remedies which are not limited to the right to reject, e.g. right to repair or replacement of non-conforming goods or digital content, right to a price reduction, refunds, and right to repeat performance of a defective service. These rights are set out in the **CRA 2015**.

- Breaches of certain types of terms (**conditions**) are, in the main, repudiatory breaches and breaches of **innominate terms** will be repudiatory breaches if the effects of the breach are serious. However, the process of identifying conditions and innominate terms is uncertain and there are risks for the non-breaching party in deciding to treat a breach as repudiatory as this may constitute wrongful repudiation.

- The repudiatory breach may be an **anticipatory breach**, i.e. breach occurs before the time for performance because, for example, one party indicates that they will not be performing. The innocent party has the usual election to **terminate**, in which event they need not wait until the date for performance before claiming damages, or **affirm**. There are risks in affirming but it may be possible to continue with performance and claim the contract price.

Introduction

This chapter examines how we identify the contractual obligations assumed by the parties in their contract, distinguishing terms (promises) and representations (non-promissory inducements to contract) and identifying both express and implied terms. It also looks at how we identify broken promises as a prelude to considering the remedies for breach of contract and whether it is possible to opt not to continue to perform further contractual obligations following the other party's breach.

Think like an examiner

There are a number of possible questions that an examiner can ask and this topic can be divided into a number of sub-areas of law, any one of which could feature as the focus of a question. However, central to this broader topic is a knowledge of the distinction between terms and representations, not least because knowledge of this is required to answer problem questions concerning misrepresentations (see Chapter 9), implied terms, and identification and the consequences of repudiatory breach (since these matters are important for future studies in commercial law). Problem questions may combine identification of terms (including implied) and the basic remedies for breach of those terms—plus the possible inclusion of remedies in the event of anticipatory repudiatory breach. It is more likely, since the **CRA 2015** and given time constraints, that examiners will focus problem questions in Contract law on commercial scenarios leaving the detail of the consumer provisions for subsequent modules.

Essay questions are more likely to focus on the circumstances in which the courts will imply terms (and this relationship with contractual construction) or a critique of the circumstances justifying the option to terminate or affirm for breach.

Terms

Practical example

During negotiations between Alex and Becky for the purchase of Alex's bicycle shop, Alex states that there are 55 bicycles in stock which are to be included in the sale contract. He adds that Becky need not count them as he guarantees that the number is correct. Becky states that she is not interested in purchasing the shop business unless the annual turnover is at least £75,000 per annum and Alex assures her that it has been in excess of that figure for each of the preceding three years. She asks if she can live in the premises above the shop and Alex tells her that that will not be a problem. In fact the written purchase contract, which they complete a month later, contains a provision limiting the use of the premises above the shop to a stockroom and expressly prohibiting their use for residential purposes. In addition, although it was not discussed and there is no provision in the contract to this effect, Becky assumed that the premises came with a parking space.

Terms

Becky has now discovered that there are only 35 bicycles in stock, the turnover has been no more than £55,000 per annum in the preceding three years, she cannot live in the premises above the shop, and there is no parking space.

Topic 1: Has a statement made in the pre-contractual negotiations become a term of the contract?

This involves distinguishing statements which constitute binding promises (terms) from representations (inducements to contract). (There is a third type of pre-contractual statement—the mere puff—but this is an advertising statement which is not intended to have any legal consequences.)

Why make this distinction at all?

Binding promises and representations which are broken or false give rise to legal remedies but they are very different remedies. The differences are highlighted in Table 5.1.

Table 5.1 The significance of the distinction between terms and representations in the context of commercial contracts

Statement	If broken/false?	Right to claim damages	Basic aim of damages	Remoteness (recovery for losses)
Term—binding promise as to truth.	Remedies for breach of contract: damages election to terminate or affirm if repudiatory breach.	Right to claim damages for breach on proof of breach.	Contractual damages seek to put the claimant in the position the claimant would have been in had the contract been properly performed (shoots forwards to compensate for lost expectation—discussed in Chapter 7).	Recovery of all losses which were within the parties' reasonable contemplations at time they made the contract as likely to be incurred in event of breach.
Representation—false statement inducing making of contract.	Remedies for misrepresentation: **rescission** (avoid contract) damages for misrepresentation.	Damages can only be claimed if the statement maker was fraudulent or negligent.	Damages for misrepresentation seek to restore the claimant to the position they were in before the misrepresentation was made (restores the status quo through the recovery of wasted expenditure).	Remoteness is likely to allow recovery of all direct losses regardless of foreseeability (fraud and **s. 2(1) Misrepresentation Act 1967**).

Therefore the right to claim damages and the measure of those damages (including recovery of consequential losses) will be quite different in a claim for breach of contract (term) and misrepresentation. Prior to the mid 1960s, and recognition of the ability to recover damages for negligent misstatements, this distinction was vital since damages could be recovered only if the untrue statement was either a term or the statement maker made the statement fraudulently (and fraud is difficult to establish). This position led to statements being interpreted as terms despite the fact that they did not appear to be binding promises of their truth.

How to distinguish a term and a representation?

Was it the intention that the statement maker was making a BINDING PROMISE as to the truth of his statement? If yes, the statement is a term. If no, it is a representation inducing the contract rather than a binding promise that it is true. The courts have developed guidelines to assist in making the distinction (see Table 5.2).

Tip

The law in this area is complicated by the fact that there are two types of promises that can be recognized as terms:

1. **a promise that guarantees a result**, e.g. A promises to pay B or A promises to deliver goods to B.
2. **a promise that reasonable care and skill has been, or will be, exercised.** This type of promise does not involve a guarantee of result and was utilized, prior to mid/late 1960s, to avoid the non-availability of damages for non-fraudulent misrepresentation. The courts found that the statement maker had made a promise to exercise reasonable care and skill. If reasonable care and skill has not been exercised, that promise will be broken and damages for breach of promise can be awarded despite the fact that there is no guarantee of result being made by that statement maker. (These promises are known as collateral warranties.)

Guidelines

Table 5.2 Making the distinction between terms and representations

Term			
	Accepting responsibility for the truth of statement (guaranteeing it is true)—it is likely to be a term, *Schawel v Reade* (1913): no need to carry out inspection of horse.	*Importance attached test.* The person to whom the statement was made: • considered the statement to be so important that he would not otherwise have contracted **AND** • he made that importance clear to the statement maker prior to that statement being made.	**Statement made by person with special knowledge of subject matter (professional or expert).** Such statements are 'collateral warranties'—**promise that the 'expert forecast' was made with reasonable care and skill rather than a promise that the forecast was correct.** (It will only be broken if there was no reasonable care and skill exercised).

Terms

****

		Bannerman v White (1861): would not purchase if hops treated with sulphur. Told they had not been.	*Dick Bentley Productions Ltd v Harold Smith (Motors) Ltd* (1965): statement by car dealers as to a car's mileage; *Esso Petroleum Co. Ltd v Mardon* (1976): statement by expert as to likely throughput of petrol station.
Representation	**Written contract makes no mention of earlier oral statement.** The assumption is that it was not intended to be included, i.e. not intended to be a term of the contract. However, it is possible to rebut this using the other guidelines, e.g. statement made by an expert during negotiations.	**Asking the other party to check the reliability of the statement or to verify it,** *Ecay v Godfrey* (1947): suggesting purchaser has independent survey.	**Statement maker has no special knowledge of the subject matter but relies on (incorrect) official document,** *Oscar Chess Ltd v Williams* (1957): sale of car *to* motor dealers. Statement that was 1948 model (relying on registration book). In fact it was 1939 model. Not a term so no remedy in damages at this time.

Practical example

Is there a claim for breach of contract (breach of one or more terms)?

(a) 55 bicycles in stock and Alex takes responsibility for the truth of this statement by telling Becky that she need not count them as he guarantees the number is correct (*Schawel v Reade*): a term—a binding promise that the statement is true. It is false so this is a breach.

(b) Importance attached test applies to Alex's statement about the turnover of the business since Becky had made the importance of this statement clear to Alex before he made it (*Bannerman v White*). This statement as to turnover is also a term so that there is a claim for breach of contract.

We will return to the other statements shortly.

Topic 2: Can we look outside the writing for terms of the contract?

What is the position if it is alleged that there is a contradictory oral statement made during negotiations?

Practical example

During the negotiations Becky asked if she could live in the premises above the shop and Alex told her that would not be a problem. This contradicts the terms of the written purchase contract. The writing provides that the premises above the shop are to be used as a stockroom and expressly prohibits their use for residential purposes. Becky says she would not have signed that written contract but for the earlier oral statement. However, is that statement (i) a term and (ii) can it override the terms of the written contract?

Definition

The **parol evidence rule** states that **if the contract is written** then the writing will constitute the whole contract and the parties cannot adduce extrinsic evidence to add to, vary, or contradict that writing.

However, it is relatively straightforward to avoid this 'rule' since it does not apply to exclude the implication of terms and, in the absence of **an entire agreement clause**, it does not apply if oral terms also exist since the contract is not then a 'written' contract. (The 'rule' is circular.)

If there is an oral statement and, on the importance attached test, it is classified as a term, then this 'term' may override inconsistent terms of the written contract

> **Couchman v Hill** (1947)
>
> An oral statement that the heifer was 'unserved' overrode a written exemption clause in the auctioneer's catalogue stating that the auctioneer was not responsible for any description of a lot.

> **City and Westminster Properties (1934) Ltd v Mudd** (1959)
>
> **FACTS:** The written new lease of a lock-up shop which the tenant was asked to sign contained a prohibition on using the premises 'for lodging, dwelling or sleeping'. The tenant was told that if he signed the lease then no objection would be made if he continued to live in the shop. He signed. The landlord later claimed that the tenant was in breach of covenant by living in the shop.
>
> **HELD:** The tenant had only signed the lease because of the oral promise and this term overrode the prohibition in the lease.

Practical example

The facts of *City & Westminster* bear a strong resemblance to the facts in the practical example concerning the contradictory oral promise that Becky could live in the premises above the shop. It follows that, in the absence of an entire agreement clause in the contract between Alex and Becky, the oral promise is a term of the contract and overrides the contradictory written prohibition.

Terms

✱✱✱✱✱✱✱✱✱✱✱

J. Evans & Son (Portsmouth) Ltd v Andrea Merzario Ltd (1976) **(CA)**

FACTS: An oral assurance was given that containers would be shipped below deck. However, the written contract gave the carriers freedom to decide the method of transportation and exempted them from loss or damage to the goods.

HELD: The oral assurance overrode the written terms. The majority considered that this was because the oral assurance was a term of the contract which was partly written and partly oral. This oral term overrode the printed conditions. The minority judge, Lord Denning MR, considered that there were two contracts, a written contract to which the parol evidence rule applied, and an oral collateral contract which prevailed. See also the collateral contract as a device to avoid **privity** issues: **Shanklin Pier v Detel Products Ltd** (1951) (Chapter 4).

Entire agreement clauses

In practice, the majority of contracts will contain an entire agreement clause. This states that all the terms of the parties' agreement are contained in the written document and there are no other terms. This prevents a party from alleging that there are separate oral terms or an oral or written collateral contract: **Inntrepreneur Pub Co. v East Crown Ltd** (2000).

Topic 3: Are there any implied terms?

Terms are implied by:

- **statute**—into contracts of certain types, often irrespective of the wishes of the parties
- **custom or as a result of trade usage/business practice**
- **the courts**—either into all contracts of a particular type on the basis that the term is a necessary incident of that type of contract, or into the particular contract as a matter of construction to give efficacy to the contract and reflect the parties' assumed intentions (as understood by the reasonable person).

Statutory implied terms

Certain terms are implied, irrespective of the wishes of the parties into contracts of specific types in order to provide protection which the law considers necessary. In contract law you are most likely to encounter the types of contract in Table 5.3 which have statutory implied terms:

Table 5.3 Types of sale and supply contracts

Type of contract	Description	Example
Contract for the sale of goods (B2B)	**s. 2(1) Sale of Goods Act 1979 (SGA 1979)**: a contract of sale of goods is a contract by which the seller transfers or agrees to transfer the property in goods to the buyer for a money **consideration**, called the price.	Purchase stationery for a business (B2B).

Sales contract (B2C)	**S. 5 Consumer Rights Act 2015 (CRA 2015)** : a contract whereby the trader transfers or agrees to transfer ownership of goods to the consumer and the consumer pays or agrees to pay the price.	Purchase of a newspaper, bottle of milk, a new sofa (B2C).
Contract for supply of services in B2B	**s. 12 Supply of Goods and Services Act 1982 (SGSA 1982)**: this is a commercial contract under which the supplier agrees to carry out a service.	Provide legal services, accountancy services.
Contract to supply a service in B2C	**s. 48 Consumer Rights Act 2015 (CRA 2015);** this is a consumer contract by which a trader supplies a service to a consumer.	Providing window cleaning or gardening service.
Mixed contracts: services and goods (work and materials)	There are two elements to such a contract. The services or work element (see above) and the transfer of goods (materials) that is incidental to carrying out that service.	Installing central heating so that the property in the valves and radiators needs to be transferred; servicing a car involving the labour of the mechanic and the new parts (goods) which are transferred in the process.
Contract for hire of goods	**B2B—s. 6 SGSA 1982**: a contract by which one person bails (hires) or agrees to bail goods to another. Under such a contract one party acquires *possession* of the other's goods. (see also **B2C—s. 6 CRA 2015**).	Hiring equipment such as a carpet cleaner or a specialist drill.

Where it applies, the **CRA 2015** refers to all consumer contracts involving sales, hire and transfer of goods as 'contracts to supply goods' (**s. 3(4) CRA 2015**).

Focusing on goods contracts and service contracts, there are implied terms as set out in Table 5.4 and Table 5.5 (B2B) and Table 5.6 and 5.7 (B2C) imposed on the seller/supplier (B2B) or trader (B2C), which you must be familiar with:

Table 5.4 Sale of Goods Act 1979 (as amended): B2B sale of goods contract

s. 12—Title	Implied term that the seller has a right to sell the goods or will have such right (in the case of an agreement to sell) when the property is to pass.
s. 13—Sale by description	Contract for sale by description—there is an implied term that the goods will correspond with the description.
s. 14(2)—Satisfactory quality	**Where the seller sells goods in the course of a business**—there is an implied term that the goods supplied are of satisfactory quality. **Section 14(2A)**: the goods meet the standard that a reasonable person would regard as satisfactory taking account of any description, the price and all other relevant circumstances. **Section 14(2C)**: this does not cover specific defects making the goods unsatisfactory where before the contract is made these were (i) specifically drawn to buyer's attention or (ii) which ought to have been revealed on examination and the buyer carried out an examination.

Terms

****

s. 14(3)—Fitness for particular purpose	**Where the seller sells goods in the course of a business**—and the buyer expressly or by implication makes known to seller any particular purpose for which the goods are required, there is an implied term that the goods are reasonably fit for that purpose, whether or not that is a purpose for which such goods are commonly supplied, except where the circumstances show that the buyer does not rely, or that it is unreasonable for him to rely, on the skill or judgement of the seller.
s. 15—Sale by sample	Where there is a sale by sample, there is an implied term that the bulk will correspond with the sample in quality—and if the sale is by sample and description (**s. 13(2)**) the bulk must correspond with both the sample and the description.

There are similar obligations relating to the 'goods' or 'materials' for B2B contracts in both (i) mixed contracts for work and materials (**ss. 2–5 SGSA 1982**) and (ii) hire (**ss. 7–10 SGSA 1982**).

Table 5.5 Supply of Goods and Services Act 1982: B2B Contract for supply of a service

s. 13—Standard of service	**Where the supplier is acting in the course of a business**—there is an implied term that the supplier will carry out the service with **reasonable care and skill**.

Table 5.6 Consumer Rights Act 2015, Part 1 Chapter 2: B2C Contracts to supply goods statutory rights

s. 9—Satisfactory quality	**Every contract to supply goods is treated as including a term that the quality of the goods is satisfactory (s. 9(1)).**
	Section 9(2): Goods should meet the standard that a reasonable person would regard as satisfactory taking account of any description, the price and all other relevant circumstances (including any public statement by trader or producer). **Section 9(3)**: Quality includes state and condition of the goods: plus fitness for all usual purposes, appearance and finish, freedom from minor defects, safety and durability are all aspects of quality. **Section 9(4)**: it does not cover anything making the goods unsatisfactory (i) which specifically drawn to consumer's attention pre-contract or (ii) where the consumer examined the goods pre-contract, which the examination ought to have revealed.
s. 10—Fitness for particular purpose	**Where the consumer makes known to the trader (expressly or by implication) any particular purpose for which the consumer is contracting for the goods, the contract is to be treated as including a term that the goods are reasonably fit for that purpose**—whether or not that is a purpose for which such goods are usually supplied, except where the circumstances show that the consumer does not rely, or that it is unreasonable for the consumer to rely, on the skill or judgement of the trader.

s. 11—Goods to be as described	**Every contract to supply goods by description is to be treated as including a term that the goods will match the description.**
s. 13—Goods to match a sample	Where the contract is to supply goods by reference to a sample that is seen or examined by the consumer before the contract is made, that **contract includes a term that the goods will match the sample** except to the extent of any differences brought to the consumer's attention pre-contract, and that the goods will be free from any defect making their quality unsatisfactory and that would not be apparent on a reasonable examination of the sample.
s. 17—Trader's right to supply the goods	Every contract to supply goods is to be treated as including a term that the trader has the right to sell or transfer the goods at the time when ownership is to be transferred, or in the case of hire of goods the trader must have the right to transfer possession of the goods by way of hire at the beginning of the period of the hire.

Table 5.7 Consumer Rights Act 2015: B2C Contract to supply a service to a consumer

s. 49—Standard of service	**Every contract to supply a service is to be treated as including a term that the trader must perform the service with reasonable care and skill.**
s. 50—Information about trader or service	**Every contract to supply a service is to be treated as including as a term anything that is said or written to the consumer by or on behalf of the trader about the trader or the service** if it is taken into account by the consumer when deciding to enter into the contract or if it is taken into account by the consumer when making any decision after entering into the contract.

Customary implied terms

Terms may be implied on the basis of an *established* custom or usage of the relevant trade (*Hutton v Warren* (1836)), unless such a term would be inconsistent with an express term of the contract. For an example of implication based on business practice, see *British Crane Hire v Ipswich Plant Hire* (1975) (see Chapter 6).

Terms implied by the courts

Courts can imply terms in law or in fact.

Terms implied in law

Terms are implied in law as a matter of policy into all contracts of a particular type, e.g. employment contracts, as a 'necessary incident' of the type of contract.

Terms

****

Liverpool City Council v Irwin (1977) (HL)

FACTS: Tenants of a council tower block claimed that the Council landlord was in breach of an implied obligation to repair and maintain the common parts of the building, i.e. to ensure the lifts and lighting worked and that the rubbish chutes were not blocked. There was nothing stated expressly on this matter in the lease.

HELD: The nature of the contract required an implied term, but it was not a guarantee obligation only an obligation to use reasonable care to keep the common parts in reasonable repair and use. The Council was not in breach of this (qualified) implied contractual obligation.

Terms implied in fact

Terms are implied in fact into the particular contract as a 'one-off' in order to give effect to the meaning the parties would reasonably understand the contract to have (construction) and as a matter of 'necessity' to make it workable.

In *Attorney General of Belize v Belize Telecom Ltd* (2009) **Lord Hoffmann stated that sometimes a process of construction would reveal that the omission of an express term was deliberate,** and the court should accept that conclusion and let the loss lie where it falls.

Implication of terms in fact recognizes terms which are 'necessary' and therefore must already exist in order to render the contract effective and workable as the parties must have intended in accordance with the rest of its terms (*Mediterranean Salvage and Towage Ltd v Seamar Trading and Commerce Inc., The Reborn* (2009)). If the instrument is a commercial contract the process of construction would involve considering whether any other meaning would fail to give effect to the parties' business purposes and render the contract workable (e.g. as in *Equitable Life Assurance Society v Hyman* (2002) and the need to avoid frustration of the parties' reasonable expectations).

The Moorcock (1889) (CA)

FACTS: The Ds had contracted to allow the Ps to load and unload at the Ds' wharf on the River Thames. It was known to both parties that at low tide any vessel at the wharf would be grounded, but there was no express provision governing this in the contract. The Ps' ship moored at the wharf and was damaged because of the condition of the river bed.

HELD: A term had to be implied whereby the Ds warranted that they had taken reasonable care to see that the berth was safe. The Ds were in breach of this term.

Practical example

As the Alex/Becky contract says nothing about the parking space and it is not even possible to argue for an oral pre-contractual promise, there can be no express term to this effect. It follows that Becky's only argument would have to be that there was an implied term that the property came with a parking space. This is not a situation where statute implies such a term; will the courts imply it?

Should all contracts for the sale of business premises necessarily contain the provision of a parking space? If not, then the implication will not be made in law.

Should this particular contract be interpreted as involving such a promise in order to make the contract work? It is far from clear that this would have been the parties' intentions. It might have been Becky's desire but this is not the same thing. A parking space is not necessary in order to make this contract workable. There can be no implied term in fact.

Tip

Arguments based on implied terms in fact are difficult to spot precisely because there is nothing explicit. Consider the decision in *Shell UK Ltd v Lostock Garage Ltd* (1976).

Shell had subsidized two of their other tied garages in the neighbourhood, but not the D's. When sued for breaking the tie (obtaining supplies of petrol elsewhere), the D alleged that the agreement was subject to an implied obligation placed upon Shell not to discriminate abnormally against the D in favour of competing and neighbouring garages so as to render the D's petrol uneconomic.

The majority of the CA refused to imply the term on the basis that it was not necessary and Shell certainly would not have considered that it was needed to make the agreement work.

Try to use this analogy when checking your problem case facts. The other difficulty with terms implied in fact (*Shell v Lostock*) is being able to formulate the desired term with sufficient precision to render it workable, even if it appears 'necessary'.

Breach
Topic 4: Is there a breach of contract? If so, what are the consequences for the parties? Is there a repudiatory breach?

Key point

A breach of contract occurs where, without lawful excuse (e.g. frustration, Chapter 8), **a party either (i) fails or refuses to perform a performance obligation** imposed upon it under the terms of the contract **or (ii) performs that obligation defectively, in the sense of failing to meet the required standard of performance.**

To determine (ii) it is necessary to identify the nature of the performance obligation imposed. There are **two types of performance obligations in contracts** which are explained in Table 5.8.

Breach

****

Performance obligations

Table 5.8 Performance obligations: strict and qualified

Strict contractual obligation	Absolute	Breach occurs (subject only to *de minimis*—minute discrepancies) where the obligation is not completely and precisely performed in accordance with its terms.	Examples: obligation to deliver by particular date; **s. 14(2) SGA 1979**—B2B goods to be of satisfactory quality and all of the statutory rights relating to goods in the **CRA 2015, Part 1 Chapter 2**.
Qualified contractual obligation	Duty to exercise reasonable care and skill	Breach occurs only where reasonable care and skill is not exercised.	Examples: contract for surgery; **s. 13 SGSA 1982 and s. 49 CRA 2015**—performance of a service; *Liverpool City Council v Irwin*.

For example, a surgeon is contracted to operate and provide breast implants. What contractual obligations do you think they would owe?

Tip

First determine the type of contract and consider the statutory implied terms.

What are the consequences of breach?

1. Subject only to the operation of an effective exemption clause excluding or limiting this right (Chapter 6), on proof of breach there is an automatic right to claim damages for breach (compensation for losses caused by that breach). The failure to perform a primary (or performance) obligation under the contract automatically gives rise to a secondary obligation to pay damages (or to pay the contract price).

2. However, unless the breach is regarded as a repudiatory breach, the contract will continue in force and both parties must continue to perform their obligations under it.

3. If the breach is repudiatory then, in addition to the right to claim damages for loss suffered, **the innocent party has a choice or election** to either (i) accept the repudiatory breach as terminating the contract (so discharging all future obligations under the contract) or (ii) affirm the contract despite that repudiatory breach so that both parties must continue with future performance (and see Table 5.9 for the correct terminology to use in relation to repudiatory breach).

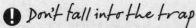 **Don't fall into the trap**

If the innocent party elects to treat the contract as terminated, it is only the *future* obligations which are discharged. The contract itself survives and its terms (such as any **exemption clauses** or **agreed damages clauses**) may be relevant for the purpose of assessing remedies.

Table 5.9 Avoid confusing your terminology

Discharge of a contract	Contract is validly formed but some event such as repudiatory breach or frustration brings future performance of the contractual obligations to an end. Performance obligations in this contract stop dead on discharge but the contract does exist.	The contract itself and its terms remain valid, e.g. exemption clauses and agreed damages clauses.
Contract not validly formed—void (e.g. for uncertainty) or voidable (and rescinded/set aside), e.g. for duress, undue influence or misrepresentation	The contract is treated as if it never existed. It is wiped from existence.	The contract and its terms do not exist, never existed, and cannot be relied upon for any purpose.

Recognizing a repudiatory breach: the classification of terms

The most likely focus of your examiner's attention will probably be reserved for the type of term broken and whether the breach of that term constitutes a repudiatory breach. The types of terms and whether their breach is repudiatory is explained in Table 5.10.

Key point

If the term broken is either a condition, or an innominate term and the effects of breach of that innominate term are serious, the breach will be repudiatory (giving rise to the option for the innocent party to terminate or affirm).

Table 5.10 Summary of types of terms

Condition	**Important term which 'goes to the root' of the contract.**	Breach of condition is a repudiatory breach so that there is always the option to terminate (repudiate) the contract or affirm.	***Poussard v Spiers*** (1876): obligation of lead singer to perform at first performance went to the root of the contract and its breach amounted to a breach of condition.

Breach

✳✳✳✳✳✳✳✳✳✳✳✳

Innominate term	It is difficult to define an innominate term other than in terms of its effect but it would seem likely that a term would be defined as innominate **where a range of possible breaches could occur, some of which may have serious consequences and some only minor.**	May or may not be repudiatory depending on how serious the consequences of the breach turn out to be. Breach will be repudiatory if the breach deprives the innocent party 'of substantially the whole benefit which it was intended he should obtain from the contract'.	***Hong Kong Fir Shipping Co. Ltd v Kawasaki Kisen Kaisha Ltd*** (1962): seaworthiness obligation could be broken in a number of different ways not all of which would be serious. Here not serious as after repairs there were still 17 of original 24 months of charter left. ***Cehave NV v Bremer Handelsgesellschaft GmbH, The Hansa Nord*** (1976): shipment of citrus pulp pellets for animal feed to be made in 'good condition'. Innominate term and effects of breach not serious since original buyer acquired the cargo and used for animal feed.
Warranty	**Less important term whose breach can be adequately compensated with a payment of damages** and is not likely to be fatal to the contractual performance as a whole.		***Bettini v Gye*** (1876): obligation to attend rehearsals for six days. Failed to attend the first three. The rehearsal obligation did not go to the root of the contract. It was only a **warranty** giving rise to a claim in damages but not to the ability to terminate the contract.

✔ Looking for extra marks?

Where an oral statement has become a 'term' on the basis of the importance attached test (*Bannerman v White, Couchman v Hill*) it will necessarily 'go to the root' of the contract and be classified as a condition.

Practical example

To return to the practical example, since the importance attached test applied to Alex's statement about the turnover of the business, the statement was not only a term but the fact that it is wrong would constitute a breach of condition, i.e. it would be a repudiatory breach giving rise to the option to terminate or affirm (in addition to the damages claim).

Difficulties with the identification of conditions in the B2B context

Statutory classification: s. 15A Sale of Goods Act 1979

Although the 'goods' obligations imposed on commercial sellers by ss. 13–15 SGA 1979 (as amended) are classified as 'conditions' in those statutory provisions, a breach may not be treated as a breach of condition and may instead be treated as a breach of warranty.

Section 15A SGA 1979 (as amended)

Where the buyer would have the right to reject (terminate) for breach of a **s. 13, 14, or 15** condition but the **actual breach is so slight** that it would be unreasonable for him to reject, the breach is not to be treated as a breach of condition but **may be treated as a breach of warranty** (i.e. *no option to terminate and limited to damages only*).

There are equivalent provisions, modifying remedies, in ss. 5A and 10A of SGSA 1982.

Party classification of a term as a condition may not be effective

---

L. Schuler AG v Wickman Machine Tool Sales (1974) **(HL)**

Use of the word 'condition' is not conclusive.

FACTS: It was a condition of an exclusive distribution contract (over a period of four and a half years) that the distributor 'shall send its representative to visit (the six largest UK motor manufacturers) at least once in every week' to solicit orders. The distributor failed to make a number of these visits and the agreement was terminated.

HELD: This term was not a condition in the sense that a single breach, however trivial, would entitle the innocent party to terminate the contract. It followed that the distribution contract had been wrongfully terminated.

These difficulties in being sure that the broken term is a condition can lead to uncertainties in terms of reacting to a breach and whether the innocent party should be treating the breach as repudiatory. When coupled with the inherent uncertainties of the innominate term and its 'wait and see' approach to a remedy, the difficulties for the innocent party are compounded.

Breaches of statutory rights relating to goods: CRA 2015

Termination (or the right to reject the goods in the context of the sale and supply of goods) may no longer be the only available remedy in the context of breaches of statutory rights (see p. 106, Table 5.6) in B2C contracts. Instead, a range of remedies may be available to the consumer depending upon the circumstances (ss. 19–24 CRA 2015: short-term right to reject, partial right to reject, right to repair or replacement, right to a price reduction or a refund in the case of a contract relating to digital content). There are also additional possible remedies for breaches of ss. 49 and 50 CRA 2015 (Table 5.7) (services contract), e.g. right to repeat performance and the right to a price reduction (ss. 54, 55, and 56). Be guided by your syllabus. These statutory provisions relating to remedies may be included in the syllabus of a consumer or commercial law module.

Topic 5: What are the options when an anticipatory repudiatory breach occurs?

Definition

An **anticipatory repudiatory breach** occurs when, after the contract was entered into, but before the time fixed for performance, one party breaches by renouncing (rejecting) their contractual obligations.

Practical example

Anticipatory repudiatory breach

By a contract entered into on 1 April, Alex employs Becky as a consultant to undertake an appraisal of his staff. This work is due to commence on 1 June. However, on 1 May Alex informs Becky that he has changed his mind and no longer needs her to perform this work. What options are available to Becky who wanted to include this prestigious assignment on her CV?

As this involves renouncing the contractual obligations, it is a repudiatory breach on 1 May. However, it is an *anticipatory* repudiatory breach since performance was not due to commence under the contract until 1 June.

Since it is a repudiatory breach there is the usual election. Becky can elect to:

(1) **Terminate the contract immediately and claim damages at the date of termination (1 May) rather than waiting until the date fixed for performance (1 June):** *Hochster v De La Tour* (1853). However, Becky will need to mitigate her loss from 1 May by looking for another assignment.

(2) **Alternatively, Becky could decide to affirm on 1 May and claim the performance due on 1 June.** In effect, she would be ignoring his statement and giving Alex a second chance to perform. If she does this and Alex still does not want her services on 1 June, Becky can accept this actual (as opposed to anticipatory) repudiatory breach despite her earlier **affirmation**. However, if Becky affirms on 1 May for the anticipatory breach, she cannot claim damages until 1 June and in the meantime runs the risk that she will lose this right of action.

What could happen in the intervening period?

1. Becky could (perhaps unwittingly) commit a breach of contract and could not then argue that the earlier anticipatory breach excused her from her obligation to perform under the contract since she had decided to keep the contract alive for all purposes (*Fercometal SARL v Mediterranean Shipping Co. SA, The Simona* (1989)).

2. Alex could rely upon supervening frustration in the period between affirmation (1 May) and the date fixed for performance (1 June), e.g. if personnel appraisals are declared illegal. Becky would then lose her right to remedies for the initial anticipatory breach (*Avery v Bowden* (1855)).

However, is it open to Becky to insist on ignoring Alex's anticipatory breach and continue with performance of the contract from 1 June on the basis that she wants to be able to put this assignment on her CV? Could she perform and then claim the contract fee?

The answer turns on the controversial decision in *White and Carter (Councils) Ltd v McGregor* which suggests that in principle she could.

White and Carter (Councils) Ltd v McGregor (1962) **(HL)**

FACTS: The Ps were to advertise the D's business on litterbins for three years. Before the date when contractual performance was to begin, the D repudiated and asked the Ps to cancel the agreement. The Ps refused and went ahead and performed their side of the agreement for the three-year period. They made no attempt to minimize their loss by finding other advertisers to take the D's place. They then sued the D for the contract price (i.e. an agreed sum rather than damages).

HELD (3:2): The Ps could continue and claim the contract price. They were not bound to accept the repudiation and sue for damages.

However, in practice there are significant limitations (Lord Reid in *White and Carter v McGregor*) which will prevent Becky from pursuing this option. These limitations are explained in Table 5.11.

Table 5.11 Lord Reid's limitations on the operation of *White and Carter*

Limitation on the ability to affirm rather than terminating and claiming damages	A party cannot affirm if it has no legitimate interest in performing the contract rather than claiming damages.
	Burden on guilty party to show this (i.e. to establish that the innocent party cannot affirm).
	The test is that affirmation 'is wholly unreasonable'. ***Clea Shipping Corp. v Bulk Oil International Ltd, The Alaskan Trader*** (1984): charterers indicated the chartered vessel would not be required. However, the owners went ahead with expensive repairs and maintained a crew ready to sail. Held that the owners had acted wholly unreasonably. ***The Puerto Buitrago*** (1976): following a repudiation by the charterers, the owners wanted to claim the charter hire (for the remaining term while the vessel was idle because repairs would cost more than the value of the vessel) rather than damages but damages would be an adequate remedy.

	But in practical terms it must be an exceptional situation where an innocent party would be denied the option to affirm, i.e. damages would be adequate and keeping the contract operating 'would be unreasonable', *Ocean Marine Navigation Ltd v Koch Carbon Inc., The Dynamic* (2003).
Limitation on the ability to perform and claim the contract price	**A party cannot perform and claim the price if it cannot continue performance without the cooperation (active or passive) of the guilty party.** *Hounslow LBC v Twickenham Garden Developments Ltd* (1971): Contractors working on a local authority site refused to accept the local authority's repudiatory breach but they could not continue performance as on repudiation they had no right to be on the site.

Isabella Shipowner SA v Shagang Shipping Co. Ltd, The Aquafaith (2012)

This case is an example of a *White & Carter* application despite these limitations.

FACTS: Charterers stated that they would redeliver the vessel early in anticipatory breach. The owners refused this early redelivery, thereby affirming, so that the charterers would be liable for the charter hire for the minimum term. The charterers claimed (i) that the owners could not affirm as they had no legitimate interest in performing rather than claiming damages and (ii) they could not claim the hire since the charter involved the cooperation of the charterer.

HELD:

(i) Affirmation would not be prevented on the basis that there was no legitimate interest in keeping the contract alive simply because damages would be an available remedy on the facts. Affirmation had to be 'beyond all reason' or 'perverse' before there was no legitimate interest in performing. That involved considering whether there was any benefit to the owners, however small, as compared to the loss to the charterers; and

(ii) The owners did not need the cooperation of the charterers to keep the ship available to them. Earning the hire was not dependent on any performance by the charterers of their obligations.

Practical example

Does Becky have a legitimate interest in affirming, i.e. in performing rather than claiming damages? She wanted to use the work to enhance her personal profile and there is nothing 'wholly unreasonable' or 'perverse' in wanting to do that. Generally, the courts will look to allow affirmation as an option. However, Becky could not perform and claim the contract price without access to Alex's premises and employees—and hence his cooperation (*Hounslow LBC v Twickenham Garden Developments Ltd*).

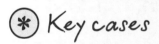

Key debates

1. Implication of terms by the courts

This is the most likely essay-style question on terms, particularly in the light of Lord Hoffmann's explanation of the basis for the implication of terms in fact in *Attorney General of Belize v Belize Telecom Ltd* and its interpretation in subsequent case law, e.g. *Marks and Spencer plc v BNP Paribas Securities Services Trust Co (Jersey) Ltd* (2014):

Kramer, 'Implication in Fact as an Instance of Contractual Interpretation' [2004] CLJ 384.

Hooley, 'Implied Terms After *Belize Telecom*' [2014] CLJ 315.

McLauchlan, 'Construction and Implication: In Defence of *Belize Telecom*' [2014] LMCLQ 203.

In addition, there is some debate about the basis for terms implied in law:

Crossley v Faithful & Gould Holdings (2004).

Peden, 'Policy Concerns behind Implication of Terms in Law' (2001) 117 LQR 459.

2. Circumstances in which termination for breach is, or should be, available

In particular, there has been some debate about opportunism and motives, so-called 'good' and 'bad' reasons justifying withdrawal from a contract:

Brownsword, 'Retrieving Reasons, Retrieving Rationality? A New Look at the Right to Withdraw for Breach of Contract' (1992) 5 JCL 83.

The author's personal favourite debate for an essay concerns the dangers of wrongful repudiation as in *Reardon-Smith Line Ltd v Hansen-Tangen* (1976), *Hong Kong Fir*, and *The Hansa Nord*, i.e. the inherent uncertainties and choices facing the innocent party if it is far from clear whether the term broken is a breach of condition, or the need to 'wait and see' the effects of breach if it is an innominate term and to make a judgement as to their seriousness.

Key cases

Case	Facts	Principle
Bannerman v White	D wanted to buy hops and said that he did not want to purchase from P if the hops had been treated with sulphur. P, seller, then confirmed (incorrectly) that the hops had not been treated with sulphur. Held: the statement was so important to the purchaser that it amounted to a contractual promise (term) by the seller.	Importance attached to the statement test indicates that the statement is a term. It is not merely that the statement is important to the recipient but that he makes this importance clear to the statement maker ahead of any statement being made.
Dick Bentley Productions Ltd v Harold Smith (Motors) Ltd (CA)	P wanted Ds, car dealers, to acquire a 'well vetted Bentley' The dealers confirmed that the particular car had travelled only 20,000 miles since being fitted with a new engine and gearbox. In fact the statement as to mileage was untrue. The statement as to mileage amounted to a warranty (term).	The statement as to mileage was made by a person professing to have specialist knowledge and therefore was a term or collateral warranty (promising that reasonable care and skill had been taken).

Key cases

****

Case	Facts	Principle
J. Evans & Son (Portsmouth) Ltd v Andrea Merzario Ltd (CA)	An oral assurance was given that containers would be shipped below deck. However, the written contract gave the carriers freedom to decide the method of transportation and exempted them from loss or damage to the goods. The goods were damaged and the carriers sought to rely on the writing. The majority of CA held that oral assurance was a term of the contract which was partly written and partly oral. This oral term overrode the written conditions.	An oral promise can be so important to the decision to enter the contract that it overrides conflicting written terms.
Liverpool City Council v Irwin (HL)	Tenants of a Council tower block claimed that the Council landlord was in breach of an implied obligation to repair and maintain the common parts of the building, i.e. to ensure the lifts and lighting worked and that the rubbish chutes were not blocked. There was nothing stated expressly on this matter in the lease. HL held that the nature of the contract required an implied term but it was not a guarantee obligation, only an obligation to use reasonable care to keep the common parts in reasonable repair and use. The Council was not in breach of this (qualified) implied contractual obligation.	Implication of term in law as a necessary incident of the type of contract. However, the implied term may be a qualified contractual obligation (reasonable care and skill) rather than a strict (guarantee) obligation.
L. Schuler AG v Wickman Machine Tool Sales (HL)	It was a 'condition' of an exclusive distribution contract (over a period of four and a half years) that the distributor 'shall send its representative to visit [the six largest UK motor manufacturers] at least once in every week' to solicit orders. The distributor failed to make a number of these visits and the agreement was terminated. The majority of HL held that this term was not a condition in the sense that a single breach, however trivial, would entitle the innocent party to terminate the contract.	The fact that a term is called a 'condition' is not conclusive.
Hong Kong Fir Shipping Co. Ltd v Kawasaki Kisen Kaisha Ltd (CA)	Breach of a 24-month charter as the ship was not seaworthy on departure. It broke down and needed repairs. The charterers terminated but the ship was returned to seaworthy condition when there were still 17 months of the original 24-month term remaining. CA held that the term broken was not a condition but an innominate term and since the effects of the breach were not sufficiently serious to justify termination, the charterers had no right to terminate when they did.	Breach of an innominate term may or may not constitute a repudiatory breach depending on whether the effects of the breach were sufficiently serious to deprive the innocent party of substantially the whole benefit they were intended to get under the contract.

Case	Facts	Principle
***White and Carter (Councils) Ltd v McGregor* (HL)**	Ps were to advertise D's business on litterbins for three years. Before the date when contractual performance was to begin, D repudiated and asked Ps to cancel the agreement. Ps refused and went ahead and performed their side of the agreement for the three-year period. They made no attempt to minimize their loss by finding other advertisers to take D's place. They then sued D for the contract price (i.e. an agreed sum rather than damages). HL (3:2) decided Ps could continue and claim the contract price. They were not bound to accept the repudiation and sue for damages.	Following anticipatory repudiatory breach the innocent party may affirm (assuming legitimate interest in continuing to perform rather than terminating and claiming damages) and can (if able to do so without the other party's cooperation) continue to perform the contract and claim the contract price (as action in debt—no duty to mitigate).

#6

Exemption clauses and unfair contract terms

- An **exemption clause** is a particular **term** which purports to exclude or limit the liability or the remedies which would otherwise be available to the non-breaching party.

- The key question is whether a particular exemption clause can be relied upon as a defence to liability or to preclude reliance on the usual remedies.

- In order to be enforceable on the facts the exemption clause must be incorporated as a term of the contract (incorporation), cover the liability that has arisen in the circumstances in which it has arisen (construction), and not be precluded from operating by legislation.

- An exemption clause can be incorporated as a result of signature, reasonable notice in a contractual document to people in general before or at the time of contracting, or as a result of a consistent course of dealing between the parties or their common understanding.

- The **Unfair Contract Terms Act 1977 (UCTA 1977)** regulates exemption clauses in B2B contracts either by rendering the clause totally unenforceable or enforceable only if it can be shown to be reasonable. The applicable test turns on the liability.

- In the context of consumer contracts, the **Consumer Rights Act 2015 (CRA 2015)** requires contract terms and notices to be fair (**s. 62**). The term or notice is regarded as unfair if, contrary to the requirement of good faith, it causes a significant imbalance in the parties' rights and obligations under the contract to the detriment of the consumer. This is the same wording as under the previous consumer legislation (Unfair Terms in Consumer Contracts

Regulations 1999) which was repealed by the CRA 2015. The assessment for fairness cannot extend to terms which (i) specify the main subject matter of the contract or (ii) relate to an assessment of the appropriateness of the price payable under the contract by comparison with the goods or services received as long as those terms are transparent and prominent. Such an unfair term is not binding at the option of the consumer.

Introduction

This chapter focuses on the use and enforceability of exemption clauses (total exclusion or limitation of liability clauses inserted into contracts). There is evidence of a greater willingness to interfere in the use of such clauses in consumer, rather than commercial, contracts. The **Consumer Rights Act 2015** extends intervention beyond exemption clauses to a larger category of unfair terms in the context of consumer contracts.

Think like an examiner

Since the key issue concerns the ability to rely upon an exemption clause as a defence to liability, examiners tend to favour problem questions on this topic. Examiners also want to be helpful. It is relatively easy for you to identify the existence of an exemption clause in the question facts where liability or remedies are denied and therefore to appreciate the area of law for discussion.

Whilst examiners appreciate that this topic can be perceived as technical and that it overlaps with knowledge of types of liabilities and the implied terms (consumer statutory rights) in the sales and supply (or consumer rights) legislation, we also know that your choice of questions to answer in the examination can make a big difference to your overall result. Law questions possess 'degrees of difficulty', just like the choice of dives in a diving competition. Exemption clauses would be at the top end of the range in terms of technicality so that in relative terms, and with clear knowledge of the basics, particularly the legislation, you can do really well in selecting to answer such a question.

✅ Looking for extra marks?

The first step should be to identify the liability on the facts, i.e. what has happened, whether it amounts to a **breach** of contract or negligence liability, and, if contractual liability, the term or terms broken.

Since this makes life so much easier when it comes to applying the legislation, this is probably essential.

❗ Don't fall into the trap

Imbalance: some students produce an excellent answer on incorporation but misjudge their timing completely (or run out of knowledge) so that they fail to consider either construction or the legislation. Remember that a good percentage of the marks will relate to the correct application of either **UCTA 1977** or the **CRA 2015**.

How to do well in exemption clauses problem answers

- Identify the liability at the outset (**and appreciate whether the clause is being relied upon against a consumer or non-consumer**).

- Consider each clause separately (if more than one) and each loss/liability issue separately.
- Follow the structure in the correct order.
- Ensure you have a reasonable working knowledge of the statutory implied terms (or consumer statutory rights) in the sale and supply of goods (or consumer rights) legislation and be precise, e.g. cite the correct section and subsection of the correct piece of legislation. Don't confuse the commercial and consumer regimes or jump between them within a single fact application.
- Ensure you balance your answer so that you leave adequate time to address the legislation.

Essay questions in this area are less popular. The likely issues are discussed at p. 139, 'Key debates'.

Structure for a problem question on exemption clauses

Step 1: Identify the exemption clause question

Are there one or more clauses in the problem facts that seem to deny responsibility, liability, or remedies?

If so, the question may well be about the effectiveness of that clause or clauses.

Step 2: What has happened?

There may be more than one incident.

Tip
This should be easy. It does not require any legal knowledge but can be seen in the facts.

Identify the legal liability attaching to each event

The liability may be liability in negligence (qualified contractual liability and/or breach of a duty of care in tort) and/or breach of strict contractual liability.

What does this mean?

If there has been a breach of contract you need to decide whether each obligation broken is a strict or qualified contractual obligation (see Table 5.8). A strict contractual obligation must be precisely performed or there will be a breach, whereas a qualified contractual obligation imposes a standard of reasonable care or skill. If this standard is met there is no breach (see Chapter 5). Qualified contractual obligations are treated as **liability in**

Structure for a problem question on exemption clauses

✱✱✱✱✱✱✱✱✱✱✱✱

negligence for the purposes of exemption clauses (see the definition of negligence in **s. 1 UCTA 1977 and/or s. 65(4) CRA 2015**).

This is the hardest part of this topic but there are only a few possibilities that you are likely to meet and these are set out in Table 6.1:

Table 6.1 Identifying types of liability

Negligence liability	Strict contractual liability
If someone has possession of your property for some purpose (cloakroom, to launder etc.) they owe you a qualified duty of reasonable care so if it is stolen due a failure to exercise reasonable care there will be liability in negligence.	Breaches of implied obligations under the sales (or consumer rights) legislation are generally STRICT (the **exceptions** are **s. 13 Supply of Goods and Services Act 1982 (SGSA 1982)** and **s. 49 CRA 2015**) so breaches of the implied obligations on the seller or supplier to supply goods which are of satisfactory quality and fit for purpose are strict contractual liability (see Chapter 5 for details of these implied terms).
Breach of **s. 13 SGSA 1982** (or **s. 49 CRA 2015**) involves a breach of a qualified contractual obligation. When carrying out a service the obligation is to exercise reasonable care and skill.	Contractual duty to supply goods or other performance by a set date and the performance is late.
Falling over an obstacle or unsafe flooring involves a breach by the occupiers of their duty to take reasonable care and skill.	

This analysis should give you one or more liabilities for each event (or loss) which has occurred. Note that sometimes there is concurrent liability, i.e. both contractual (strict) and negligence liability (usually result of breach of duty of care in tort) on the facts.

White v John Warwick & Co. Ltd (1953)

A tricycle was hired but it had a defective saddle. This involved both a breach of a strict contractual obligation (to supply a tricycle reasonably fit for the purpose, **s. 9 SGSA 1982**) and a failure to take care to ensure that the tricycle was safe (negligence liability).

Step 3: The core question—can the exemption clause operate as a defence to this liability?

The clause must:

- **be incorporated as a term**
- **cover what has happened**
- **not be rendered ineffective by the operation of legislation.**

❶ *Don't fall into the trap*

Don't forget to state that the crucial question is whether the clause can be relied upon as a defence to the liability—and what must be established for it to do so.

Advice: it is important to follow these steps sequentially. Students often do less well than they think with exemption clauses problem questions because they rush into the legislation when the clause was either not incorporated as a term (e.g. reasonable notice was given too late) or the clause does not cover the liability which has occurred in the circumstances in which it occurred— and so cannot be relied upon in any event.

1. Is the clause incorporated as a term?

(i) Is it contained in a signed *contractual* document?

The document that is signed must be of a type that would normally be expected to contain contractual **conditions**. Signing a time sheet was not sufficient as it merely evidenced performance under an existing contract: *Grogan v Robin Meredith Plant Hire* (1996).

Yes—incorporated. If a party signs a written document containing contractual terms then they are bound by those terms—even if they have not read them: *L'Estrange v Graucob Ltd* (1934) and *Peekay Intermark Ltd v Australia & New Zealand Banking Group Ltd* (2006). The only exception occurs where the signature was obtained as a result of fraud or misrepresentation (*Curtis v Chemical Cleaning & Dyeing Co.* (1951)).

No—go to (ii).

(ii) Has reasonable notice of the existence of the clause been given in a contractual document—and in time?

Where the exemption clause is contained in an unsigned document (e.g. a ticket) or notice or is referred to in such a document, incorporation can be achieved by reasonable notice.

- **Is the clause contained in a contractual document?**

Chapelton v Barry U.D.C. (1940) **(CA)**

FACTS: Deckchairs were displayed in a pile as available for hire. The tickets, which might have been obtained later from the deckchair attendant, purported to exclude liability. Was the exemption contained in a contractual document so that the Council could rely on it?

HELD: The ticket was not a contractual document, but only a voucher or receipt for money paid. Therefore the Council could not rely on the exemption contained in the ticket.

Structure for a problem question on exemption clauses

✳✳✳✳✳✳✳✳✳✳✳

> *Revision Tip*
>
> When assessing whether the document is a contractual document:
>
> (i) The fact that it may be called a 'receipt' is not conclusive.
>
> (ii) The *time* when the contract is made seems to be important in determining whether the document is contractual. The display of deckchairs in **Chapelton** was a standing **offer** so that **acceptance** took place when the deckchair was removed from the pile. The ticket could be obtained much later and was therefore only a receipt to prove payment rather than part of the contract formation process.

- **Does the document contain writing so that people in general (*Thompson v London, Midland & Scottish Railway*) would reasonably assume that writing to include terms and conditions?**

An indication of where conditions can be found in another document is sufficient notice, e.g. 'subject to conditions on timetables': *Thompson v London, Midland & Scottish Railway* (1930) and *O'Brien v MGN Ltd* (2001). The particular clauses do not need to have been read by the other party. However, the writing must be supplied or reference must be made to a place where it can be obtained (*Sterling Hydraulics Ltd v Dichtomatik Ltd* (2006)).

- **Has notice of the existence of the clause been given before or at the time of contracting?** (*Olley v Marlborough Court Ltd* (1949); *Thornton v Shoe Lane Parking Ltd* (1971)).

If yes, go to (iii). If no, go to (iv).

> *Revision tip*
>
> You will need to analyse the formation of the contract, i.e. the offer and acceptance. Notice will be in time where the situation resembles the purchase of a train ticket at a railway station since the offer is said to be made by the ticket issuer and to be accepted by the passenger if the passenger accepts the ticket containing the terms without objection, although it is accepted that the passenger is unlikely to have read those terms. However, where a ticket is issued by an automatic ticket machine, since the machine is the standing offer and acceptance occurs when the passenger enters the booking details, any terms on a ticket which is dispensed will be too late to be incorporated (see the judgment of Lord Denning MR in **Thornton v Shoe Lane Parking Ltd**).

Thornton v Shoe Lane Parking Ltd (1971) **(CA)**

FACTS: There was a notice at the entrance of a car park stating that parking was to be 'at owner's risk'. Entry was controlled by means of an automatic barrier and a machine before the barrier dispensed tickets which were 'issued subject to conditions displayed on the premises'. There was a notice inside the car park stating that the car park owners were not liable for injury to customers.

HELD: The exemption on the ticket (referring to exemption from liability for personal injury) came too late. The offer in the notice at the entrance was accepted when the motorist drove up to the machine.

Structure for a problem question on exemption clauses

✳✳✳✳✳✳✳✳✳✳✳

If a contract is made orally and is followed later by a written document, notice on this occasion will be too late: *Grogan v Robin Meredith Plant Hire.*

(iii) A higher standard of incorporation will apply if the particular clause is considered to be onerous or unusual

> **Interfoto Picture Library Ltd v Stiletto Visual Programmes Ltd** (1988) **(CA)**
>
> **FACTS:** A clause imposed a fee of £5 per day for the late return of photographic transparencies. There were 47 of these transparencies and they had been kept inadvertently for an additional two weeks and a charge of £3,783.50 had been imposed. Had the clause been incorporated as a term of the contract?
>
> **HELD:** Since the clause was particularly onerous and unusual, it had to be fairly and reasonably brought to the other's attention in order to be incorporated. This had not been achieved and incorporation had not occurred.

(a) **Is the clause onerous or unusual?** If yes, go to (iii)(b). If no, the clause will be incorporated by reasonable notice.

> **Thornton v Shoe Lane Parking Ltd** (1971)
>
> Clause absolving the proprietors of a car park from liability for personal injury, as opposed to damage to the cars, was considered unusual and so calling for special attention.

> **AEG (UK) Ltd v Logic Resource Ltd** (1996) **(CA)**
>
> **FACTS:** The clause stated that a purchaser of goods had to pay the cost of returning any defective goods. This is not an unusual clause but, with the knowledge of the supplier, the particular contract involved the purchase of the goods for export to an Iranian customer.
>
> **HELD (majority):** The clause was onerous and unusual in the particular context in which it was used.

> **O'Brien v MGN Ltd** (2001)
>
> **FACTS:** The clause in a document relating to a scratch-card competition stated that if there was more than one winner lots would be drawn to determine the prize winner.
>
> **HELD:** It was neither onerous nor unusual.

(b) **Has the onerous or unusual clause been fairly and reasonably brought to the attention of the other party** (e.g. *J. Spurling Ltd v Bradshaw* (1956), Lord Denning's 'red hand')? If yes, the clause is incorporated. If no, the clause will not be incorporated and cannot be relied upon as a defence to the liability identified at step 2.

Structure for a problem question on exemption clauses
✳✳✳✳✳✳✳✳✳✳

(iv) Has the clause been incorporated as a result of a consistent course of dealing including the clause between these parties?

It is easier to find the consistency in dealings between commercial parties. If yes, the clause is incorporated. If no, the clause will not be incorporated and cannot be relied upon as a defence to the liability identified in step 2.

2. Construction: Does the clause on its natural and ordinary meaning cover the liability in question in the circumstances in which it occurred?

Revision tip

Do not spend too long on construction as it is often easily established due to the width of today's exemption clauses. Equally it may be a matter of general language, e.g. 'injury or damage' does not cover loss due to theft. Deal only with any construction issues that are raised by the facts, e.g. if there is a limitation clause, if there is negligence liability, or a fundamental breach has occurred and it is necessary to consider whether the clause covers it.

The following *may* need to be considered but you should ensure each is relevant on the facts before raising it:

(i) Is the clause ambiguous? If so, the ambiguity will be construed against the party relying on the clause

Houghton v Trafalgar Insurance Co. Ltd (1954): car insurance policy reference to 'excess load' was ambiguous and therefore construed against the insurers to mean excess weight rather than too many passengers. It followed that the insurance policy remained enforceable. (Note: There are often policy issues underlying outcomes in construction cases, i.e. the need to protect consumers.)

(ii) Is there any inconsistent undertaking which may prevent reliance on the clause?

If an exemption clause is inconsistent with another term of the contract or with an oral undertaking given before or at the time of contracting, the exemption clause will be overridden (*Mendelssohn v Normand Ltd* (1970): inconsistent oral undertaking by garage attendant promising to lock a car whereas the exemption clause purported to exclude any liability for the loss of vehicle contents).

(iii) Limitation clauses (clauses limiting liability to a fixed figure as opposed to denying any liability) are construed more favourably than total exclusion clauses which deny all liability

For example, a limitation clause will cover negligence liability if the clause is 'clear and unambiguous': *Ailsa Craig Fishing Co. Ltd v Malvern Fishing Co. Ltd* (1983).

Structure for a problem question on exemption clauses

(iv) Is the wording of the clause wide enough to cover a fundamental or serious breach of contract?

If the breach is fundamental, i.e. affecting the very purpose and substance of the contract, then very clear words will be required for the clause to cover it. However, it is common for exemption clauses to be drafted generously (leaving it for the legislation to control the ability to rely on the clause).

Photo Production Ltd v Securicor Transport Ltd (1980) **(HL)**

FACTS: A contract involving the provision of security services for a factory contained a wide exemption clause exempting the security provider from loss. The security firm's employee started a fire on the premises and the factory owner suffered significant loss.

HELD: As a matter of construction, on its natural and ordinary meaning the clause in the contract did cover such a deliberate act.

(v) Where there is negligence liability on the facts (see p. 123, 'Step 2'), it is necessary to determine whether the clause covers this negligence liability or whether the clause is limited to providing a defence to the strict contractual liability only

- If there is only negligence liability on the facts then the clause must be construed as covering that negligence liability (*Alderslade v Hendon Laundry Ltd* (1945): loss of handkerchiefs to be laundered involved only a breach of a duty to exercise reasonable care).

- If there is both negligence and strict contractual liability on the facts then the clause will cover BOTH negligence and strict contractual liability only if the clause expressly purports to cover the negligence (uses the word negligence or a synonym of negligence) (*Monarch Airlines Ltd v London Luton Airport Ltd* (1997): 'neglect or default' amounted to express reference to negligence so that the clause covered negligence liability in addition to the strict liability—breach of a statutory duty in relation to the airport runway).

- If such express language of negligence is not used then the clause will be construed so that it covers only the strict contractual liability and it cannot operate as a defence to liability in negligence (*White v John Warwick & Co. Ltd* (1953): both strict contractual liability and negligence involved in hiring tricycle with defective saddle and the CA held that the exclusion clause had to be construed as covering only the strict contractual liability and not the negligence).

Bear in mind that in the light of the *West Bromwich* principles of contractual construction (*Investors Compensation Scheme Ltd v West Bromwich Building Society (No. 1)* (1998)), the court will not permit a construction in relation to negligence liability which would be at odds with the commercial purpose of the contract: *HIH Casualty & General Insurance Ltd v Chase Manhattan Bank* (2003) and *Kudos Catering (UK) Ltd v Manchester Central Convention Complex Ltd* (2013).

You should now be left with either:

- strict *and* negligence liability (word negligence used in the clause) or
- strict liability only or
- negligence liability only

and will therefore know which liabilities (or liability) should be considered in UCTA—(the correct section of UCTA to look at)—and whether s. 65 CRA 2015 is relevant in the consumer context.

3. Does legislation prevent the use of the exemption clause as a defence to this liability on these facts?

Be clear which piece of legislation you need to apply to the facts. The applicable piece of legislation:

- the Unfair Contract Terms Act 1977 (UCTA 1977) **or**
- the Consumer Rights Act 2015 (Part 2, Unfair Terms) (CRA 2015)

depends on the nature of the contract, so it is essential to determine whether the contract is B2B or B2C. Table 6.2 explains the key differences between the two pieces of legislation.

Table 6.2 Summary of scope and effect of the legislation

UCTA	Since the CRA 2015, **UCTA applies only to B2B contracts, i.e. where one business is using an exemption clause against another business (irrespective of the respective sizes of those businesses).**
	Depending on the liability which the clause seeks to exclude or limit, **UCTA** renders the clause in question either totally unenforceable or only enforceable if it can be shown to be reasonable (**s. 11 reasonableness requirement**).
CRA	**The CRA applies to B2C contracts only—contracts between a trader and a consumer**. The Act defines 'a trader' and 'a consumer'.
	'Trader' is a person acting for purposes relating to that person's trade, business, craft or profession.
	'Consumer' means an individual acting for purposes that are wholly or mainly outside that individual's trade, business, craft or profession. It will be difficult to establish this (see ***Overy v Paypal (Europe) Ltd*** (2012)).
	The CRA has potentially wide application since it regulates 'unfair terms' in general. Such 'unfair terms' are not binding on the consumer, i.e. the consumer can avoid the application of an unfair exemption clause.

The Unfair Contract Terms Act 1977 (UCTA 1977)

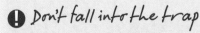

❶ Don't fall into the trap

Make sure you use appropriate terminology. Since the ability to rely on a particular exemption clause as a defence depends on the context in which it is used and the liability which has occurred on the particular facts, it is inappropriate to use overly dramatic terminology. Each case turns on its own particular facts and if a particular clause is unenforceable on the facts it may not follow that the same clause used in a different context would be similarly unenforceable. It is therefore preferable to avoid terminology such as **void** or 'invalid'.

Step 1: Does the Act apply?

UCTA applies to 'exemption clauses' covering business liability (and since the CRA 2015 it does not cover any exemption clauses that would be covered by that Act, i.e. in contracts between a trader and a consumer). 'Exemption clause' has an extended definition within s. 13(1). You may therefore need to consider the following where it is not clear that the clause is excluding or limiting liability:

- Does the clause state that there is to be no liability unless some condition is complied with such as identifying and reporting a defect within seven days? If yes, it is covered by UCTA. OR

- Does the clause exclude or limit any right or remedy that would otherwise be available such as the right to claim **damages**? If yes, it is covered by UCTA. OR

- Does the clause exclude or restrict rules of evidence or procedure? If yes, it is covered by UCTA. OR

- Does the clause exclude or limit the obligation or duty? In other words, does the clause deny that there is any contractual promise or responsibility, e.g. a general disclaimer? If yes, it is covered by UCTA. (*Smith v Eric S. Bush* (1990): a contract for a mortgage valuation of a property contained a clause stating that there was 'no acceptance of responsibility for the valuation' being provided. Since this disclaimer purported to prevent any duty of care from ever arising it fell within s. 13(1) and UCTA regulation would apply to it.)

Step 2: To determine how the Act applies in an individual case we need to identify which section of the Act applies to the liability sought to be excluded

This involves:

- looking at what happened and the liability which arose (see p. 123, 'Step 2')

- assessing which of these liabilities is covered by the clause (see p. 129, 'Construction, point (v)')
- applying the relevant section of UCTA.

Is there negligence liability?

Section 1 UCTA states that negligence includes:

(1) breaches of contractual obligations which impose a duty to exercise reasonable care and skill (qualified contractual liability)

(2) breach of a duty of care in tort.

> There will therefore be liability in negligence where a valuer fails to take care when carrying out a valuation of a property: *Smith v Eric Bush*.

Section 2 UCTA (negligence) must be applied where negligence is a liability on the facts and the clause has been construed (see p. 129, 'Construction point (v)') to cover that negligence.

Identify the loss caused by the negligence. (Remember that you have already identified the loss or damage at step 2—what has happened?)

> **Section 2(1):** death or personal injury resulting from negligence. This liability cannot be excluded or limited.
> **Section 2(2):** other loss or damage (property damage or economic loss). This liability can only be excluded or limited if the party seeking to rely on the clause establishes that the clause is reasonable (**s. 11**).
> Case example of **s. 2(2)** application is *Smith v Eric Bush*: financial loss resulting from negligent valuation. It followed that the valuer could rely on the disclaimer only if it could establish that the clause was reasonable.

Is there liability for breach of contract (i.e. strict contractual obligations)?

1. Does the liability which it is sought to exclude or limit involve a breach of any implied obligation relating to goods in the sale and supply of goods legislation?

Is the contract a contract for the sale of goods or for work and materials and is the term broken a breach of ss. 13, 14, or 15 SGA 1979 (or appropriate equivalents) relating to goods obligations, e.g. a breach of s. 14(2) SGA 1979 where the goods sold are not of satisfactory quality?

If no, consider the application of s. 3 UCTA (question 4 below). If yes:

2. Is the contract a contract for the sale of goods (s. 6 applies) or for the supply of work and materials (s. 7 UCTA applies to attempts to exclude implied obligations concerning the goods in a work and materials contract)?

✅ Looking for extra marks?

You can impress your examiner by being able to identify the type of contract (as well as the correct liability) and applying the correct section of UCTA—ss. 6 or 7. See Chapter 5 discussion of types of contracts and implied terms.

3. Does the applicable section (s. 6 or s. 7) allow the liability in respect of the goods to be excluded or limited?

By s. 6(1A) (sale of goods contracts) or s. 7(1A) (work and materials contracts), the implied terms as to conformity with description, satisfactory quality, fitness for purpose, or correspondence with sample (ss. 13–15 SGA 1979 and equivalents) **can be excluded or limited but only if the clause in question can be shown to be reasonable.**

Go to the reasonableness requirements (s. 11).

4. Other strict contractual liability and the application of s. 3

- If the breach is a breach of some other term of the contract (i.e. other than one of the implied terms as to the goods in the sales and supply legislation), **does s. 3 apply to the clause?**

Section 3 will apply to a B2B contract where one of the businesses is dealing on the other's written standard terms of business.

In general terms a set of standard terms will remain standard as long as there has been no negotiation of the exemption clauses although other terms, such as the price, may have been the subject of negotiation. This is all subject to the proviso that there must have been no substantial (or material) alterations to the standard form: *Yuanda (UK) Co. Ltd v WW Gear Construction Ltd* (2010).

Note that if s. 3 applies, it can be applied to:

(a) clauses allowing for substantially different contractual performance, e.g. allowing terms to be changed AND

(b) clauses allowing the party in breach to tender no performance at all (i.e. denials of any contractual obligation in the first place).

If s. 3 applies, the clause can be used to exclude or limit the strict contractual liability but only if the clause is shown to be reasonable (s. 11).

If s. 3 does not apply, then the clause is not subject to UCTA control at all.

The Unfair Contract Terms Act 1977 (UCTA 1977)

✳✳✳✳✳✳✳✳✳✳✳

The reasonableness requirement (s. 11)

If the clause has to be shown to be reasonable (**s. 11**) before it can be relied upon to exclude or limit the liability, can that burden be discharged by the party seeking to rely on the clause (**s. 11(5)**)?

Revision tip

Sections 2(2), 3, 6(1A), and 7(1A) all require that the clause is shown to be reasonable if it is to be relied upon.

❶ *Don't fall into the trap*

Don't rush into automatically applying the reasonableness test without showing that it is the applicable test for the liability in question. Since the **CRA 2015** has excluded consumer contracts from the application of **UCTA**, it is likely that there will be more applications of the reasonableness test as the context is B2B.

The test is whether the clause is 'fair and reasonable' when judged at the time the contract is made (as opposed to in the light of the breach) and on the basis of the circumstances which were, or ought reasonably to have been, known to or in the contemplation of the parties (**s. 11(1)**).

Reasonableness is determined by adopting a balancing test and placing factors on either side of that balance (per Lord Bridge in *George Mitchell v Finney Lock Seeds* (1983)). It follows that each case turns on its own facts and findings have no real precedent value.

Assessing reasonableness under s. 11

Traditionally the courts have favoured a finding of reasonableness of a clause where:

- The clause is contained in a commercial contract between commercial parties of equal bargaining power. The courts adopt a policy of non-intervention with the parties' agreement (*Photo Production Ltd v Securicor Transport Ltd* and *Watford Electronics Ltd v Sanderson CFL Ltd* (2001)). The courts take the view that 'commercial parties of equal bargaining strength . . . should generally be considered capable of being able to make contracts of their choosing and expect to be bound by their terms' (per Tuckey LJ in *Granville Oil & Chemicals Ltd v Davies Turner & Co Ltd* (2003)).

- The clause is a **standard operating clause in the particular industry** and has been negotiated by the relevant trade bodies.

- Where it is possible to cover the risk excluded by the exemption clause with **insurance** which could more economically, and should reasonably, be taken out by the non-breaching party, e.g. *Photo Production Ltd v Securicor Transport Ltd*: insurance cover should be taken out by the owner who would be the person directly sustaining any loss, particularly as the fee for service was modest. See also *Regus (UK) Ltd v Epcot Solutions Ltd* (2008).

- The fact that a breaching party's resources are limited may favour the reasonableness of a limitation clause (**s. 11(4)**).

- Where there was an inducement to agree to accept the exemption clause, such as a lower price (**Sched. 2 (b)**).

- If there is a realistic possibility that an alternative contract could have been entered into without the existence of the exemption clause (**Sched. 2 (a)**).

- Where the goods which are the subject of the exemption clause have been manufactured to customer's special order (i.e. bespoke) (**Sched. 2 (e)**).

Traditionally the courts have favoured a finding of unreasonableness where:

- There has been an imbalance in the parties' bargaining positions in favour of the party seeking to rely on the clause (**Sched. 2(a)**).

- A party's negligence may weigh in the balance against the reasonableness of a clause designed to protect that party, e.g. suppliers in *George Mitchell v Finney Lock Seeds* had been negligent in supplying incorrect seed. In the 'soft drinks' cases, *Bacardi-Martini Beverages Ltd v Thomas Hardy Packaging* (2002), and *Britvic Soft Drinks v Messer UK Ltd* (2002), the supply of carbon dioxide for use in carbonated drinks had been contaminated with benzene. This possibility had not been contemplated when drafting the exemption clause denying liability for breaches of implied terms as to satisfactory quality and fitness for purpose. It followed that this risk had not been accepted. In addition the contamination was the result of negligence on the part of the manufacturer and therefore this risk should not be transferred in the circumstances.

- If the insurance cover could more easily and cost effectively have been secured by the party in breach. In the commercial context the reasonableness of a supplier taking out insurance cover in relation to the fitness of products it supplies may depend on what that party knows of the intended uses for those products. Equally, a purchaser of products might not be expected to take out insurance cover in relation to latent defects in those products: *Balmoral Group Ltd v Borealis (UK) Ltd* (2006).

- If the clause is ignored in practice that may be evidence that it is regarded as unreasonable, e.g. *George Mitchell*.

George Mitchell (Chesterhall) Ltd v Finney Lock Seeds Ltd (1983) **(HL)**

FACTS: In breach of a contract for the supply of a specific cabbage seed, the wrong type of seed was supplied and the crop failed resulting in actual loss of over £60,000. However, the contract contained a limitation clause limiting the supplier's liability to the purchase price (roughly £200).

HELD: Although the breach involved the supply of a different product, the clause was construed to cover it. This clause was unreasonable in the circumstances and could not be relied upon by the supplier.

Where a clause provides that there will be no liability unless a condition is complied with, (i) it will fall for assessment under **UCTA** due to the **s. 13(1)** extended definition and (ii) the question is whether it is reasonable and practicable to expect compliance with the condition imposed: **R. W. Green Ltd v Cade Brothers Farms** (1978): clause required rejection, claim or complaint within three days of the arrival of the potato seed. However, the defect that occurred (seeds infected with a potato virus) would not be discoverable simply by inspecting the seed. It followed that this clause was unreasonable and could not be relied upon as a ground for denying liability.

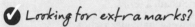

✅ *Looking for extra marks?*

An examiner will always be impressed if you are able to come to some reasoned conclusions, however tentative, on whether the clause is likely to be viewed as reasonable, although it is important to provide reasons by reference to application of the factors listed here.

The Consumer Rights Act 2015, Part 2 (Unfair Terms)

Does the Act apply to the contract?

This new regime regulating unfair terms in consumer contracts applies to contracts between traders and consumers (see Table 6.2 for definitions) and replaces the revoked Unfair Terms in Consumer Contracts Regulations 1999.

Significantly, a 'consumer' must be an individual (and therefore not a company or other legal entity) and that consumer must be acting for purposes which are 'wholly or mainly' outside that individual's business or profession, although the trader has the burden of disproving this position.

How does the Act regulate?

The **CRA 2015** requires contract terms and notices in consumer contracts to be fair (**s. 62**) but not all terms can be assessed for fairness. The assessment for fairness cannot extend to terms which (i) specify the main subject matter of the contract or (ii) relate to an assessment of the appropriateness of the price payable under the contract by comparison with the goods or services received as long as those terms are transparent and prominent. Transparency relates to the way in which the term is expressed (plain and intelligible language—and written terms need to be legible). Prominence relates to the way in which the term is presented. The term is prominent if it is brought to the attention of the consumer so that an average consumer would be aware of it. (Apart from the fact that this is questionable as overlapping with incorporation by reasonable notice, **s. 64(5)** then defines 'average consumer' as 'reasonably well-informed, observant and circumspect'.)

The Consumer Rights Act 2015, Part 2 (Unfair Terms)

With the exception of the need for the excluded terms to be transparent and prominent, this exclusion from the assessment for fairness existed under the previous legislation and caused difficulties in distinguishing between 'core' and 'ancillary' terms. It seems likely that this will continue.

Director General of Fair Trading v First National Bank plc (2001) **(HL)**

FACTS: A term of a loan agreement issued by the Bank provided that if the debtor defaulted on the loan, contractual interest on the outstanding debt remained payable until the debt was discharged. The debtor was taken to court and the judgment debt was ordered to be paid by instalments. However, the judgment debt and instalments did not include the contractual interest so that having paid the instalments the debtor would find that he still owed money in respect of the interest. It was argued that the term could not be challenged as unfair under the previous regulations since the contractual interest term was a 'core term' relating to the price of the goods and therefore the regulations did not apply.

HELD: The interest term was ancillary and not 'core'. It was not concerned with the price since it was not concerned with the Bank's remuneration for the service supplied.

However, in *Office of Fair Trading v Abbey National plc* (2009), the Supreme Court held that the Regulations could not be applied to bank charges since these charges were part of the 'core bargain'.

The terms listed in Sched. 2, Part 1 (terms which may be unfair—the 'grey list') cannot be subject to exclusion from the fairness evaluation.

Is the term in question unfair?

The term or notice is regarded as unfair if, contrary to the requirement of good faith, it causes a significant imbalance in the parties' rights and obligations under the contract to the detriment of the consumer (s. 62(4)). (This is the same wording as under the previous regulations so that previous interpreting case law will remain relevant.)

What guidance is there on judging whether a term is 'unfair'?

Section 62(5) contains some guidance regarding how the unfairness of a contractual term shall be assessed. It is necessary to take into account:

* the nature of the subject matter of the contract, and
* all the circumstances existing when the term was agreed, together with all the other terms of the contract or any other contract on which it depends.

Part 1 of Sched. 2 contains an 'indicative and non-exhaustive list of terms which MAY be regarded as unfair' (s. 63(1)). This lists 20 examples. (Advice: look at this list and identify the trends in regulation.)

The Consumer Rights Act 2015, Part 2 (Unfair Terms)
****

Section 65 CRA 2015 states that a trader cannot by a term of a consumer contract or a consumer notice either exclude or restrict liability in negligence for death or personal injury. (This corresponds to s. 2(1) UCTA which now applies only in the B2B context).

When, contrary to the requirement of good faith, does a term cause a significant imbalance in the parties' rights and obligations to the consumer's detriment?

Director General of Fair Trading v First National Bank plc

(For facts see p. 137, 'How does the Act regulate?')
The CA had concluded that the interest term was unfair to the debtor because of the element of unfair surprise, i.e. the judgment debtor would think that the entire debt had been repaid only to discover that interest was also owed. On appeal the HL disagreed and held that the term was not unfair as it stood. The expectation is that interest will be payable on money owed and any unfairness stemmed not from this term but from the fact that the judgment debt instalments did not incorporate the interest due on top of the capital sum owed.

The HL dealt separately with 'significant imbalance' and 'good faith'.

(a) There would be **significant imbalance** if the term was weighted in its substance (content) so heavily in favour of the trader that the parties' rights and obligations under the contract were tilted significantly in favour of that trader, e.g. a discretion or power granted to trader or imposition of a disadvantage, risk, or duty on the consumer. To determine this substantive fairness it is necessary to assess the particular term in the context of the contract as a whole, e.g. there might be a balancing provision in favour of the consumer.

(b) Good faith meant 'fair and open dealing':

   - **Openness** is procedural and requires the terms to be clearly and legibly expressed with no concealed pitfalls or traps. In particular, prominence needs to be given to terms which might operate to the disadvantage of the consumer.

   - **'Fair dealing'** refers to the fact that the trader should not seek to take advantage of the inequality of bargaining position and the consumer's lack of experience or knowledge. It follows that 'fair dealing' is both procedural and substantive since the substance of a term is relevant to whether advantage has been taken.

What is the consequence if the term is 'unfair' under the CRA 2015?

If a term is 'unfair', it is not binding on the consumer (s. 62(1) CRA 2015), although the contract can continue without that term (if this is possible) (s. 67).

Duty of court to consider fairness of terms

Where there are proceedings before a court which relate to a terms of a consumer contract and the court considers it has sufficient legal and factual material to do so, that court must consider whether the term is fair even if none of the parties has raised this as an issue or indicated that it intends to do so (**s. 71**).

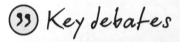 Key debates

Essay questions in this area are less common but will now tend to focus on:

> **The differing treatment of exemption clauses and unfair terms in commercial and consumer contracts, the history of the legislation and an evaluation of the provisions in the CRA 2015**

This debate involves evaluating different policy objectives in these different contexts and how the main distinction was seen in the differing approaches to the application of the reasonableness requirement in **UCTA**. Such a debate will involve looking at the differing scope of **UCTA** and the scope of the previous Regulations, together with the problems of overlap and odd distinctions relating to 'consumers' as 'companies' for the purposes of protections via **UCTA** but not the Regulations. Difficulties are posed for 'small businesses' by a simple B2B or B2C divide where 'consumers' are defined as 'individuals'. It will be necessary to analyse the position with regard to regulation (and protection) in commercial and consumer contracts to determine whether there is appropriate regulation for the respective contexts and parties under the current legislation. In other words, has the recent legislative reform achieved its objectives? How clear, for example, is the drafting in the **CRA 2015**? Has it assisted with the 'core and ancillary terms' distinction?

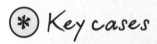 Key cases

Case	Facts	Principle
Chapelton v Barry Urban District Council **(CA)**	Deckchairs were displayed in a pile. The tickets for their use, which might have been obtained later, from the deckchair attendant, purported to exclude the Council's liability. CA held that the clause had not been incorporated as a term of the contract since the ticket was only a receipt for money paid and not a contractual document.	Incorporation: reasonable notice in time. The offer was the pile of deckchairs and acceptance was removing a deckchair from that pile. The ticket might come later and so was not part of the contract formation process.

Key cases

✳✳✳✳✳✳✳✳✳✳✳

Case	Facts	Principle
Thornton v Shoe Lane Parking Ltd (CA)	Notice at the entrance of a car park stating that parking was to be 'at owner's risk'. Entry was controlled by means of an automatic barrier and a machine before the barrier dispensed tickets which were 'issued subject to conditions displayed on the premises'. A notice inside the car park stated that the car park owners were not liable for injury to customers. CA held that the exemption on the ticket came too late. The offer in the notice at the entrance was accepted when the motorist drove up to the machine.	Incorporation by reasonable notice and automatic machines. The notice at the entrance, which was incorporated, was interpreted so that it did not cover personal injury, only damage to or loss from cars.
Interfoto Picture Library Ltd v Stiletto Visual Programmes Ltd (CA)	A clause imposed a fee of £5 per day for the late return of photographic transparencies. There were 47 of these transparencies and they had been kept inadvertently for an additional two weeks and a charge of £3,783.50 had been imposed. CA held that this term had not been incorporated since it was particularly onerous and unusual and therefore had to be fairly and reasonably brought to the other's attention, which had not happened.	A higher standard of incorporation will apply if the particular clause is considered to be onerous or unusual.
Photo Production Ltd v Securicor Transport Ltd (HL)	A contract involving the provision of security services for a factory contained a wide exemption clause exempting the security provider from loss. The security firm's employee started a fire on the premises and the factory owner suffered significant loss. HL held that as a matter of construction on its natural and ordinary meaning the clause in the contract did cover such a deliberate act. However, since this was a commercial contract, the fee was modest compared to any potential liability and the factory owner was expected to have insurance cover. The parties should be free to allocate their own risks.	Construction of exemption clauses: natural and ordinary meaning with clear words needed to cover a breach of this nature. Commercial contracts where the parties are of equal bargaining power: in general the parties are free to allocate responsibility for contractual risks through the use of exemption clauses.
Director General of Fair Trading v First National Bank plc (HL)	Bank's loan agreement provided that if the debtor defaulted on the loan, contractual interest on the outstanding debt remained payable until the debt was discharged. The judgment debt was ordered to be paid by instalments but it did not include the contractual interest so that, having paid the instalments, the debtor would find that he still owed money in respect of the interest. HL rejected argument that 'interest' was a core term relating to price for the service supplied so that it could be assessed within the legislation regulating unfair terms. Nevertheless, HL concluded that any unfairness to consumers resulted from the inability to add the contractual interest to the judgment debt and not from the term itself.	Legislation governing 'unfair terms': scope of application and meaning of core terms which could not be assessed for fairness as compared to ancillary terms (which could be) and approach to determining unfair contract terms in consumer contracts.

#7

Remedies for breach of contract

Key facts

- Compensatory **damages** (financial compensation) are the principal remedy for **breach** of contract. Specific enforcement is available only in limited circumstances when damages would not be an adequate remedy, e.g. ***Beswick v Beswick*** (Chapter 4).

- Contractual damages aim to compensate the claimant for losses suffered, as opposed to seeking to punish the defendant. The aim of damages is to protect the claimant's contractual expectation and put the claimant into the position they would have been in had the contract been properly performed and had the breach not occurred. Compensation for lost expectation may include an award of damages to compensate for expenditure wasted as a result of the breach.

- The lost expectation may be measured in terms of the difference between what the claimant expected to get and what was actually received. However, this loss may extend beyond the financial interest in performance to include purely subjective expectations in performance (the 'consumer surplus') and in such circumstances the cost of repair or replacement may be appropriate to achieve compensation if this would be reasonable (not out of all proportion to the benefit to be obtained) and if this expense represents an actual loss incurred.

- Non-pecuniary losses are generally not recoverable in a claim for breach of contract. However, there are some exceptional circumstances where pleasure, enjoyment, or peace of mind are recognized as being part of the expectation so that their loss is compensated.

Key facts

*********** *

- There are other limitations on the claimant's ability to be fully compensated such as the 'duty' to take reasonable steps to minimize loss (**mitigation**), the fact that losses which are too remote a consequence of the breach cannot be recovered (**remoteness**), and the possibility that a damages award may be apportioned (reduced) to take account of the claimant's own negligence (**contributory negligence**).

- The parties may agree in advance on the damages to be payable in the event of breach (**agreed damages clauses**). However, in certain circumstances the courts will strike down these clauses if they are penal (or punitive). It is necessary to distinguish those clauses operating as penalties from those which constitute enforceable liquidated damages. In addition, there are a number of anomalies surrounding the operation of the rule which strikes down penal clauses.

Introduction

The principal remedy for breach of contract in English law is **damages** (compensation for loss suffered as a result of the breach) and, as we saw in Chapter 5, there may also be an option to **terminate** or affirm where the breach in question is repudiatory. In the context of consumer contracts there may be a range of possible remedies if the **Consumer Rights Act 2015 (CRA 2015)** applies and statutory rights under a sale of goods, digital, or services contract have not been met.

Damages, as a common law remedy, are available as of right on proof of breach. This chapter focuses primarily on the basis on which those damages are calculated.

There are, however, other potential remedies although syllabuses frequently place less emphasis on these given the constraints of a modular teaching structure.

Other remedies

Debt claim

In a practical sense the most important alternative remedy is recovery of the contract price (debt claim; action for an agreed sum) which is relevant where the breach is non-payment of the price or other monetary sum due under the **terms** of the contract. This claim is for a liquidated (known) figure so that the difficulties of calculation of compensation for losses suffered are avoided. The claim in *White and Carter (Councils) Ltd v McGregor* (1962) was an action in debt and there was therefore no duty on the innocent party to mitigate by seeking to minimize the loss suffered.

A debt claim may be combined with a claim for damages where there is additional (unliquidated) loss.

Restitutionary claims

Restitution allows for the recovery of money paid or the value of benefits conferred on the guilty party on the basis that the guilty party should not be unjustly enriched at the injured party's expense.

- It must be shown that the D was enriched by the receipt of some benefit, e.g. money, realizable financial benefit, or has been saved a necessary expense.
- It must be shown that the D was enriched at the expense of the claimant.
- It must be unjust for the D to retain the benefit without compensating the claimant.

Recovery of money paid

An action for money had and received where there has been a *total* **failure of consideration (no contractual performance)** is an example of a restitutionary claim, e.g. price paid

Introduction

✳✳✳✳✳✳✳✳✳✳✳

for non-existent wreck of an oil tanker in *McRae v Commonwealth Disposals Commission* (1951). The price could be recovered in restitution as the payer had received no part of the performance in return.

Quantum meruit

Another type of restitutionary claim is recovery on a *quantum meruit* for the reasonable value of a non-financial benefit which the innocent party has provided and which is not otherwise recoverable since there is no express contractual provision for remuneration (*British Steel Corp. v Cleveland Bridge & Engineering* (1984), discussed in Chapter 2). The basis of recovery is that the guilty party would otherwise secure a benefit that it did not have to pay for.

Specific performance

Specific performance is an order which compels the party in breach to perform its obligations, whereas an **injunction** is generally prohibitory in the sense that it is an order preventing the breach of an obligation in the contract.

Key facts concerning the remedy of specific performance

- Unlike damages for breach which are available as of right and are the primary remedy for breach, specific performance is an equitable remedy available only at the court's discretion and subject to the usual 'rules of equity' such as 'coming to equity with clean hands', 'equity will not assist a volunteer' (someone who has not provided consideration).

- The court is only willing to exercise that discretion if damages would not be an adequate remedy. Damages will be an adequate remedy if it is possible to use the compensatory damages to purchase a substitute so specific performance is limited to unique goods, including the sale of land. Equally damages may not be an adequate remedy on the facts, e.g. *Beswick v Beswick* (1968) (for facts see Chapter 4).

- It is unlikely that such an order would be made if it would involve the court in *supervision* over a period of time (*Ryan v Mutual Tontine Westminster Chambers Association* (1893)).

- Similarly, in *Co-operative Insurance Society Ltd v Argyll Stores (Holdings) Ltd* (1997), the House of Lords (HL) held that a covenant in a lease of retail premises to keep open for trade during usual hours of business was not specifically enforceable because the courts would not make an order requiring a person to carry on a business. Any such order would require constant supervision and might cause injustice if keeping the business open involved the D in a loss.

- A court will not usually order specific performance of a contract involving personal services, such as a contract of employment (*Warren v Mendy* (1989)).

Damages for breach of contract

Think like an examiner

The topic of damages for breach of contract may feature in a set of problem facts, often in combination with terms and breach and usually requiring an assessment of recovery and quantum in the light of issues of remoteness, mitigation, and contributory negligence—sometimes with an issue relating to the recovery of damages for disappointment and distress. These questions will always be based on an understanding of the compensation principle and how that might be applied on the facts, e.g. identifying the lost expectation and considering how to compensate for it. You may be asked whether your assessment would be different in the light of a clause in the contract which appears to specify the basis of the damages in advance (agreed damages clause). These problem questions can be deceptive and the approach to answering them often causes students unnecessary angst.

Alternatively, essay questions are popular with examiners since it is relatively straightforward to draft an essay question focusing on whether damages for breach of contract compensate fully for losses caused by a breach. You will soon discover that they don't. Other essays may focus on specific limitations on recovery such as remoteness or on the approach to agreed damages clauses and the penalty rule.

This can seem like a large area of law but, as with all things, it is more manageable when broken down. There are a number of topics:

Topic 1: the compensation principle and how the lost expectation is measured

Topic 2: the limitations on the ability of a claimant to be fully compensated: remoteness, mitigation, contributory negligence, recovery of damages for disappointment and distress

Topic 3: the law governing agreed damages clauses and the application of the penalty rule.

Topic 1: The compensation principle and how the lost expectation is measured

The aim of contractual damages is to compensate the claimant for the loss they have suffered as a result of the D's breach of contract. Damages are therefore assessed by reference to the claimant's loss so that the claimant cannot recover more than their actual loss. Damages are restricted to nominal damages in the event that the claimant suffers no loss since the aim is not to punish the D even if they have profited from the breach: *Surrey County Council v Bredero Homes Ltd* (1993): developer breached original planning permission granted by the Council by building five extra houses. The Council did not suffer any loss as a result of the breach and damages were nominal.

Damages for breach of contract
✳✳✳✳✳✳✳✳✳✳

Key point

Parke B (at p. 855) in *Robinson v Harman* (1848): 'The rule of the common law is that where a party sustains a loss by reason of a breach of contract, he is, so far as money can do it, to be placed in the same situation, with respect to damages, as if the contract had been performed.'

It follows that contractual compensation focuses on what the claimant expected to receive and compensates the claimant for its loss.

Tip

Causation is an element in establishing liability, i.e. linking the breach to the loss which occurs. It is important not to forget this link once the loss has been established and **before** seeking to measure that loss.

Actual loss

Starting with an identification of the actual loss is key to the determination of the applicable measure of damages to compensate for it. In *Golden Strait Corporation v Nippon Yusen Kubishika Kaisha, The Golden Victory* (2007), the HL, by a majority of 3:2, held that damages may be reduced where subsequent events are known to the court at the date of the court hearing (and assessment of quantum) and those events would have reduced the actual loss suffered. Contractual principles required the innocent party (ship-owner) to be placed in the position that it would have been in if the contract had been properly performed. If the breach had not occurred, the Gulf War would have led to the exercise of the termination clause in March 2003 and no damages could be recovered for loss after that date.

Measuring lost expectation

We saw in Chapter 5 that a breach occurs either as a result of the non-performance of the contractual promise or its defective performance. In either case the starting point for measuring loss is the difference in value between what a party expected to receive and what that party in fact received due to the breach.

Damages for non-performance

Practical example

Florence and Adam are both car dealers. Florence buys a new car from Adam for £20,000. However, Adam fails to deliver the car. The measure of damages will be the extra cost to Florence, if any, of obtaining a substitute car, over and above the contract price. This is based on the market value of that substitute car on the date of the non-delivery. If that market price is £23,000 then the damages will be the extra £3,000 to ensure the contractual expectation of acquiring the car is fulfilled (**s. 51(3)**

Sale of Goods Act 1979 (SGA 1979)—non-delivery by a commercial seller in a contract for the sale of goods). If the market price is £20,000 or less than £20,000, only nominal damages will be awarded as there is no loss.

What if the breach is Florence's? Adam tries to deliver the car and obtain the £20,000 contract price but Florence refuses to take delivery and pay. Adam is left with a car which he is expected to sell in the market (mitigation—reasonable steps to keep his loss to a minimum). His damages will be the difference between the contract price and the market price on the date of Florence's non-acceptance (**s. 50(3) SGA 1979**—non-acceptance by the buyer in a contract for the sale of goods). If the market price has fallen to £17,000 then Adam's damages will be £3,000. If the market price is static at £20,000 or has risen, there is no loss. Given that products, particularly new cars, often have standard prices there may well be no loss—other than the loss of the profit that Adam would have made on the sale.

Since Adam is a car dealer and had a number of these cars (so that supply was greater than demand), he could argue that he has lost his profit on the sale to Florence (i.e. profit on this one extra sale). This lost profit will be recoverable where, as in this example, supply is greater than demand (*W. L. Thompson Ltd v Robinson (Gunmakers) Ltd* (1955): breach resulted in a lost sale of a car where these cars were readily available).

Cancellation of a contract to supply services

The measure of damages is the difference between what the contractor expected to receive had the contract been properly performed and what they actually received. If the contract had gone ahead as planned, the contractor would have received the price but would have needed to cover its fixed costs and the costs of performing the contract, leaving the net profit. It follows that the measure of damages would, subject to mitigation, normally be the net profit on the contract.

Damages for defective performance

The starting point for the measure of damages is the difference between the value of the performance **as promised** and the value actually received.

Practical example

Florence buys a car from Adam for £20,000. The market value of the car at the date of the contract to purchase (assuming it is as promised) is £22,500. Adam impliedly promises that the car is fit for purpose and of satisfactory quality. It is not (defective performance), and consequently its actual value is only £18,500.

Promised value (£22,500) - What actually received (£18,500) = £X (£4,000).

Is it ever possible to recover the cost of putting right the non-performance or defective performance rather than being limited to the difference in value?

This 'cost of repair' or 'cost of achieving the contractual performance' may greatly exceed the difference in value measure of damages.

Damages for breach of contract

✳✳✳✳✳✳✳✳✳✳✳✳

Practical example

Morgan agrees to sell Nazola a plot of land at the back of his garden. Nazola in turn agrees to comply with his request that she build a 6-foot-high red-brick wall as a boundary between the plots to ensure privacy. Morgan is very specific that the bricks should be red since he likes red bricks. It is clear that if Nazola either fails to build the wall or fails to build the wall in accordance with the contractual requirements then Morgan will have lost his contractual expectation (his 'consumer surplus': Harris, Ogus, and Phillips (1979) 95 LQR 581). It is equally clear that a damages award based on the difference in value between the land with or without a wall, or at a lower height or different bricks, might fail to adequately compensate Morgan. On the other hand, although we might see a justification in awarding Morgan cost of repair damages to build the wall to ensure privacy, we might well consider it wasteful if a 5-foot red wall had been erected or a 6-foot yellow wall and Morgan was insisting on the cost of knocking both down and rebuilding to meet his specific requirements.

When can the cost of repair be awarded?

Ruxley Electronics and Construction Ltd v Forsyth (1996) (HL)

FACTS: The D employed the P to build a swimming pool and specified the maximum depth and depth at a point for diving. The swimming pool depths did not meet these requirements but were safe and there was no difference in value as a result. The D argued that he should be able to recover £21,560 to demolish and rebuild the swimming pool to the depths specified in the contract.

HELD (agreeing with the trial judge): The cost of demolition and rebuilding was refused. Instead the HL awarded damages of £2,500 for loss of amenity (recognizing concern over diving depth).

- Recovery of cost of replacement had to be **reasonable, i.e. not out of all proportion to the benefit to be obtained**.
- **Intention to rebuild** was relevant to assessing the loss for which compensation was required—and hence was relevant to the reasonableness of awarding cost of replacement.

Tip

Cost of replacement tends to be relevant to land and buildings on land. It has the effect of guaranteeing the result of the obligation. It follows that in order to recover cost of repair on the *Ruxley* criteria, the obligation broken needs to be a strict obligation, e.g. to build a wall in accordance with the contractual specification (see Chapter 5, p. 110, Table 5.8, 'Standards of performance'). If, on the other hand, a surveyor is employed to survey a property but fails in his duty to exercise reasonable care and skill (breach of qualified obligation)—so missing property defects which need to be rectified—only difference in value damages can be recovered (*Watts v Morrow* (1991)). If cost or repair were recoverable the obligation broken would have been treated as if strict or a guarantee.

Consumer contracts and breaches of statutory rights relating to goods

In a consumer contract falling within the **CRA 2015**, the right to repair or replacement of:

- non-conforming goods (breaches of satisfactory quality, fitness for purpose, description, correspondence with sample or correspondence with a model seen and examined pre-contract) in a consumer contract; or

- goods incorrectly installed where installation forms part of the consumer contract and installation was the trader's responsibility; or

- non-conforming digital content in a consumer contract,

is specifically provided for as a remedy available to the consumer rather than the option to reject and claim damages. But this remedy cannot be disproportionate when compared to other available remedies (**s. 23(3) and (4) CRA 2015**).

Recovery for wasted expenditure

Wasted expenditure damages: it is possible to recover damages to compensate for expenditure which has been incurred in preparing for or performing the contract—and which has now been wasted as a result of the breach. This is now accepted as compensating for loss of expectation but achieving that calculation by restoring the claimant's position pre-breach rather than by calculating forwards to successful performance: *Omak Maritime Ltd v Mamola Challenger Shipping Co., The Mamola Challenger* (2010).

1. This *must* be the measure of damages where it is impossible to say what successful performance would have looked like, or been measured as

---

McRae v Commonwealth Disposals Commission (1951) **(High Ct Australia)**

FACTS: The Commission sold an oil tanker, said to contain oil, and lying at a particular location. The P paid £285 for the tanker and fitted out a salvage expedition but could not find the tanker.

HELD: Although the Commission was in breach of contract, since the promised tanker did not exist it was not possible for the P to establish its lost expectation (or profit on the oil). Instead the P recovered:

(i) £285—price paid for the wreck (restitution—total failure of consideration) and

(ii) £3,000—cost of salvage expedition (wasted expenditure).

Anglia TV v Reed (1972) **(CA)**

The same applied to the profits on a film being made for television which had to be cancelled when the lead actor pulled out of the filming. It was not possible to say what the profit would have been

---

as the film had not been made or sold to any television company. However, the Court of Appeal (CA) held that the film company could recover for the expenditure they had wasted ahead of the breach—and even before the D was contracted to appear, since he would have been aware that costs had already been incurred and these costs were likely to be wasted if the film did not proceed.

2. In other cases the claimant has a choice

The claimant has a choice whether to claim lost expectation (in a forward/profit sense) or lost expectation (in a wasted expenditure sense) BUT the claimant **cannot claim wasted expenditure loss** (and will be limited to lower expectation loss) if the expenditure would have been wasted anyway under the terms of the contract (so called 'bad bargains').

This is because to award wasted expenditure in such circumstances would amount to putting the claimant in a better position than they would have been in if the contract had been properly performed. Bad-bargain losses flow from the fact that the claimant made this contract on these terms rather than from the breach.

C & P Haulage Co. Ltd v Middleton (1983) **(CA)**

The D had a contractual licence to use the Ps' garage. The Ps wrongfully ejected the D but the D saved on this rent as he was permitted to use his own premises. Instead he sought the costs of fixtures for the garage but these were not recoverable under the terms of the contract. Therefore these wasted expenses were not caused by the breach but by the terms of the contract.

Equally, since the overall principle of calculation is compensation for losses suffered and the types of losses must be looked at as a whole, where the result of the breach is positive (no loss of expectation) and the effects of breach wipe out any wasted expenditure, there can be no wasted expenditure recovery. To do otherwise would put the claimant in a better position than if the contract had been performed and the breach had not occurred.

Omak Maritime Ltd v Mamola Challenger Shipping Co., The Mamola Challenger (2010)

Charterer repudiated charter but the owner was able to rehire at a higher rate (no lost expectation). The judge rejected the claim for wasted expenditure in preparing the vessel for the original charter on the basis that it would put the owners in a better position overall (due to the rehire receipts) than they would have been in had the contract been properly performed. This wasted expenditure, unlike the position in *C & P Haulage*, was caused by the breach (on the basis that these costs would have been covered by the hire) but the overall position meant that they could not be recovered separately because there was no loss of hire.

What is the applicable burden of proof?

There is a presumption in favour of the innocent party (the claimant) to the effect that the claimant would have recovered their wasted expenditure had the contract been properly performed. It was for the defendant (the guilty party) to seek to rebut this by showing that the claimant's expenditure would not have been recovered (*CCC Films v Impact Quadrant* (1985) and *Omak Maritime Ltd v Mamola Challenger Shipping* Co.).

Topic 2: Limitations on the ability to be fully compensated for lost expectation (Table 7.1) and put in the same position as if the contract had been properly performed

Table 7.1 Limitations on compensation for lost expectation

Remoteness	A claimant cannot recover for a loss which is too remote a consequence of the breach, i.e. although caused by the breach, the loss in question is too far away from what would have been contemplated to result.	Losses can only be recovered if they were **within the reasonable contemplation of the parties** *at the time of making the contract* as the probable result of its breach (*Hadley v Baxendale* (1854).
Mitigation	Innocent party cannot recover for any loss which he failed to take reasonable steps to minimize. What are reasonable steps in the circumstances is a question of fact (*Payzu Ltd v Saunders* (1919): Ps should have paid cash to acquire future goods at the contract price).	*Pilkington v Wood* (1953): reasonable steps did not extend to requiring P to bring onerous legal proceedings against the vendor of a house in order to protect D solicitor from the consequences of his negligence. Where steps are reasonable but increase the loss, the full extent of that loss can be recovered: *Banco de Portugal v Waterlow & Sons Ltd* (1932) (decision to exchange all notes increased the loss but was reasonable in the circumstances). But if the mitigation wipes out the loss then there is no recovery and limited to nominal damages for the breach: *British Westinghouse v Underground Electric* (1912).
Contributory negligence	Claimant's damages award **may** be reduced to take account of **claimant's own fault** in contributing to the loss suffered. Whether it does, depends on **nature of D's breach of contract**.	*Vesta v Butcher* (1989): apportionment if D's breach was a breach of a qualified contractual obligation ('fault': Law Reform (Contributory Negligence) Act 1945), but no apportionment for claimant's negligence if D breached a strict contractual obligation (*Barclays Bank plc v Fairclough Building Ltd* (1995) and *Hi-Lite Electrical Ltd v Wolseley UK Ltd* (2011).

Damages for breach of contract

✳✳✳✳✳✳✳✳✳✳✳✳

Damages for disappointment and distress	Non-pecuniary losses are generally not recoverable in breach of contract claim.	There are limited instances only when damages for disappointment and distress can be recovered in contractual claims.

Limitation 1: Remoteness of loss

Hadley v Baxendale (1854)

FACTS: The Ps engaged the Ds, a firm of carriers, to transport their broken mill shaft to Greenwich so that it could be used as a pattern for a new one. Carriage was delayed and the Ps lost profits in operating the mill as a result of the delay.

HELD: These profits were not recoverable since this loss depended on the fact, which the carriers did not know, that there was no spare shaft at the mill enabling it to operate. The loss of profits was therefore too remote a consequence of their delay in carriage, i.e. it was not in the contemplation of **both** parties at the time they made the contract as the probable result of a delay in the carriage. It would have been different if the carriers had been told that there was no spare mill shaft since any delay would inevitably have extended the shutdown.

Alderson B: the damages 'should be such as may fairly and reasonably be considered either *arising naturally* i.e. *according to the usual course of things, from such breach of contract itself, or such as may reasonably be supposed to have been in the contemplation of both parties at the time they made the contract as the probable result of the breach of it'*.

Losses are either 'normal loss' or 'abnormal loss'

(i) The D is liable for such losses as occur 'naturally' or as a result of the 'usual course of things' after this sort of breach of contract (Normal Loss) since both parties are taken to have knowledge of normal losses (and assume responsibility for it).

(ii) The D will be liable for losses that did not arise naturally (Abnormal Losses— dependent on special facts) but only if these losses were actually within the contemplation of both parties at the time they made the contract, i.e. both parties must have had actual knowledge of the special facts giving rise to the loss in order to assume responsibility for it.

Koufos v Czarnikow Ltd, The Heron II (1969) (HL): normal loss

FACTS: Ship-owners chartered a vessel to the charterers for the carriage of sugar from Constanza to Basrah knowing that the charterers were sugar merchants, the cargo was sugar, and that there was a sugar market at Basrah. The route taken meant that arrival was delayed and the market price of sugar fell. The charterers sought damages based on the difference in market price for their sugar caused by the delay.

HELD: Although the ship-owners did not actually know of the intention to sell the cargo immediately on arrival, the HL considered that this must have been within their reasonable contemplations as probable so that the market fall was normal loss, within remoteness and recoverable.

Victoria Laundry (Windsor) Ltd v Newman Industries Ltd (1949) **(CA): normal loss and abnormal loss**

FACTS: The Ps operated a laundry business and purchased a boiler for dyeing fabrics which they told the Ds, suppliers, would be put to immediate use in their business. The boiler was delivered late and the Ps sought loss of profits.

HELD: The Ps were able to recover their normal loss of profits on the use of the boiler in the period of the delay (normal loss when equipment purchased for a business) but not the loss of profits on some government contracts which they 'could have accepted' had the boiler arrived on time. This loss was abnormal loss depending on these special facts and was too remote since there was no evidence that the Ds knew of the intentions with regard to these special contracts.

Type of loss: provided the *type* of loss caused by the breach is within the reasonable contemplation of the parties, the extent of it need not be.

H. Parsons (Livestock) Ltd v Uttley Ingham & Co. Ltd (1978) **(CA)**

Illness to pigs due to eating mouldy pig nuts caused by the failure to ventilate the food hopper was within the parties' reasonable contemplations, so that the fact that some of the pigs died from a rare intestinal disease, e-coli, did not need to be specifically within the parties' contemplation.

Transfield Shipping Inc. v Mercator Shipping Inc., The Achilleas (2008) **(HL)**

FACTS: Time charterers were late in redelivery of the vessel. The owners had rechartered the vessel and managed to agree an extension of the cancelling date under the new charter but only on the basis that the new charterers received a reduction in the daily rate of the hire. The charterers argued that damages for their late redelivery were limited by the remoteness principles to the difference between the charter rate and the market rate at the time of redelivery for the period of the overrun since they had no knowledge of the terms agreed under the new charter. The owners wanted to claim their actual loss.

HELD: Recovery was limited to the difference between the charter rate and market rate since the charterers had not assumed responsibility over the renegotiated recharter terms. (Their Lordships had differing approaches so that it is necessary to be familiar with each if tackling an essay question examining remoteness.)

Lord Hoffmann considered that the actual loss (i.e. the actual terms) could not be contemplated and it would not be reasonable to hold the charterers liable for this risk. This must particularly have been the case given that damages limited to the difference in market rate for the overrun were accepted as the appropriate measure in the shipping market.

Limitation 4: No recovery in contract for non-pecuniary losses

Contractual damages may under-compensate an innocent party because she can recover only for economic (pecuniary) loss in contract and not for physical loss or disappointment (*Addis v Gramophone Co. Ltd* (1909)).

Damages for breach of contract
✷✷✷✷✷✷✷✷✷✷

Exceptions to the rule that damages for distress are not recoverable

1. *Watts v Morrow* (1991), per Bingham LJ at 1445: ***damages for distress were recoverable where 'the major or important' object of the contract*** (prior to *Farley v Skinner (No. 2)* it needed to be 'the very object') **was:**

    *   **to obtain some form of pleasure or peace of mind** (*Jarvis v Swans Tours* (1973) QB 233: package-holiday contract, damages for disappointment were recoverable when the contract failed to comply with brochure promises since 'enjoyment' was part of the lost expectation) **or**

    *   **to relieve a source of distress** (*Heywood v Wellers* (1976): solicitor employed to obtain a non-molestation injunction so avoiding this was part of the contractual expectation).

Farley v Skinner (No. 2) (2001) **(HL)**

FACTS: Potential purchaser specifically asked surveyor whether property he intended to purchase would be seriously affected by aircraft noise. The surveyor's report stated that this was unlikely. However, there was noise as the property was close to navigation beacon outside Gatwick. In **Watts v Morrow** the CA had rejected an argument that survey contract was a contract whose *very object* was to provide peace of mind.

HELD: 'Peace of mind' only needed to be a major or important object and not the sole object of the contract and, since the purchaser had specifically asked for a report on this matter, it had become an important part of the contract. Damages for distress were recoverable.

Hamilton Jones v David & Snape (a firm) (2003)

A **major or important object** of the contract with solicitor was to ensure for client's peace of mind that her ex-husband could not remove their children from the jurisdiction, although the **very object** of the contract in accordance with legislation was the protection of those children.

Commercial contracts: despite this relaxation in the basic test for the exception to operate, damages for distress will *not* normally be recoverable where the object of the contract is the carrying on of a commercial activity with a view to profit **since the major object of such a contract will be to make a profit** (*Hayes v Dodd* (1990)).

2. **It is possible to recover in contract for distress consequent on physical inconvenience or discomfort loss where that physical inconvenience or discomfort is directly caused by the breach,** i.e. the breach leads to a physical conclusion which itself gives rise to distress (*Perry v Sidney Phillips & Son* (1982) and *Watts v Morrow*).

Practical example

David manufactures bicycles at his factory in Burton Green. David contracts with the Burton Green Hotel for himself and his employees to enjoy a special spa day at the hotel following a tripling in bicycle sales. The hotel's brochure details the facilities available on the day, the lavish lunch and the beauty and relaxation treatments which 'will be provided for all guests'. The total cost of the day for David and 20 members of staff is £2,500. David pays this in advance.

The day is a disaster as the spa has been double-booked. There are no beauty and relaxation treatments available for David and his party. The lunch consists of a few lettuce leaves and a table-spoon of cottage cheese. David wishes to know if he can recover some compensation.

Clearly there are a number of breaches of contract, although not a total failure of consideration since the party has had some use of the facilities for the day. David will therefore want to be compensated for his loss (and will argue that he should be able to recover for the loss suffered by others in his party). This is a 'party convenience' contract calling for special treatment: Lord Wilberforce in *Woodar v Wimpey*, so David should be able to recover for the loss of the party. *Can you envisage any circumstances in which the individual employees might (in theory—since promisee action is more convenient) have a direct right of enforcement under the* **Contracts (Rights of Third Parties) Act 1999?** See Chapter 4.

The damages will therefore be the difference between the value of what was promised and what was received by David and his party. It is clear that this loss was within both parties' reasonable contemplations and David could not reasonably mitigate if these problems only came to light on arrival on the day booked for the spa day.

He will wish to recover damages for disappointment and distress for himself and his party and can do so as this contract falls within the pleasure/holiday contract exception (*Jarvis v Swans Tours, Jackson v Horizon Holidays*). Pleasure or enjoyment was part of the contractual expectation and was denied by the breach.

Topic 3: Agreed damages clauses

What is an agreed damages clause?

The parties may provide in their contract for the amount of damages to be paid upon breach. There are advantages for both parties in the use of such clauses:

- The innocent party does not have to prove its loss and need not be concerned with limitations on recovery such as remoteness and mitigation.

- The clause provides clear notice of the extent of the risk upon non-performance.

- Agreed damages clauses should avoid much of the disruption to the continuing relationship between the parties and the associated costs of a dispute on quantum.

Damages for breach of contract

✳✳✳✳✳✳✳✳✳✳✳✳

It follows that agreed damages clauses are generally regarded as efficient and desirable. However, there is a danger that where the damages payable are set too high, the clause will have a punitive effect, which would be contrary to the essential compensatory aim of contractual damages.

Key point

The distinction between clauses which will be enforced and those which will not is expressed as a distinction between **liquidated damages clauses** (enforceable) and **penalty clauses** (unenforceable and the courts instead award damages based on unliquidated principles to compensate for actual loss). Table 7.2 explains the distinction and the consequences of classification.

Table 7.2 Agreed damages clauses

Type of clause	Valid?	Nature	Consequences
Liquidated damages clause	√	Genuine attempt to pre-estimate the loss which will be suffered by breach.	If a liquidated damages clause, the liquidated sum will be payable whether the actual loss is greater or smaller than this stipulated sum. *Cellulose Acetate Silk Co. Ltd v Widnes Foundry (1925) Ltd* (1933): 'penalty' for late performance at rate of £20 a week. Actual loss of £5,850 but liquidated damages so limited recovery to 30 weeks x £20 = £600.
Penalty clause	X	Not a genuine pre-estimate of the loss suffered in the event of breach but is extravagant and unconscionable designed as a threat to compel the other to perform by penalizing that other for non-performance, i.e. predominant function is deterrence (*Makdessi v Cavendish Square Holdings BV* (2013)). *Jobson v Johnson* (1989)): D had contracted to purchase shares in a football club but if he defaulted on payment of any instalment of price he had to retransfer the shares for only £40,000. He defaulted when he had paid £140,000 of the purchase price. CA held the retransfer clause was not a genuine pre-estimate of the loss on breach, but an unenforceable penalty.	Penalty clause is unenforceable so that claimant can recover its actual loss.

Damages for breach of contract

Distinguishing liquidated damages and penalty clauses

This is a question of construction depending upon the parties' intentions but guidelines (see Table 7.3 for a summary) were laid down by Lord Dunedin in ***Dunlop Pneumatic Tyre Co. Ltd v New Garage & Motor Co. Ltd*** (1915).

Table 7.3 Lord Dunedin's recommendations

Terminology used is not conclusive, e.g. ***Cellulose Acetate***.
Decide if the clause was **a genuine pre-estimate of the likely loss at the time contract was made rather than in the light of the breach.** The estimate does not have to be correct, i.e. does not need to be the same as the actual loss as long as it was a genuine and sensible estimate of the likely loss resulting from that breach.
In commercial contracts made 'at arms' length' the clause is likely to have been intended by the parties as enforceable liquidated damages clause: ***Philips Hong Kong Ltd v AG of Hong Kong*** (1993). Account should not be taken of unlikely hypothetical breaches, since it would be very difficult to draft a clause that would *never* operate in a penal way. The courts should uphold the parties' agreement.
It is a penalty if the sum stipulated is much greater than the possible loss resulting from the breach.
It is a penalty if the breach is **non-payment** and the agreed figure is greater than the price due.
Where a single sum is payable for a variety of different breaches it might be thought that it should be considered a penalty because it is difficult to see how it could be a genuine pre-estimate of likely loss in the case of all of these types of breaches. But in the commercial context the courts should ignore trifling breaches when applying this guidance: ***Cenargo Ltd v Izar Construcciones Navales SA*** (2002). It follows that if an agreed damages amount increases in proportion to the seriousness of different breaches then it is more likely to be considered as liquidated damages.
Situations where it is difficult to estimate the loss are just the situations where the amount in the clause was likely to be 'the true bargain between the parties' and hence a liquidated damages clause.

The CA in ***Makdessi v Cavendish Square Holdings BV*** considered that a clause that was extravagant in amount, and so not a genuine pre-estimate of loss, might still be rescued from unenforceability as a penalty if it could be shown to be 'commercially justified' in the sense of fulfilling a balancing commercial purpose in the contract as a whole (and ensuring that a commercial bargain was reached). On the facts there was no commercial justification and the clause was held to be a penalty. (This case is on appeal to the Supreme Court.)

The penalty rule applies only where the sum specified as agreed damages is payable on breach and not where it is payable in the event of some other event

This means that even if the agreed sum is penal in nature (i.e. excessive amount or threat to compel performance), it will be enforceable (i.e. payable) where it is payable on an event

Damages for breach of contract

✱✱✱✱✱✱✱✱✱✱✱✱

other than breach (*Alder v Moore* (1961): declaration that professional footballer would not play football again and that if he did, he would be subject to a £500 penalty. He played football again and argued that he did not need to repay the £500 since it was an unenforceable penalty payable on breach. Held: it was not a sum payable on breach (i.e. a promise not to play with the £500 repayable if he did), but a positive obligation to repay £500 if he played again. It followed that it was enforceable and had to be repaid).

The penalty rule will not normally apply to prevent a deposit being forfeited by the payer in the event of that payer's breach of contract

---

Practical example

Nazia has agreed to buy Laura's house and on exchange of contracts pays her a 10 per cent deposit. This deposit is normally forfeited in the event that Nazia (the payer) changes her mind and withdraws from the purchase. However, it might be argued that this sum is an unenforceable penalty which is payable on breach, particularly if Laura has suffered little in the way of loss due to the breach. Nevertheless, although the deposit may exceed the actual loss and so could be considered 'penal' in nature, it will normally be forfeited and cannot be recovered (***Howe v Smith*** (1884)).

However, the deposit must be reasonable in amount. If it is unreasonable then the penalty rule may apply to it (*Workers Trust and Merchant Bank Ltd v Dojap Investments Ltd* (1993)). In *Workers Trust*, a deposit of 25 per cent had been demanded when the prevailing local rate was 10 per cent. The Privy Council considered the deposit to be unreasonable and therefore repayable.

Template problem question covering damages

David manufactures bicycles at his factory in Burton Green. He wishes to manufacture a new model of bicycle with optimal electronic settings and performance. However, he needs to purchase specialist machinery for this purpose. The only manufacturer of this electronic equipment in the UK is Creative Maximum Performance plc (CMP).

(a) David therefore enters into a contract with CMP plc for the manufacture and delivery of this specialist equipment by 1 July, intending to put it into production and produce the new model bicycles in time to supply the Christmas market. The equipment costs £50,000. However, he does not disclose these specific intentions to CMP plc as he wishes future expansion and the new products plan to remain confidential in order to be ahead of the competition. CMP plc knows only that David manufactures bicycles.

The contract between David and CMP plc contains the following clause: 'In the event that the equipment is not supplied by 1 July, CMP plc will pay, by way of agreed compensation, £5,000 for every day by which delivery is delayed.'

(b) Having made the contract to acquire the specialist equipment, David enters into a contract with Eclipse plc, a chain of bicycle shops, for the supply of 5,000 new model bicycles a week for 20 weeks at a contract price of £1,000,000, with the first delivery commencing on 1 August.

The equipment was eventually delivered by CMP plc but was 35 days late. David was unable to meet the initial deliveries under the Eclipse contract and Eclipse has advised that it plans to sue for 'substantial damages'.

CMP claims that the clause in its contract with David is unenforceable.

Advise David.

Is the agreed compensation clause in the contract between David and CMP enforceable liquidated damages or an unenforceable penalty? You need to (i) explain the consequences to each finding, i.e. if liquidated damages then this sum is payable and (ii) apply the principles in *Dunlop v New Garage & Motor* to determine the classification, bearing in mind that this is a commercial contract and, although CMP is the only manufacturer of this equipment in the UK, there is no evidence that this was not an arms' length negotiation.

If it is a liquidated damages clause then CMP must pay £5,000 x 35 days (*Cellulose Acetate Silk*) which is £175,000. The contract price is £50,000. It may follow that it would be a penalty clause (threat to compel performance) but it is difficult to imagine that its insertion was down to David given CMP's market position. It would be a penalty if breach were non-payment (see *Dunlop v New Garage*). However, the position depends on whether £5,000 a day could be seen as a genuine pre-estimate of the loss due to a day's delay judged at the date of the contract. We know the contract price but would need to consider evidence of David's operating costs and production to determine this.

If we assume (if only because it makes the question more interesting) that the clause is a penalty, it is unenforceable and we would need to discuss the calculation of unliquidated damages in the usual way. David's lost expectation due to delay would be his lost profits on putting the new equipment into use in his business (*Victoria Laundry v Newman Industries*: normal loss of profit). Could David recover for his lost profit on the Eclipse contract and other costs if sued by Eclipse for failure to deliver? This is a loss which is dependent on special facts (abnormal loss) but CMP has no knowledge of the special facts and therefore of the fact that loss over and above normal lost profits is likely to result. It follows that to the extent that the loss on this contract exceeds normal lost profit on the use of the equipment it will be too remote to be recoverable. However, recovery is probably not impacted by any failure to mitigate since David would have found it difficult to secure an alternative supplier of the equipment, there being no other supplier in the UK.

David may therefore be keen to argue that the agreed compensation clause is a liquidated damages clause.

Key debates

****

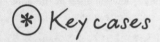

There are numerous possible essay-style questions on damages for breach and you should be led by the emphasis in the syllabus of your module. The 'limitations on compensation' question allows the examiner to test the full range of principles for determining compensation but it is equally difficult for a student to produce an exceptional or unusual answer in the absence of specific readings and analysis. You should therefore ensure that you (i) understand the terminology so that you answer the question set, (ii) cover the relevant ground, and (iii) have read a range of articles and readings. It is vitally important to have the readings to ensure depth to your analysis where the essay focuses on a more specific element of damages, e.g. remoteness, or recovery of non-pecuniary loss or cost of repair damages (*Ruxley*).

1. **Remoteness** has proved popular in recent years as a result of the controversies surrounding the decision in *The Achilleas* (and the assumption of responsibility test) when compared to the principles in *Hadley v Baxendale*.

   Lord Hoffmann, '*The Achilleas*: Custom and Practice or Foreseeability?'[2010] Edin LR 47.

   Kramer, 'The New Test of Remoteness in Contract' (2009) 125 LQR 408.

2. **Cost of repair damages**: *Ruxley* and consideration of the approach taken by Lord Scott in *Farley v Skinner (No. 2)*.

3. **Debate about the differing approaches to agreed damages clause in commercial and consumer contracts or a more general critique of the penalty rule.** As to the latter, see the excellent discussion in Morgan, *Great Debates: Contract Law*, 2nd ed (Palgrave Macmillan, 2015), 234–42.

For further readings see Poole, *Textbook on Contract Law*, 12th edn (Oxford University Press, 2014), pp. 395–6.

Key cases

Case	Facts	Principle
Ruxley Electronics and Construction Ltd v Forsyth (HL)	D employed P to build a swimming pool and specified the maximum depth and depth at a point for diving. The swimming pool depths did not meet these requirements but were safe and there was no difference in value as a result. HL rejected D's argument that he should be able to recover £21,560 to demolish and rebuild the swimming pool to the depths specified in the contract. HL agreed with trial judge and awarded £2,500 for loss of amenity.	Cost of repair damages will be available (to avoid a windfall) only where the cost of repair or replacement was reasonable (not out of all proportion to benefit to be obtained) and there was an intention to repair.

Case	Facts	Principle
McRae v Commonwealth Disposals Commission (High Ct Australia)	The Commission sold an oil tanker, said to contain oil, and lying at a particular location. It could not be found. P sued for breach and recovery of lost profits on tanker. Commission alleged **common mistake** (both thought the tanker existed). Held that the Commission was in breach of contract since it had promised that the tanker was lying at the location (had taken this risk so not common mistake) but since it was not possible to establish the lost profit on non-existent oil, P was limited to recovering the price paid and the cost of the salvage expedition.	Where lost profits are too speculative to prove, a claimant will be limited to recovering for wasted expenditure.
Omak Maritime Ltd v Mamola Challenger Shipping Co., The Mamola Challenger	Charterer repudiated charter but the owner was able to rehire at a higher rate (no lost expectation). The judge rejected the claim for wasted expenditure in preparing the vessel for the original charter on the basis that it would put the owners in a better position overall (due to the rehire receipts) than they would have been in had the contract been properly performed.	Although the contract did not prevent recovery of the wasted expenditure (no provision as in **C & P Haulage v Middleton**), its recovery would not be permitted if overall it would put the claimant in a better position than if the contract had been performed. This case recognizes wasted expenditure as an element of expectation recovery.
Hadley v Baxendale	Ps engaged Ds, a firm of carriers, to transport their broken mill shaft to Greenwich so that it could be used as a pattern for a new one. Carriage was delayed and Ps lost profits in operating the mill as a result of the delay. However, the lost profits were too remote a consequence of the delay to be recovered since they depended on the special fact that there was no spare mill shaft and this fact was not known to the carriers.	Remoteness rule in contract: the loss must fall within the reasonable contemplations of both parties as liable to result in the event of breach. This loss of profits was not in the contemplation of **both** parties at the time they made the contract as the probable result of a delay in the carriage since the carriers had no notice of this fact.
Victoria Laundry (Windsor) Ltd v Newman Industries Ltd (CA)	Ps operated a laundry business and purchased a boiler for dyeing fabrics which they told Ds, suppliers, would be put to immediate use in their business. The boiler was delivered late and Ps were able to recover their normal loss of profits on the use of the boiler in the period of the delay but not the loss of profits on some government contracts which they 'could have accepted' had the boiler arrived on time. This loss was abnormal loss depending on these special facts and was too remote since there was no evidence that Ds knew of the intentions with regard to these special contracts.	Remoteness: normal loss can be recovered as both parties have imputed knowledge of such loss. However, abnormal loss is dependent on special facts and both parties must have actual knowledge of these special facts for the loss to fall within their contemplations.

Key cases

✳✳✳✳✳✳✳✳✳✳

Case	Facts	Principle
Farley v Skinner (No. 2) (HL)	Potential purchaser specifically asked surveyor whether property he intended to purchase would be seriously affected by aircraft noise. Surveyor's report stated that this was unlikely. However, there was noise as the property was close to navigation beacon outside Gatwick. HL held that damages for distress and disappointment were recoverable since the purchaser had specifically asked for a report on noise, making 'peace of mind' a major or important object of the contract. *Obiter*, such damages would have been recoverable for distress consequent on physical inconvenience, i.e. resulting from the aircraft noise.	Exceptional situations when damages for distress and disappointment can be recovered have been extended so that 'contracts to obtain some form of pleasure or peace of mind' no longer need to be the sole purpose of the contract as long as they are major or important objects.
Dunlop Pneumatic Tyre Co. Ltd v New Garage & Motor Co. Ltd (HL)	Dunlop supplied tyres to dealers and the dealers received discounts for agreeing not to sell the tyres at below Dunlop's list price. If they did, they had to pay £5 per tyre 'by way of liquidated damages'. The dealer sold the tyres at below list price and pleaded that the clause was an unenforceable penalty. Held it was an enforceable liquidated damages clause. Since any pre-estimate of loss would be difficult, this was just the situation where the sum agreed should be enforced as the parties' bargain.	Making the distinction between liquidated damages and penalty clauses: see Lord Dunedin.

#8

Contractual impossibility and risk: Frustration and common mistake

Key facts

- Where the contract **terms** expressly or impliedly allocate the risk of a contractual event (such as the existence of the contractual subject matter) to one party and that event occurs, that party cannot rely on the impossibility of performance as an excuse to a claim for non-performance or **breach** of that contract.

- However, in the absence of a contractual allocation of the risk, a contract may be **void** (of no effect from the very beginning) if unknown to the parties at the time the contract was made, it was impossible to perform from the outset (**common mistake**). Non-performance in such circumstances is excused since there is no valid contract to perform.

- Circumstances falling short of impossibility, such as mistakes as to the quality of the subject matter rather than as to its existence, do not render the contract void and the contract must therefore be performed in accordance with its terms or the non-performing party will be in breach.

- This is an 'all or nothing' principle, i.e. a contract is valid or void. The courts have no equitable jurisdiction to set aside the contract for a fundamental mistake as to quality.

- Equally, in the absence of a contractual allocation of the risk, if an event occurs after the contract has been made which renders further performance of the contract 'impossible' and that event occurs without the fault of either party, the contract will be discharged by **frustration** and the non-performing party has an excuse for that non-performance.

- If the subsequent event which renders further performance impossible can be attributed to one of the contractual parties, that party will be in breach and cannot rely on frustration as a defence to a claim based on non-performance.

Key facts

✳✳✳✳✳✳✳✳✳✳ ✳

- Where a contract is discharged by frustration both parties are excused performance of their future obligations and the application of the **Law Reform (Frustrated Contracts) Act 1943 (LR(FC)A 1943)** determines what happens to advance payments (such as deposits) due before the frustrating event, and claims for reimbursement for contractual expenses and performance conferred prior to frustration.

- The legal treatment of initial and subsequent impossibility is very different. It is important to appreciate this and to attempt to explain the difference in treatment.

Introduction

This chapter examines the law's response to events that render performance of the contract impossible for reasons beyond the responsibility of the contracting parties, and so provide an excuse for non-performance.

Practical example 1

Alex agrees to sell his bicycle (named make and model) to Becky and to deliver it on Friday. However, the day after the agreement was made, the government passed emergency legislation which required the compulsory requisition of all bicycles in private ownership, and so prevented Alex from performing.

Should Alex be liable for his failure to perform, assuming that the contract is silent as to this risk? What happens if Becky has already paid the price for the bicycle or paid a deposit?

This type of impossibility occurs *after* the contract was made (subsequent impossibility) but it is also possible to envisage the impossibility existing from the outset, albeit in quite limited circumstances.

Practical example 2

Alex agrees to sell his bicycle to Becky and to deliver it on Friday. However, unknown to Alex and Becky at the time when they make this contract, Alex no longer has such a bicycle since a few hours earlier Alex's mother had inadvertently driven her car over it and destroyed it beyond repair. Both Alex and Becky thought there was such a bicycle in existence, but unknown to both it did not exist at the time they made the contract of sale.

Does Alex need to refund the price or any deposit that Becky has paid?

This type of impossibility exists from the outset and is known as initial fundamental impossibility (the subject matter of the contract does not exist).

Risk allocation

The law's response to impossibility is to look to what the contract says is to happen in the circumstances that have occurred (an express provision allocating the risk to one of the parties), e.g. there may be a *force majeure* clause placing the risk of events such as strike, riot, flood, or fire on one of the parties. In these circumstances the express provision will govern and any dispute between the parties tends to concern construction issues concerning this provision (interpreting the scope of the words used; see Chapter 6).

Introduction
✱✱✱✱✱✱✱✱✱✱✱

Metropolitan Water Board v Dick Kerr & Company Ltd (1918) **(HL)**

FACTS: Contractual provision allowed engineer to grant an extension of time in relation to contract to build reservoir in six years if contractor had been 'unduly delayed or impeded' by 'any difficulties, impediments or obstructions whatsoever and howsoever occasioned'.

HELD: This did not cover a government prohibition on construction of the reservoir as a consequence of the First World War.

William Sindall plc v Cambridgeshire County Council (1994) **(CA)**

The Court of Appeal (CA) held that the contract allocated the risk of the existence of a sewer on development land to the purchaser. The purchaser could not avoid the contract and recover the purchase price by relying on mistake as to the existence of the sewer.

If the contract says nothing as explicit, then the court may consider that the contract terms and context impliedly places the risk of the existence of the subject matter on the seller. In such circumstances the non-existence of the 'promised' subject matter will constitute a breach. This is what happened in *McRae v Commonwealth Disposals Commission* (1951): sale of wreck of oil tanker stated to be at a specified location. The seller impliedly promised that the wreck was located there. Its absence was a breach of contract, entitling the purchaser to obtain **damages**.

Default legal doctrines where there is no allocation of the risk

It is only where there is no express or implied allocation of the risk of this event in the contract that the default legal doctrines—frustration (subsequent impossibility) and common mistake (initial impossibility)—may come into play in instances of impossibility of performance.

Think like an examiner

So, how do examiners approach this area of law? Essay-style questions are popular, not least because the academic interest in these topics far outweighs their significance for the practising lawyer (see p. 183, 'Key debates').

Some tutors and examiners adopt a less contextual approach to the law of mistake than appears in this book and amalgamate problem questions on the law of mistake. This involves blurring the distinction between those mistakes which prevent agreement being reached (**mutual mistake** (cross-purposes) and **unilateral mistake**, see p. 36, Table 2.1) and instances of fundamental common mistake (Table 8.1) where, although an agreement has clearly been reached (as in the Alex and Becky contract to sell the destroyed bicycle: p. 165, 'Practical example 2'), both parties enter that contract based on the same fundamentally mistaken assumption, i.e. that the bicycle is in existence so that its ownership can be transferred.

Table 8.1 Nature of common mistake

Mistake which nullifies the agreement reached.	Both parties are mistaken.	Each party makes the same mistake, e.g. both believe subject matter of the contract exists when it does not—***Couturier v Hastie***.

It is possible to construct a problem question based only on establishing whether there is a sufficiently fundamental common mistake, usually including a mistake as to quality (discussed at p. 169, 'Mistakes as to quality'). It can be difficult to spot the issue as being one which concerns a quality. You need to look out for references to particular types of the goods in question, e.g. types of teas, types of pottery, paintings by famous artists (see p. 169, 'Don't fall into the trap'). Use the case law facts as your guide. By comparison, problem questions based on subsequent impossibility, identifying the fact that the frustration doctrine can operate on the facts and assessing the consequences for the parties, are relatively common in examination papers.

Initial impossibility and the excuse of common mistake

Assuming that there is no express or implied provision allocating the risk of the event in question to one party, **if a contract was entered into under a *fundamental* common mistake, then the contract will be void at common law for mistake (of no effect from the very beginning). If a contract is void, then the parties are clearly excused from all performance.**

This occurs where the event renders performance in accordance with the contract terms an *impossibility*, e.g. unknown to the parties the subject matter of the contract does not exist (*res extincta*), or both parties believe the property that the seller purports to sell belongs to the seller when in fact it already belongs to the buyer (*res sua*—the thing was already his; *Cooper v Phibbs*). In both instances there can be no transfer of title/ownership of the goods or property so that the basic premise of the contract is always impossible.

Res extincta: Mistake as to the existence of the subject matter

Couturier v Hastie (1856) **(HL)**

FACTS: Seller sold corn, which was believed to be in transit on board a ship, to the buyer. Unknown to both, the cargo had already been sold because it had begun to ferment on route. Thus the subject matter had ceased to exist before the time of the contract.

HELD: Since the contract was for the sale of existing goods, the contract was void and the buyer was not liable to pay for the corn. (This proposition can now be seen in **s. 6 of the Sale of Goods Act 1979 (SGA 1979)**: where there is a contract for the sale of specific goods, and the goods without the knowledge of the seller have perished at the time when the contract is made, the contract is void.)

Initial impossibility and the excuse of common mistake

✱✱✱✱✱✱✱✱✱✱

Compare this with *McRae v Commonwealth Disposals Commission* (see p. 166, 'Risk allocation'), where the seller was impliedly taken to accept the risk of the non-existence of the tanker.

Another useful example to mention in your answers is *Griffith v Brymer*.

Griffith v Brymer (1903)

FACTS: When a contract was made at 11 a.m. on 24 June 1902 to hire a room to view the coronation procession of Edward VII (the subject matter of the contract), neither party was aware that at 10 a.m. on 24 June the decision had been taken to cancel the procession due to the King's surgery.

HELD: This went to the root of the hire contract, which was therefore void. The plaintiff could therefore recover the £100 hire charge he had paid. Compare this decision with **Krell v Henry** (see p. 175, 'The final possibility').

Returning to practical example 2 concerning initial impossibility. This is a common mistake (both parties make the same mistake) as to the existence of the subject matter at the date of the contract. It is similar to *Couturier v Hastie* and **s. 6 SGA 1979** would apply.

Practical example 2

Alex agrees to sell his bicycle to Becky and to deliver it on Friday. However, unknown to Alex and Becky at the time when they make this contract, Alex no longer has such a bicycle since a few hours earlier Alex's mother had inadvertently driven her car over it and destroyed it beyond repair. Both Alex and Becky thought there was such a bicycle in existence, but unknown to both it did not exist at the time they made the contract of sale.

Does Alex need to refund the price or deposit that Becky has paid?

The contract is void and it follows that the price or deposit must be refunded.

Res sua: Mistake as to ownership of the subject matter of the contract

---

Cooper v Phibbs (1867) **(HL)**

FACTS: A fishery belonged to a nephew but he thought it was owned by his uncle so that, on his uncle's death, he entered into an agreement to rent the fishery from his uncle's daughters.

HELD: The nephew was entitled to have the contract set aside. (Although this suggests that the agreement was **voidable** so that the court needed to intervene with an appropriate order, the agreement was clearly void as this is true impossibility.)

Mistakes as to quality

It may be contended that a mistake made by both parties as to some quality (mistake as to quality), which both mistakenly believe the goods possess, *should* render the contract void because both would not otherwise have contracted, e.g. both believe that a picture is painted by a famous artist such as Constable although neither party makes express reference to their belief.

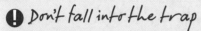

❶ Don't fall into the trap

Don't fall into the trap of confusing s. 14(2) SGA 1979 (and the equivalent provision in consumer sale and supply contracts, s. 9(1) CRA 2015) 'satisfactory quality' with the position where the goods or subject matter do not possess *a particular quality* which both parties thought the goods possessed.

'Satisfactory quality' refers to a minimum quality level in a broad sense, whereas mistakes as to quality refer to a characteristic of the goods—e.g. a particular type of pottery, a particular quality or type of tea, whether a service agreement could be terminated only by paying compensation to the director, the relative positions of vessels.

Summary: Other possible remedies if the goods do not possess a particular quality that had been anticipated

- Was the quality a term of the contract or otherwise part of the contractual description in a sale of goods by description (**s. 13 SGA 1979 (B2B)** or **s. 11 CRA 2015 (B2C)**) (i.e. there was a promise that the goods possessed this quality)? In the context of consumer contracts covered by the CRA 2015, s. 11(4) provides that any information relating to the 'main characteristics of the goods' that is supplied by the trader falling within the Consumer Contracts (Information, Cancellation and Additional Charges) Regulations 2013 (SI 2013/3134) will constitute 'a term' (or promise). In these circumstances, there will be a remedy for breach of contract.

- Did the vendor state that the goods possessed a particular quality and this had the effect of inducing the contract? If so, there may be a remedy in misrepresentation—**rescission** and/or damages for misrepresentation (Chapter 9) or, in the context of consumer contracts, remedies under the Consumer Protection from Unfair Trading Regulations 2008 (CPRs 2008) as amended (discussed Chapter 9).

- **If no statement of fact was made, then the last-resort remedy of mistake may be attempted.**

However, an argument based on common mistake as to quality is most unlikely to succeed. Unless the quality is made a term (promise) of the contract, the absence of this quality will not make the contract **impossible to perform in accordance with its terms** (*Bell v Lever*

Initial impossibility and the excuse of common mistake

****

Brothers Ltd (1932) and *Great Peace Shipping Ltd v Tsavliris Salvage International Ltd* (2002)). If there is such a promise relating to the quality, there will be an action for breach of contract. Link this back to *Smith v Hughes* (1871), Chapter 2, and the principle of '*caveat emptor*' (let the buyer beware): it was a contract for 'oats' in the absence of any statement that the oats being sold were 'new' or 'old' or a statement from the buyer that he wanted only 'old' oats.

Leaf v International Galleries (1950) **(CA)**

FACTS: Both the gallery selling a painting and the purchaser of the painting believed the painting was by Constable.

HELD *Obiter*: In the absence of any assumption of risk, e.g. a promise by the gallery, the contract remained valid despite the parties' mistake. The parties were agreed in the same terms on the same subject matter.

---

❶ Don't fall into the trap

Don't fall into the trap of thinking that what matters is whether the parties would have contracted had they known the truth. They usually would not, but this is not the applicable legal principle. Equally, in English law the value associated with the mistake is not determinative, e.g. the fact that a picture is bought and sold at a high price does not mean that any common mistake that it was painted by a famous artist must be fundamental and render the contract void.

There are two key cases concerning common mistake as to quality.

---

1. Bell v Lever Bros. Ltd (1932) **(HL)**

FACTS: £30,000 compensation was paid to an employee to terminate his service contract with the company. This was a common mistake as to quality since both parties thought that the service contract could only be terminated with compensation, when in fact no compensation was required.

HELD 3:2: The compensation agreement was not void for such a mistake as to quality.
Nevertheless there are *dicta* in *Bell v Lever Bros.* suggesting that a contract may be void if the mistake as to quality is sufficiently fundamental, Lord Atkin commenting that:

> **a mistake as to quality will affect assent if it is as to the existence of some quality which makes the thing without the quality *essentially different* from the thing as it was believed to be.**

However, Lord Atkin then gave some examples of situations where the mistake as to quality would not be sufficiently fundamental, i.e. where the parties are taken to agree in the same terms on the same

---

subject matter so that there is no 'essential difference'. **These examples are so restrictive that it is difficult to envisage situations where the mistakes will be sufficiently fundamental to render the contract void.** For example: A buys a picture from B: both A and B believe it to be the work of an old master and a high price is paid. It turns out to be a modern copy. A has no remedy in the absence of **representation** or **warranty** (contractual promise).

---

2. *Great Peace Shipping Ltd v Tsavliris Salvage (International) Ltd* (2002) **(CA)**

The CA accepted that the test of whether the contract performance would be 'essentially different from the performance that the parties contemplated' **amounted to whether performance in accordance with the contractual terms or adventure is impossible due to the common mistake.** Only if it is impossible will the contract be void. ('Essential difference' therefore equates to the strict test of impossibility of performance.)

FACTS: A ship suffered structural damage at sea. The Ds (salvage service) sought the closest vessel which both the Ds and the Ps (owners of '*The Great Peace*') thought was '*The Great Peace*' at about 35 miles distance. The Ds therefore hired this ship on the basis of terms which required them to pay a charge if the contract was cancelled. In fact the vessels were 410 miles apart. The Ds cancelled the contract once they had found an alternative vessel (although they did not cancel straight away) but refused to pay the cancellation charge pleading the mistake.

HELD: The test was narrow and this mistake was not fundamental since performance was not impossible. '*The Great Peace*' would have arrived in time to provide several days of stand-by service and the contract had not been cancelled until an alternative vessel had been arranged.

It follows that impossibility of terms or adventure will rest on the facts and context of each individual case. For example: it may not have been possible for '*The Great Peace*' to have provided any part of the contracted for salvage services had it been 4,000 miles away from the damaged ship. If cancelled on discovery, such a contract would be void for fundamental common mistake as to quality. In other words, there would then be a total failure of consideration.

The CA also refused to follow its own previous decision in **Solle v Butcher** (1950) and held there was no equitable jurisdiction to set aside the contract on terms for mistake as to quality. The advantage of this remedy was that it offered great flexibility and discretion to the courts to do justice on the facts (see p. 183, 'Key debates').

Compromise agreements

In the context of agreements to compromise claims which were alleged to have been entered into under common mistakes as to quality, subsequent courts have considered that since the compromise agreements remained capable of performance despite the mistakes, they could not be void: *Brennan v Bolt Burdon* (2004) and *Kyle Bay (t/a Astons Nightclub) v Underwriters Subscribing Under Policy Number 019057/08/01* (2007): mistake as to insurance cover held had led to compromise agreement on reduced terms but the compromise was capable of being performed. (Consider why this conclusion has practical significance for compromise agreements and their sanctity.)

Subsequent impossibility: Frustration doctrine and discharge of the contract

A contract may be **automatically discharged** (so that the parties are excused further performance of their contractual obligations) if, during the currency of the contract, and **without the fault of either party, some event occurs which renders further performance:**

- **impossible**
- **illegal**
- **radically different so that the purpose of both parties is no longer possible and the contract becomes essentially different.**

In a problem question you first need to identify the issue as involving subsequent impossibility and ensure that the contract does not contain any express allocation of this risk which applies, e.g. *force majeure* clause. (Bear in mind that this is unlikely as the examination question would then be about breach—and simple breach at that.)

Let us look again at **practical example 1** concerning the bicycle:

Alex agrees to sell his bicycle (named make and model) to Becky and to deliver it on Friday. However, the day after the agreement was made, the government passed emergency legislation which required the compulsory requisition of all bicycles in private ownership, and so prevented Alex from performing.

Should Alex be liable for his failure to perform, assuming that the contract is silent as to this risk? What happens if Becky has already paid the price for the bicycle or paid a deposit?

Note: This contract became illegal after it was made. It was not illegal at inception.

Having noted that there is no risk allocation provision (or *force majeure* clause), there are two questions to address:

1. **Is this a frustrating event so that the frustration doctrine will apply?** It will be necessary to rule out 'fault' on the part of any party since the frustration doctrine applies only where the event is 'external' and occurs without the fault of either party.

2. **What effect does the frustrating event have on the contract and the parties' obligations under it? How does the law allocate the risk of the event?**

Issue (1) is often relatively straightforward (as in the bicycle example) since the examiner is often keen to test how well you understand the effects and the application of the legislation, the **LR(FC)A 1943.**

Is this a frustrating event so that the frustration doctrine will apply?

The first possibility: Is further performance impossible?

(a) Has the subject matter of the contract been destroyed by an external occurrence or is otherwise permanently unavailable for the contract term? *Taylor v Caldwell* (1863): hire of music hall for concerts but before the concert dates the hall was destroyed by fire. Another example would be the sinking, or requisitioning of a hired (chartered) ship for the remainder of the contract term.

Example

If in practical example 2 Alex's mum had reversed over his bicycle **after he had made the contract** with Becky, the contract would be frustrated by the destruction of its subject matter. Since she had reversed over it **before the contract was made**, it is initial impossibility based on the absence of subject matter.

(b) If there is an agreed means of performing the contract and this becomes unavailable, the contract will be frustrated, e.g. *Nickoll & Knight v Ashton, Edridge & Co.* (1901): shipment to be made on a specified ship which was stranded at sea. (Compare the position where there is no agreed means of performance, only a contractual expectation, e.g. that shipment will be made via the Suez Canal as this was the quickest route: *Tsakiroglou & Co. Ltd v Noblee Thorl GmbH* (1962)—contract not frustrated when the Suez Canal was closed.)

(c) Is this a personal contract (requiring performance by a named individual) where, ahead of the performance, the performer dies or has a permanent illness preventing performance on the date in question? *Robinson v Davison* (1871): contract to play the piano at a concert on a particular day. The pianist was unable to play due to illness and this was successfully pleaded as a defence to a claim of breach of contract.

(d) What if the subject matter, agreed means of performance, or performer (in a personal contract) is only temporarily unavailable? This may amount to impossibility if the interruption is of such a nature and likely duration as to undermine the possibility of further performance when assessed in relation to the contract as a whole and render the contract 'radically different', e.g. *Morgan v Manser* (1948): contract to manage comedian from 1938 for ten years was frustrated from the time when the comedian was called up for the army in 1940. He was not demobilized until 1946.

Jackson v Union Marine Insurance Co. Ltd (1874)

FACTS: Ship sailed from Liverpool to Newport on 2 January. It was to 'proceed with all possible dispatch' and load a cargo of iron rails in Newport for transport to San Francisco. However it ran

---

Subsequent impossibility: Frustration and discharge
****

> aground en route to Newport on 3 January and was not got off until 18 February, and was not repaired until the end of August. The charterers had purported to terminate the charter on 15 February.
>
> **HELD:** The charter contract was frustrated. The resumed voyage would have been a very different voyage to the spring voyage contemplated by the charterers.

Compare with *Edwinton Commercial Corporation v Tsavliris Russ (Worldwide Salvage and Towage) Ltd, The Sea Angel* (2007): purpose already largely performed when vessel unlawfully detained.

Rix LJ in *The Sea Angel* at [111]:

> In my judgment, the application of the doctrine of frustration requires a multifactorial approach. Among the factors which have to be considered are the terms of the contract itself, its matrix or context, the parties' knowledge, expectations, assumptions and contemplations, in particular as to risk, as at the time of contract, at any rate so far as these can be ascribed mutually and objectively, and then the nature of the supervening event, and the parties' reasonable and objectively ascertainable calculations as to the possibilities of future performance in the new circumstances. Since the subject matter of the doctrine of frustration is contract, and contracts are about the allocation of risk, and since the allocation and assumption of risk is not simply a matter of express or implied provision but may also depend on less easily defined matters such as 'the contemplation of the parties', the application of the doctrine can often be a difficult one. In such circumstances, the test of 'radically different' is important: it tells us that the doctrine is not to be lightly invoked; that mere incidence of expense or delay or onerousness is not sufficient; and that there has to be as it were a break in identity between the contract as provided for and contemplated and its performance in the new circumstances.

Returning to practical example 1

The day after the agreement was made, the government passed emergency legislation which required the compulsory requisition of all bicycles in private ownership, and so prevented Alex from performing. The terms of the contract require Alex to deliver the bicycle on Friday but he no longer has the bicycle and the circumstances indicate that the requisition will continue beyond Friday. The requisition may initially be temporary, but in relation to the contract terms it seems permanent and equivalent to the unavailability of the subject matter through no fault of either party.

The second possibility: Is further performance illegal?

If, during the currency of the contract, a change in the law renders further performance illegal, the contract will be frustrated for subsequent impossibility: *Denny, Mott & Dickson v James B. Fraser & Co. Ltd* (1944): the Control of Timber Order 1939 frustrated a trading agreement involving timber.

A contract may also be frustrated by *temporary* illegality, as in *National Carriers Ltd v Panalpina (Northern) Ltd* (1981): a lease of a warehouse for ten years from 1974 was not frustrated when the local authority closed the street (so there was no vehicular access) for 20 months from 1979. The interruption was only 20 months out of ten years and there were still three years to run after the interruption ceased. On the other hand, in *Metropolitan Water Board v Dick, Kerr & Co.* (1918) a contract was made in 1914 to construct a reservoir in six years. In 1916 the Minister of Munitions ordered the contractor to stop. The HL held that this interruption was of such a character and likely duration as to frustrate the contract for supervening illegality. The resumed contract would be very different in nature.

The final possibility: Has the common purpose of both parties been ended by the subsequent event?

In some circumstances frustration may occur where further performance, though technically possible, would become something radically different from that originally envisaged by **both** parties, i.e. the event has destroyed the purpose of the contract for both parties.

Krell v Henry (1903) **(CA)**

FACTS: A contract to hire rooms was advertised as rooms to view the coronation procession of Edward VII. The coronation was subsequently cancelled due to the King's illness and surgery.

HELD: The contract of hire was frustrated since the CA considered the viewing of the procession was the 'foundation of the contract' for *both* parties.
   It is not enough that the purpose of only *one* party is destroyed. Vaughan Williams LJ gave an example to explain this:

> Suppose a person hires a cab to go to Epsom on Derby Day and Derby Day is cancelled. The contract is not frustrated since seeing the races is not the foundation of the contract for BOTH parties. It is only the hirer's purpose. The cab driver's purpose is to drive to Epsom and back.

(But if, for example, a person buys a coach ticket for an excursion to Epsom 'to see the races on Derby Day' the common basis of both is to see the races. Therefore if the races are cancelled the contract is frustrated.)

   Compare *Krell v Henry* with *Griffith v Brymer* (1903), see p. 168, 'Res extincta' (decided on the basis of common mistake because, unknown to the parties, the procession had already been cancelled at the time the contract was entered into).

   Krell v Henry can also be contrasted with the CA decision in *Herne Bay Steam Boat Co. v Hutton* (1903) where there were two purposes to the contract—one of which was still possible.

Herne Bay Steam Boat Co v Hutton (1903) **(CA)**

FACTS: The Ds had chartered steamboat from the Ps to take out a party:

- to view the naval review, and
- for a day's cruise around the fleet.

The naval review was cancelled because of the King's illness but the fleet remained.

HELD: The contract was not frustrated since the review was not regarded as the foundation of the contract and the cruise around the fleet was still possible.

Subsequent impossibility: Frustration and discharge
****

Limitation on frustration

A contract is not frustrated by an event, which leaves it possible to perform, but which makes it more burdensome to one party

---

Davis Contractors Ltd v Fareham UDC (1956) **(HL)**

FACTS: The Ps agreed to build council houses for D Council in eight months. The work took 22 months and the Ps argued that the contract was frustrated by the long delay, which was due to a severe manpower and materials shortage.

HELD: The contract had not been frustrated. Lord Radcliffe: 'It is not hardship or inconvenience or material loss itself which calls the principle of frustration into play. There must be as well such a change in the significance of the obligation that the thing undertaken would, if performed, be a [radically] different thing from that contracted for.'

Tsakiroglou & Co. Ltd v Noblee Thorl GmbH (1962) **(HL)**

Contract was not frustrated by the closure of the Suez Canal as the seller could perform by shipping the goods via the Cape of Good Hope, although that would be more expensive and would take longer.

Was the frustrating event foreseen by the parties—or by one of the parties—and not provided for?

If **one** party foresaw or should have foreseen the 'frustrating event', the doctrine of frustration does not apply and that party may be liable for breach of contract. *Walton Harvey Ltd v Walker & Homfrays Ltd* (1931): the Ds were aware of the possibility of compulsory purchase of the premises on which the sign had been erected under the terms of the agreement with the Ps. The Ps had no such knowledge. The Ds could have expressly provided against this risk but they did not.

What if the parties should have foreseen the event but neither made express provision to deal with it? Is this a risk allocation or does the doctrine of frustration apply?

There have been two positions:

1. There is HL authority supporting the conclusion that the contract would not be frustrated in these circumstances. In *Davis Contractors* the shortage of labour and materials was foreseeable but, since there was no express contractual provision to provide for it, the contractors had taken this risk on themselves and the contract was not frustrated. Equally, in *Amalgamated Investment & Property Co. Ltd v John Walker & Sons Ltd* (1977), the contract to purchase commercial property was not frustrated by the decision to list the property, since there was a risk that the building might be listed and this was a risk that the purchaser had to bear.

2. However, there are *dicta* in *Tatem Ltd v Gamboa* (1939), and comments by Lord Denning in *The Eugenia* (1964), suggesting that the frustration doctrine might still

apply where an event was foreseen but not provided for (although on the facts in *The Eugenia* it did not).

In *Edwinton Commercial Corporation v Tsavliris Russ (Worldwide Salvage and Towage) Ltd, The Sea Angel* (2007), the risk of government detention of a salvage vessel given environmental concerns was foreseeable but Rix LJ considered that foreseeability did not necessarily rule out the application of the frustration doctrine. He noted that 'the less that an event, in its type and impact, is foreseeable, the more likely it is to be a factor which, depending on other factors in the case, may lead on to frustration'.

Practical example 1

The government passing emergency legislation to compulsorily requisition all bicycles in private ownership is unforeseeable, so this issue need not detain our application.

Was the event attributable to the fault of one of the parties—or was it the result of a choice made by one of the parties?

The frustration doctrine only applies where the frustrating event comes about without the fault of either party. Therefore, if it was brought about by the fault of one of the parties, that party will be in breach and the frustration doctrine will not apply. (This is commonly known as 'self-induced frustration' but it is actually breach.) For example, in *The Eugenia*, in breach of contract, the vessel had gone into the Suez Canal without the owner's consent and had become trapped when the canal had been closed. Charterers claimed the contract had been frustrated but the CA held that this was their own fault.

(a) Self-induced frustration can occur if a party deliberately elects to pursue a course of conduct rendering performance impossible, such as making a choice over which vessels were to receive licences for nets and claiming that the charter of trawlers from the Ps had been frustrated by the absence of the necessary licences (*Maritime National Fish Ltd v Ocean Trawlers Ltd* (1935)). It followed that the Ds were not excused the payment of hire for these trawlers.

(b) More surprisingly (so that this has become an examiners' favourite), the mere existence of a choice may be sufficient to establish self-induced frustration.

J. Lauritzen AS v Wijsmuller BV, The Super Servant Two (1990) **(CA)**

FACTS: The contract permitted performance by either of 2 vessels, the *'Super Servant One'* (SS1) and the *'Super Servant Two'* (SS2). The Ds allocated the work to SS2 and employed SS1 on other contracts. When the SS2 sank the Ds claimed that this frustrated the contract.

HELD: Since it was Ds' decision not to use the alternative vessel, the sinking of SS2 could not automatically bring the contract to an end.

What effect does the frustrating event have on the contract and the parties' obligations under it? How does the law allocate the risk of the event?

The effect of frustration is to automatically discharge the contract as to the future (i.e. each party is excused from future obligations).

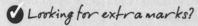

✅ Looking for extra marks?

1. This is a principle of common law (and has nothing to do with the **LR(FC)A 1943**).

2. Frustration does **not** render the contract void—rather it discharges future obligations (like termination for **repudiatory breach**). It is a grave error to state otherwise in an examination or coursework as the examiner will assume that you are confused on a fundamental issue.

3. However, the discharge of a contract for frustration happens automatically on frustration (although a court will later confirm this), whereas termination (discharge of future obligations) for repudiatory breach is dependent on the election of the innocent party (Chapter 5).

What about the position of obligations which had arisen prior to frustration, expenses incurred and any performance conferred?

At common law (prior to the **LR(FC)A 1943** and the common law remains applicable where the Act has no application):

- Obligations arising before the frustrating event remained binding and the loss was said to lie where it fell. It followed that advance payments paid or due to be paid before the frustration could not be recovered or remained payable (*Chandler v Webster* (1904)), unless there had been a total failure of consideration, i.e. the payer had received no part of the contracted for performance (*Fibrosa SA v Fairbairn Lawson Combe Barbour Ltd* (1943)). However, in cases of total failure of consideration, where the advance payment has to be returned by the payee, there was no provision to attempt to recompense the payee who had incurred expenses in preparing to perform the contract.

- If payment under a contract was to be made on the completion of the work and frustration occurred before the work was completed, then no payment (or any part of it) could be recovered at common law.

Appleby v Myers (1867)

FACTS: The Ps had contracted to install and maintain all machinery in the D's factory, payment to be made upon completion. Before the task of installation had been completed, the factory and machinery were destroyed by fire and the contract was frustrated.

HELD: The future payment obligation was discharged by frustration and the Ps could recover no part of it.

The Law Reform (Frustrated Contracts) Act 1943

1. Recovery of advance payments

Section 1(2): recovering money paid in advance:

> **Payer's rule**: money paid before the frustrating event is recoverable and money payable before the frustrating event ceases to be payable (irrespective of whether there has been a total failure of consideration).
>
> **Payee's rule**: however, if the party to whom the sums are paid or payable, incurred **expenses before discharge in performance of the contract**, the court **may** award him such expenses up to the limit of the money paid or payable before the frustrating event.

Practical example

(1) Henry, the purchaser, pays £500 in advance. Isabel, the seller, has already incurred £350 in expenses for the purpose of performing the contract before the frustration occurs. Henry is prima facie entitled to the return of his £500, but *the court may* allow Isabel to retain *up to* £350 as expenses.

(2) If Henry has paid £500 in advance and Isabel has incurred £800 as expenses, the maximum Isabel can recover as expenses is £500 (the amount paid in advance).

Thus the maximum amount of recovery under **s. 1(2)** is the amount of the advance payment. The court possesses a discretion within this advance payment figure.

Of course, **s. 1(2)** does not provide that the performing party (Isabel in the example) will be entitled to retain **all** of her expenses from the advance payment amount.

> #### *Gamerco SA v I.C.M./Fair Warning (Agency) Ltd* (1995)
>
> **FACTS:** A concert by the group 'Guns N' Roses' at a stadium in Madrid had to be cancelled due to safety issues affecting the stadium. The Ps were promoting the concert and had already paid $412,000 on account and were under an obligation to pay, but had not yet paid, a further $362,500. The Ps had also incurred expenses of $450,000 prior to the cancellation and the Ds had expenses of $50,000.
>
> **HELD:** On the basis that the contract was frustrated, the Ps were able to recover the advance payment of $412,000 and did not need to make the further payment of $362,500 already due. Although the court had a 'broad discretion' to allow the Ds to set off their expenses under the proviso to **s. 1(2)**, having particular regard to the expenses incurred by the Ps which would be lost, no deduction for the Ds' expenses was made under the proviso.

Practical example

On 1 July Sarah engages Tyler, a painter and decorator, to paint the outside of her house for £900, payable on completion. The painting work is to commence on 16 July and it is estimated that it will take five days. It is agreed that Sarah will pay Tyler £200 on or before 10 July to cover the costs of hiring scaffolding and purchasing the masonry paint. Sarah paid the £200 on 9 July. Tyler started work on 16 July but on 18 July (to take a simple example) the government passes legislation rendering domestic house painting illegal. This frustrates the contract.

What is the position with regard to payment of the price? Can Sarah recover the £200 advance payment? Can Tyler claim to retain all of the £200 and recover for other expenses he has incurred since starting work of an additional £75?

(a) The obligation to pay the balance of the price (£700) has been automatically discharged by the frustration.

(b) In accordance with **s. 1(2) LR(FC)A 1943**, Sarah can prima facie recover the amount of the advance payment (£200), unless the court in its discretion allows Tyler to keep up to £200 (amount of the advance payment) to cover his expenses. Let us suppose that Tyler is able to establish that he has expenses of this amount (or more) and the court exercises its discretion to allow him to retain it all.

(c) Tyler cannot claim to recover any more than the amount of the advance payment under **s. 1(2)**.

Tips

1. **Section 1(2)** is popular with examiners (probably because **s. 1(3)** is more complex in its application and only likely to apply in limited circumstances). You should express the application of **s. 1(2)** as meaning that prima facie the advance payment is recoverable by its payer but that the court *'acting in its discretion' may* allow the payee to retain up to £X (whatever figure may be given as the expenses—or the lower figure of the advance payment) to cover the payee's expenses. This may involve some simple maths but you should not panic. As in the example above, the figures will be straightforward and the examiner is looking primarily for the correct principles—correctly expressed.

2. If there is no advance payment then expenses cannot be recovered under **s. 1(2)**.

2. Recovery for performance prior to frustration

Key points

A performing party can recover for his pre-frustration performance but:

(a) **only where this performance confers a valuable benefit on the party receiving performance**

(b) recovery is subject to the court's discretion.

Section 1(3) limitation: There must be a tangible benefit to the recipient which remains after the frustration

There was no **s. 1(3)** claim in *Gamerco v I.C.M.* in respect of the Ps' expenditure incurred in preparing the stadium because the expenditure had not resulted in any benefit to the Ds at the time of discharge for frustration.

Practical example:

In the painting example Tyler may argue that his painting work has left him out of pocket, over and above the £200 expenses he has recovered. Can he recover for this work? He can seek to argue that he has conferred a valuable benefit (partially painted house) on Sarah prior to the frustration. How will the court approach such a claim?

Section 1(3): Performance conferring a valuable benefit

If a party has conferred a valuable benefit before the frustration, the court may award him a just sum to recompense him for the benefit he has conferred. This cannot be greater than the value of that benefit to the party receiving it.

In deciding on the just sum, the court must consider all the circumstances of the case and in particular:

(a) **whether the benefited party (Sarah in the painting example), has incurred expenses in the performance of the contract before the time of discharge** (including the fact that Sarah made an advance payment to Tyler of £200 which Tyler was allowed to retain under s. 1(2)—Tyler cannot recover the same figure twice)

(b) **the effect of the frustrating event on the benefit received.**

BP Exploration Co. (Libya) Ltd v Hunt (No. 2) (1979)

The P oil company had agreed to explore for oil and develop the D's oil concession in Libya on the basis of being entitled to share in oil revenues if oil was discovered. The P spent considerable sums drilling for oil before finding oil in commercial quantities. However, the Libyan government then expropriated the concession.

The P sought a 'just sum' under **s. 1(3) LR(FC)A 1943** in respect of the benefit obtained by the D as a result of the P's performance of the contract prior to frustration.

Robert Goff J considered that the purpose underpinning the **LR(FC)A 1943** was the prevention of unjust enrichment, i.e. one party unfairly acquiring a benefit which he would not otherwise have to pay for. Accordingly, he identified the following as the steps to determine a 'just sum' to award:

- **Identify the valuable benefit that the D has received.**

The benefit, he said, was the end product of the services and not the services themselves.

On the facts in *BP v Hunt*, the benefit was not the services of exploration but the end product (i.e. the increased value of the concession due to the discovery of oil).

In the painting example, the valuable benefit would be the partially painted house received by Sarah rather than Tyler's work in painting.

Subsequent impossibility: Frustration and discharge
****

- Value the benefit to the party receiving it.

Such value forms the upper limit of any award.

The court would therefore need to determine how much the partially painted house was worth to Sarah, particularly given the fact that it cannot be finished due to the prohibition on such painting. Let us say that the court values this benefit to Sarah as being worth £500.

According to the judge, at this stage the court would need to take account of the expenses already recovered by Tyler under **s. 1(2)** from the advance payment (or the fact that Sarah has already paid £200 towards the painting). (It is arguable that **s. 1(3)** states that this is a factor to bring into account at the next stage. The positioning is important since the figure produced at the stage of valuing the benefit forms the upper limit of any award of a just sum.) This leaves a figure of £300 (£500–£200) as the value of the benefit and the upper limit of any award made.

- Then the court may award such sum, not greater than the value of such benefit to the D, as the court considers just having regard to all the circumstances of the case, i.e. the just sum.

As a basic measure, the claimant should get the reasonable value of his performance (as long as this is not more than the value of the benefit to the D). In any event, the court cannot award more than the contract price.

Let us suppose that the court considers that the reasonable value of Tyler's painting work is £600 at the time when the frustration intervenes. The just sum awarded to Tyler could not be more than £300 since Sarah should not have to pay any more than the value of the painted house to her (and we have concluded that was £300, after taking account of the money already paid for expenses).

Consequences of the approach adopted by Robert Goff J

Goff J considered that the Act was concerned with preventing unjust enrichment which meant allowing recovery of no more than the value of any benefit received from performance. He defined 'benefit' as the end product of services. It follows that, on this view, if there is no valuable benefit because the effect of the frustration is to destroy it, then there can be no **s. 1(3)** award of a 'just sum'.

Practical example

What if, on the facts of the painting contract, the frustration was not illegality but the destruction of Sarah's house due to a freak forest fire?

Sarah is left with no valuable benefit if the benefit is the end product of the services (painted house) and not the services themselves. Tyler could not recover any 'just sum' under **s. 1(3)** and

---

would be seriously out of pocket. His recovery would be limited to the recovery of expenses under the **s. 1(2)** proviso. He is fortunate therefore that there was an advance payment since no expenses could be recovered had there been no such pre-payment.

You should now be able to advise on the parties' positions in the simple bicycle example at the beginning of this chapter: practical example 1.

Should Alex be liable for his failure to perform, assuming that the contract is silent as to this risk? What happens if Becky has already paid the price for the bicycle or paid a deposit?

At common law the frustration will discharge both parties' future obligations and that includes Alex's obligation to deliver the bicycle. Becky's advance payment (full price or deposit) is prima facie to be returned to her (**s. 1(2) LR(FC)A 1943**) unless the court, in its discretion, allows Alex to retain any part of that payment to cover his expenses. On these facts we have no evidence of any expenses.

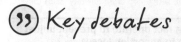 Key debates

---

1. The denial in *The Great Peace* of any equitable jurisdiction to set aside (rescind) a contract for common mistake as to quality
....

Until 2002 where a contract was entered into as a result of a common mistake which was not sufficiently fundamental at common law to render the contract void (i.e. mistakes as to quality), that contract might still be treated as voidable in equity and be set aside on terms. This possibility was recognized by the CA (the judgment of Denning LJ) in *Solle v Butcher* (1950) and allowed for great flexibility of remedy in such cases. However, in order to be voidable in equity the mistake needed to be 'fundamental' and it proved to be particularly difficult to justify the position that a mistake was not sufficiently fundamental at common law to render the contract void but could be sufficiently fundamental to set it aside in equity (Evans LJ in *William Sindall plc v Cambridgeshire County Council* (1994)).

A key debate is whether the *Great Peace* denial of such an equitable jurisdiction can be justified on a historical analysis and it is clearly unhelpful in terms of the flexibility of remedy.

See Chandler, Devenney, and Poole, 'Common Mistake: Theoretical Justification and Remedial Inflexibility' [2004] JBL 34 and the New Zealand Contractual Mistakes Act 1977.

---

2. The legal treatment of 'impossibility'
....

The effects of common mistake and frustration are very different although both operate in a general sense to excuse further performance.

- **Common mistake**: the contract will be void for common mistake (at common law) but in very narrow circumstances based on there being a total failure of consideration; otherwise it seems that the contract remains valid. Where the contract is void (*res extincta*), each party hands back anything received under the void contract but there is no means of redressing any other financial consequences (compare the **LR(FC)A 1943**). There is also no possibility of recovering damages in mistake cases.

Key cases
****

It may be possible to justify such an 'all or nothing' conclusion based on the very limited circumstances in which common mistakes can occur and therefore the potentially limited impact on third parties. Equally, it would seem that a common mistake might be discovered quite quickly and before significant performance has occurred (see Tettenborn, 'Agreements, Common Mistake and the Purpose of Contract' (2011) 27 JCL 91, arguing that mistake should not be raised once performance has begun). The same might not be true of frustration which can occur towards the end of a contract term where payment is due on completion.

* **Frustration** (subsequent impossibility) discharges the contract for the future and there is a statutory adjustment of the parties' positions regarding pre-frustration obligations in accordance with the **LR(FC)A 1943** and Goff J's interpretation of the Act as aimed at preventing unjust enrichment.

In practice, there can be very fine distinctions of timing and fact which distinguish the application of the doctrines, e.g. *Amalgamated Investment & Property Co. Ltd v John Walker & Sons Ltd* (1977): the operative date was taken to be the date of the listing of the property although the decision to list had, unknown to the parties, been taken before the date of the contract of purchase. Similar facts led to different outcomes based on timing in *Krell v Henry* (1903) (frustration) and *Griffith v Brymer* (1903) (mistake because unknown to both parties the *decision* to cancel the procession had already been taken).

---

3. The basis of the LR(FC)A 1943: whether s. 1(2) and (3) in fact operate to prevent unjust enrichment or whether the purpose of the Act should be to apportion losses

Haycroft and Waksman 'Frustration and Restitution' [1984] JBL 207, and McKendrick, 'Frustration, Restitution and Loss Apportionment' in Burrows (ed.), *Essays on the Law of Restitution* (Clarendon, 1991), argue that the aim of the Act should be the apportionment of losses. It is arguable that this may underpin the broad discretion in *Gamerco v I.C.M.* (1995) (at least as far as this was a means to redress losses in the limited context of the **s. 1(2)** expenses proviso). It would follow that on this interpretation the benefit would not be the end product of the services but the services themselves.

See also the excellent discussion of this question in Morgan, *Great Debates: Contract Law*, 2nd edn (Palgrave Macmillan, 2015), Chapter 5.

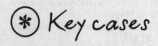 (✱) *Key cases*

Case	Facts	Principle
Couturier v Hastie (HL)	Seller sold corn, believed to be in transit, to the buyer. Unknown to both, the corn had been sold en route. HL held: since the contract was for the sale of existing goods and they did not exist at the time of sale, the contract was void and the buyer was not liable to pay for the corn.	*Res extincta*: unknown to both parties the subject matter of the contract had ceased to exist by the time they made the contract so the contract was void for initial impossibility.

Case	Facts	Principle
Bell v Lever Bros. Ltd (HL)	£30,000 compensation was paid to an employee to terminate his service contract with the company. This was a common mistake as to quality since both parties thought that the service contract could only be terminated with compensation, when in fact no compensation was required. HL held that the compensation agreement was not void for such a mistake as to quality.	Mistake as to quality will not generally render the contract void as parties are agreed in the same terms on the same subject matter. Only if the mistake as to quality is fundamental—i.e. renders the subject matter 'essentially different'—will the contract be void, and this is interpreted restrictively.
Great Peace Shipping Ltd v Tsavliris Salvage (International) Ltd (CA)	Ds (salvage service) sought the closest vessel when a ship was damaged at sea. Both Ds and Ps (owners of *'The Great Peace'*) thought it was *'The Great Peace'* at about 35 miles distance and the ship was hired. The ships were 410 miles apart (mistake as to quality). CA held this mistake was not fundamental since performance of obligation to reach destination and 'stand by' was not impossible.	CA accepted that the test of whether the contract performance would be 'essentially different from the performance that the parties contemplated' amounted to whether performance in accordance with the contractual terms or adventure is impossible due to the common mistake. This is the most important recent case on common mistake and CA discussed the development of the law and denied any equitable jurisdiction to set aside on terms for 'fundamental' common mistake as to quality.
Krell v Henry (CA)	A contract to hire rooms advertised as rooms to view the coronation procession of Edward VII was frustrated when the coronation was subsequently cancelled due to the King's illness and surgery. CA considered the viewing of the procession as the 'foundation of the contract' for **both** parties.	A contract may be frustrated if the common purpose of **both** parties has been destroyed by the event. It is not enough that the purpose of only **one** party is destroyed or if there are two purposes and one remains (*Herne Bay Steam Boat Co. v Hutton*).
Davis Contractors Ltd v Fareham UDC (HL)	Contractors argued that a construction contract was frustrated because they were unable to acquire manpower and materials in a period of shortages after the Second World War and they could therefore recover on a *quantum meruit* basis for performance to date. HL held that the contract had not been frustrated.	The shortages had made the contract more onerous to perform but had not altered the fundamental nature of the contractual performance. The shortages should have been foreseen so, in the absence of a risk provision, this was a risk which fell on the contractor.

Key cases

✱✱✱✱✱✱✱✱✱✱

Case	Facts	Principle
Gamerco SA v I.C.M./ Fair Warning (Agency) Ltd	Concert by the group 'Guns N' Roses' at a stadium in Madrid had to be cancelled due to safety issues affecting the stadium. Ps, promoters, had already paid $412,000 and had incurred expenses of $450,000 prior to the cancellation. Ds had expenses of $50,000. Held: contract was frustrated and Ps could recover advance payment under **s. 1(2) LR(FC)A 1943**. There would be no deduction for Ds' expenses under the proviso bearing in mind that Ps had expenses of $450,000 which they had no way of recovering.	**Section 1(2) LR(FC)A 1943** and the exercise of the discretion to permit expenses to be retained before the return of an advance payment to the payer.
BP Exploration Co. (Libya) Ltd v Hunt (No. 2) (Robert Goff J)	P oil company had agreed to explore for oil and develop D's oil concession in Libya. P spent considerable sums drilling for oil and found it. However, the Libyan government then expropriated the concession. P sought a 'just sum' under **s. 1(3) LR(FC)A 1943** for the benefit it had conferred on D prior to frustration. Held the contract had been frustrated and the Act applied.	The decision is of greatest significance for what is said in the judgment about the purpose of the Act (prevention of unjust enrichment) and calculation of a just sum under **s. 1(3)**.

#9

Misrepresentation

Key facts

- Where the making of a contract has been induced by a false statement of fact (either a statement or conduct in the pre-contractual negotiation process or, on occasion, silence or an omission), the party induced to contract (the misrepresentee) has a remedy for this **actionable misrepresentation**.

- Misrepresentation renders the contract **voidable** so that the misrepresentee should be able to set aside (rescind) the contract and be restored to the position that misrepresentee was in before the contract was made. This may involve an additional award of **damages** for misrepresentation.

- However, the ability to rescind will be lost where any of the bars to **rescission** apply, e.g. if the misrepresentee has affirmed the misrepresentation or failed to avoid the contract in a timely manner. In such circumstances, the only way for the misrepresentee to be restored to their original position is by means of an award of damages.

- The measure and recovery of damages for misrepresentation is determined by the state of mind of the misrepresentor, and whether the misrepresentor was fraudulent (damages in the tort of deceit), negligent (common law damages for negligent misstatement, or damages for negligent misrepresentation in accordance with **s. 2(1) of the Misrepresentation Act 1967 (MA 1967)**), or wholly innocent (damages in lieu of rescission where rescission would otherwise have been available).

- Controversially the judicial interpretation of **s. 2(1) MA 1967** means that damages awarded under this section are based on the principles governing the measure of damages for fraud due to the 'fiction of fraud'.

Key facts

✳✳✳✳✳✳✳✳✳

- Following the amendments to the **Consumer Protection from Unfair Trading Regulations 2008 (CPRs 2008)** made by the **Consumer Protection Amendments Regulations 2014, SI 2014/870**, after 1 October 2014 consumers who entered into a contract for the sale or supply of a product by a trader or who entered into a contract to sell a product to a trader (e.g. selling their car to a car dealer) or made a payment to a trader for the supply of a product, and that trader engaged in a prohibited practice in relation to the product (e.g. a misleading action—misrepresentation) have an extended range of specific consumer 'rights to redress' under the CPRs (right to unwind, right to a discount, and specific right to damages). This regime is separate to the consumer's general remedies but the consumer cannot make a claim twice in respect of the same conduct. In addition, there is an amendment to **s. 2 MA 1967** which removes the ability of consumers to recover damages under that legislation where they have a right to redress under the CPRs in respect of the misrepresentation. This is an important removal of a consumer remedy of damages and makes it more likely that the CPR remedies will be used in practice in B2C misrepresentation claims.

Introduction

This chapter examines the identification of actionable misrepresentations which affect the fairness of the process by which a contract was entered into and render that contract **voidable** for misrepresentation (liable to be set aside and the parties restored to their pre-contractual positions). The discussion distinguishes between remedies available for the different types of pre-contractual statements.

Practical example 1

Ranjit and Scott operate taxi businesses. Following a period of negotiations, Ranjit agreed to purchase one of Scott's taxi cabs after Scott told him that it had been fitted with a brand new engine only a month earlier and that the oil had been changed. In fact, the Canley Garage had warned Scott that the engine would need replacement within weeks and that, although the oil had been changed, there was an oil leak. Scott decided that the new engine and fixing the oil leak would cost too much money and that he would attempt to sell the cab to another firm. The cab broke down on the journey from Scott's premises and was taken to Canley Garage where Ranjit discovered the need for a new engine and the existence of the oil leak. Can Ranjit get his money back and recover the costs of towing the broken down cab to the garage?

Practical example 2

Following a period of negotiations, Tamzin agreed to purchase Umar's bicycle shop and business as a result of Umar's statement that the turnover in the last accounting year had been £75,000. Umar had made this statement following a quick glance at the annual accounts but was not very good with figures. He offered to allow Tamzin to take the books away to be checked but she said that 'she trusted him' and did not bother. A few months after the purchase, Tamzin discovers that the true turnover figure was only £25,000 and the business is struggling. Can she avoid the purchase, secure damages for any expenditure she has wasted in the meantime, and claim for lost profits?

Think like an examiner

Problem-style questions involving one or more actionable misrepresentations are easily drafted, particularly scenarios where the misrepresentations induce the purchase of a small business such as a public house, restaurant, newsagent shop, or beauty salon, and are therefore a relatively common inclusion in Contract Law examination papers. The technicality of the law on remedies also allows the better students to shine. (You will be in this position once you have digested this chapter and its helpful hints.)

Actionable misrepresentation
✷✷✷✷✷✷✷✷✷✷✷✷

❗ Don't fall into the trap

On occasions, statements which appear to be misrepresentations are in fact broken contractual promises (**terms**) so that the focus of the question should be on identifying the type of term and remedies for **breach** of contract (see Chapter 5). Examiners may set questions involving statements which are both terms and misrepresentations. This necessarily requires a judgement as to best remedies.

Even if you are convinced that the question concerns only actionable misrepresentations, your first paragraph should explain the legal principles and application which lead you to conclude that the statements are representations and not terms. A kind examiner will leave various hints in the problem question facts.

Tips

Indications that the statements are representations and not terms:

- Examiners frequently include a statement that the written contract is silent on the pre-contractual statements. This statement of silence suggests that it was intended that no binding promise as to the truth of those statements was being made.
- A statement suggesting that the other party (usually a prospective purchaser) should check the accuracy of any statements being made, e.g. by inspecting accounts (see *Redgrave v Hurd* (1881)), or having an independent assessment of a car, is more likely to be a representation (*Ecay v Godfrey* (1947)).
- A statement made by a consumer about his own goods is more likely to be a representation, and a statement of fact since the consumer-owner of goods is in the better position to know the truth about any statement relating to those goods: *Smith v Land & House Property Trust Ltd* (1884).

Actionable misrepresentation

Having confirmed that the statement(s) are representations, proceed to establish that the statement is an actionable misrepresentation.

Important fact

Only a **false statement of fact** (not opinion, not future intention and not abstract law) made by one party to the other **which induces the other to enter into the contract**, can constitute an actionable misrepresentation rendering the contract voidable (liable to be set aside) and give rise to possible remedies for misrepresentation.

Step 1: Is there a false statement?

❗ Don't fall into the trap

A statement may be true, so you must be very careful to analyse all of the facts of your problem before launching into a discussion of *mis*representation. (Note however that a statement may

> be true when made but can become untrue before the contract is entered into due to a change of circumstances. There may then be a misrepresentation in failing to disclose that change of circumstances.)

This false statement can be an actual statement but it can also include **conduct (encouraging a false belief) or an omission (failing to speak when there is a duty to do so).**

Conduct

Gordon v Selico Co. Ltd (1986): covering up patches of dry rot so that they could not be seen on the inspection of a flat.

Silence or omission to speak

As a general rule, silence does not amount to a misrepresentation since there is no general duty in pre-contract negotiations to disclose material facts not known to the other party: *Keates v Cadogan* (1851).

- However, if the statement is a **half-truth** (what is said is true but it is misleading since it fails to present the whole picture), there is a misrepresentation. *Dimmock v Hallett* (1866): a statement that farms on the land to be sold were let to tenants but both had given notice to quit. The misrepresentation was in the failure to disclose the notices to quit.
- If the statement was true when made but, due to a change of circumstances, has become false by the time that it is acted upon, the representor's failure to disclose the change in circumstances is a misrepresentation. *With v O'Flanagan* (1936): failure to disclose vendor's illness occurring prior to the contract and the impact of this on the medical practice being sold. Equally in *Spice Girls Ltd v Aprilia World Services BV* (2002), the sponsor had not been informed that a member of the group had decided to leave despite this being known to all members of the group.

Step 2: Is it a statement of 'fact'?

This is a requirement since only a fact can be true or untrue.

1. Statements of belief or opinion

Statements of belief or opinion are not statements of fact—or at least they are not where it is clear to both parties that the statement maker has no basis in fact for the belief or opinion stated. *Bisset v Wilkinson* (1927): both vendor and purchaser knew that the land had not previously been used for sheep farming so the vendor's statement of belief relating to the number of sheep the land would support was clearly not a statement of fact.

Actionable misrepresentation

✳✳✳✳✳✳✳✳✳✳✳✳

However, if either:

- the statement maker is in a stronger position to know the truth (usually because the statement relates to their property or other facts within their control) (*Smith v Land & House Property Corporation* (1884)); or
- the statement maker is an expert (*obiter* in *Esso Petroleum Co. Ltd v Mardon* (1976))

then it is assumed that the statement maker knows of facts to justify any statements of their 'opinion'. On this basis if they are false, such statements are implied misrepresentations of fact.

Finally, if the opinion is not honestly held, there is a statement of fact. For example, Alex, who is selling a picture, says that he believes the picture to be an original when he actually believes it to be a copy. This would be a misrepresentation of fact, although the difficulty would be proving the belief.

2. Statements of future conduct or intention

A false statement by a person as to what they will do in the future or as to what they intend to do, is not a misrepresentation. However if at the time of stating the intention the person did not in fact have any such intention (again this would need to be established in evidence) then it is a misrepresentation, since a present intention is a fact that can be falsely described.

> **Edgington v Fitzmaurice** (1885) **(CA)**
>
> **FACTS:** Directors of a company sought to raise money and stated that they intended to use funds raised to purchase company assets and develop its trading potential, whereas they intended all along to use the money to pay off existing liabilities.
>
> **HELD:** The statement of intention was a misstatement of fact.

Abstract statements of law

Abstract statements of what the law is cannot be statements of fact. However, statements of law are rarely abstract but statements of law as applied to a particular set of facts. Where there is factual context, statements of law will be statements of fact. *Pankhania v Hackney London Borough Council* (2002): statements concerning the legal status of the current occupier of a property to be sold which impacted the ability to eject that occupier.

Step 3: Does the statement, conduct, or omission induce the other party to enter into the contract?

The false statement of fact must induce the contract, i.e. it must actually be relied upon: *Horsfall v Thomas* (1862). These case facts seem similar to *Gordon v Selico* (concealment of dry rot) since in *Horsfall* there was a concealment of a defect in a gun. However, whereas in

Gordon the flat had been inspected and the concealment not discovered so that the concealment induced the contract, in *Horsfall* the defect was discoverable on inspection and there had been no inspection. It followed that in *Horsfall* the concealment (misrepresentation) could not have induced the contract.

There must be knowledge of the statement

It follows that there must be knowledge of the existence of the statement in order to be induced by it and normally that means that the statement must have been made to the party induced: *Peek v Gurney* (1873). However, if it can be shown that the statement maker knew that the statement would be passed onto someone else, it is passed on (so that there is knowledge of it), and then that person is the party actually induced to contract, there will be liability in misrepresentation to the party induced despite the fact that they were not the original addressee of the statement (*Pilmore v Hood* (1838) and *Clef Aquitaine SARL v Laporte Materials (Barrow) Ltd* (2001)).

Where a claimant relies on their own judgement or investigations, as a general principle, they will not be induced by the misrepresentation

Attwood v Small (1838)

FACTS: False statements as to the earning capacity of a mine were confirmed by the purchasers' independent experts.

HELD: The purchasers could not rely on the vendors' false statements as constituting actionable misrepresentations since they had not relied on these but on the statements made by their own experts.

Tip

Do not place too much reliance on ***Attwood v Small*** since, following ***Edgington v Fitzmaurice***, there can be reliance where the representation was not the only reason inducing the claimant to contract. ***Attwood v Small*** would therefore only have application where the purchasers rely entirely on their own experts and not at all on the previous statements.

Think like an examiner

Redgrave v Hurd (1881) is useful for examiners in testing knowledge of inducement and introducing later discussion of contributory negligence.

This case is authority for the fact that where a misrepresentation is made (e.g. false statement about turnover or profits) and the misrepresentee is given the opportunity to test the accuracy of the statement (e.g. in the account books) but does not take it, the misrepresentation will still be considered as an inducement since it will still be an active influence. This relates to establishing the actionable misrepresentation. This authority can be put another way in terms of legal principle:

> Constructive notice will not suffice to prevent inducement: the knowledge of the true position must be actual.

However, there may still be a price to be paid for failing to inspect accounts or failure to check a statement, but this relates to any damages award. The damages awarded may be reduced to take account of the misrepresentee's contributory negligence in contributing to their own loss.

Step 4: Was the misrepresentation material to the decision to contract?

Whereas the question of whether the misrepresentee was induced is subjective (i.e. it depends on the actual state of mind of the misrepresentee), the statement must also relate to a matter which would have influenced the reasonable man (objective test) to contract, as opposed to something which has no obvious connection. Where the misrepresentation is fraudulent, inducement may be assumed from materiality: *Barton v County NatWest Bank Ltd* (1999).

Actionable misrepresentations in Practical examples 1 and 2

Example 1
There is a false statement relating to the 'brand new engine' and it is a false statement of fact since, although Scott is not an expert on cab maintenance, he is clearly 'in a better position to know the truth' as the cab owner and so is impliedly stating that his statement is based on fact (*Smith v Land & House Property*). It appears that the oil has been changed (so this is a truthful statement) but there is no mention of the 'oil leak'. Is the failure to mention the oil leak an actionable misrepresentation? It may be a half-truth (what is said is true but it is misleading since it fails to present the whole picture: *Dimmock v Hallett*). Changing the oil will be defeated if it is leaking.

Both statements appear to be material and are relied upon in deciding to contract.

Example 2
There is a false statement of fact concerning the turnover of the business made by the business owner (better position to know the truth). It still operates as an inducement to contract since Tamzin does not check the accounts and therefore places reliance on the turnover figure (*Redgrave v Hurd*). (Tamzin appears to be contributorily negligent in failing to check the accounts but this can only be relevant to the damages award and cannot impact on the finding that there is an actionable misrepresentation.)

Type of misrepresentation

Having established one or more actionable misrepresentations, you can now consider what type of misrepresentation each statement might be.

There are three types depending on the state of mind of the misrepresentor: fraudulent, negligent, or innocent (see Table 9.1). We have already noted that the statement must be false; this may either be because the statement maker always knew it was false or because the statement maker's belief in the truth of their statement turns out to be misplaced.

Table 9.1 Types of misrepresentation

Type	Definition	Detail
Fraudulent	Absence of an honest belief that the statement is true. Statement is made (i) knowing it is false, or (ii) not believing it is true, or (iii) recklessly—not caring whether it is true or false.	Claimant has to establish this on the evidence. ***Derry v Peek*** (1889) ***Thomas Witter Ltd v T.B.P. Industries Ltd*** (1996): Jacob J stated that 'recklessness' meant dishonesty: making a statement (so asserting its truth) not knowing whether it is true or false—and not caring.
Negligent	An honest belief that the statement is true but the statement maker has failed in their duty to use reasonable care and skill to check accuracy and so failed to appreciate it is false.	There are two types of damages claim for negligent misrepresentation: (i) negligent misstatement at common law (claimant needs to establish the defendant's negligence) (ii) negligent misrepresentation under **s. 2(1) MA 1967** (defendant has to establish that they were not negligent). This statutory damages claim has greater practical significance where there is a contract with the statement maker (as is likely to be the case in all Contract Law assessments and exams). Bear in mind the exclusion of this remedy where the **CPRs 2008** apply.
Innocent	An honest belief that the statement is true where that belief is based on reasonable grounds. However, the statement turns out to be false.	The remedy of rescission (where available) is most likely to be lost in such circumstances and damages awarded in lieu (instead) applying the discretion in **s. 2(2) MA 1967**. Again, these damages in lieu will not be available as a remedy in a B2C situation where the **CPRs 2008** apply.

Practical examples 1 and 2

Sometimes examiners give you hints about the state of mind of the statement maker, e.g. compare Scott's state of mind in example 1 with Umar's state of mind in example 2. In example 1 (taxi cab), it is clear that Scott knows that the cab has not had a new engine fitted and that there is an oil leak, i.e. there is a deliberate lie and failure to speak which induces the sale to Ranjit (fraudulent misrepresentation). However, in example 2 (sale of the bicycle shop), it appears that Umar is honest but careless (negligent misrepresentation) and Tamzin is also negligent in failing to take the opportunity to check the accounts.

What remedies are available for the misrepresentation?

****

> **Tip**
>
> Even if you are uncertain, it is often possible to rule out one or more possible types of misrepresentation by a careful reading of the facts the examiner presents.

What remedies are available for the misrepresentation?

The basic remedy is **rescission** since the contract is **voidable**. This involves setting aside the contract—handing back the property received under the contract and the return of the price paid.

> **Tip**
>
> Remember that the aim of remedies for misrepresentation is to put the parties in the position they were in before the misrepresentation was made which induced the contract. If rescission is either unavailable (see bars to rescission, Table 9.3) or does not fulfil this aim then a claim for damages for misrepresentation (wasted expenditure) should be considered.

> **Examination tip**
>
> Ensure you spend sufficient time considering the remedies for misrepresentation since it is likely that many of the marks will be awarded for this discussion. An ability to identify actionable misrepresentations is not sufficient to provide advice. The range of available remedies for each type of misrepresentation in the B2B context is considered in Table 9.2.

Table 9.2 Remedies which may be available for misrepresentation (assume not a B2C contract and that the **CPRs 2008** do not apply)

All types of misrepresentations	Rescission alone.	Rescission is available and rescission alone restores the parties to their original positions—therefore no additional loss.	As there is no additional loss there will be no claim for damages (although see innocent misrepresentation and **s. 2(2) MA 1967**).
Fraudulent or negligent misrepresentation	Rescission.	AND if there is additional loss suffered	Damages (wasted expenditure)—usually **s. 2(1) MA 1967**.
Fraudulent or negligent misrepresentation	**Where rescission has been lost.**	Damages alone (substantial damages to restore parties to original positions).	Usually damages under **s. 2(1) MA 1967**.

Innocent misrepresentation	Where rescission is available.	Rescission may be too drastic a remedy.	The court may exercise its discretion under **s. 2(2) MA 1967** to award **s. 2(2)** damages instead of rescission.
Innocent misrepresentation	Where rescission has been lost.	No rescission and therefore no damages instead of rescission.	Possible indemnity only.

Step 1: Always start by considering whether rescission is possible—since the circumstances may indicate that the remedy has been lost

Table 9.3 Bars to rescission

Affirmation	Knows about the misrepresentation but continues performance of the contract or acts in such a way that an unequivocal intention to continue performance can be implied from conduct.	**Examiners tend to set facts involving similar second chances or second journeys.** *Long v Lloyd* (1958): purchase of lorry. Took it out on first journey and defects were discovered identifying misrepresentations had been made. P accepted D's offer to pay part of the costs of repair. P then took the lorry on a second journey after the repair and this was held to be **affirmation**.
Lapse of time	Period from the date of the contract (non-fraudulent misrepresentations) and from date when fraud could reasonably have been discovered (fraudulent).	Lapse of time may be evidence of affirmation. *Leaf v International Galleries* (1950): picture represented (non-fraudulent) to be 'Salisbury Cathedral' by Constable. Five years later the purchaser attempted to sell it and discovered it was not by Constable. The Court of Appeal (CA) held that rescission had been lost as not exercised within a reasonable time.
Restitution impossible	It has become impossible to restore the parties to their original positions, e.g. if the subject matter has deteriorated or changed.	There is an equitable discretion in cases of substantial **restitution** to order rescission whilst allowing for a financial adjustment to take account of inability to make full restitution: *Erlanger v New Sombrero Phosphate Co.* (1878). *Clarke v Dickson* (1858): purchaser of shares in a mining company could not have rescission once he had worked out the mine. Rescission of a contract to purchase goods cannot be rescinded once the goods have been consumed. *Thomas Witter Ltd v T.B.P. Industries Ltd* (1996): changes to a business purchased as a result of misrepresentation prevented restitution.

What remedies are available for the misrepresentation?
****

Third party rights	Rescission is a personal right against the representor and the misrepresentee cannot claim the return of property so as to defeat rights acquired by the bona fide third party purchaser.	If A obtains goods from B as a result of misrepresentation and sells them to C, who takes in good faith, B cannot later rescind on learning of the misrepresentation in order to recover the goods from C. See mistake as to identity (discussed Chapter 2) and **s. 23 Sale of Goods Act 1979 (SGA 1979)**).
Damages instead of rescission under s. 2(2) MA 1967	The court has a discretion under **s. 2(2)** to award damages instead of rescission that is otherwise available in the case of innocent or negligent misrepresentation. If the court exercises this discretion, then the right to rescission is lost and **s. 2(2)** damages are awarded instead.	This discretion is most likely to be exercised in the case of an innocent misrepresentation where rescission is seen as too drastic a remedy.

These bars (with the exception of **s. 2(2) MA 1967**) apply generally to the remedy of rescission (i.e. they are not limited to rescission for misrepresentation): for example, *Halpern v Halpern* (2007): bars to rescission (restitution impossible) also apply to remedy of rescission for **duress**.

Practical examples 1 and 2

Can Ranjit and Tamzin get their money back and avoid the contracts they have entered into in examples 1 and 2?

In example 1, Ranjit discovers the misrepresentations quickly and there seems to be no journey after discovering the true position (compare *Long v Lloyd*). If he acts immediately he should therefore be able to rescind the contract and get his money back.

However, in example 2 (purchasing a business), it is rarely as simple since the business will often operate for a period before the misrepresentation is discovered and rescission sought. We are told that a few months have elapsed since the purchase so that it may be impossible for Tamzin to hand the business back in its original position (*Thomas Witter v T.B.P. Industries Ltd*). In addition, third party rights may have intervened. (Even if rescission is possible in example 2, it seems unlikely, given the nature of the misrepresentation and its consequences, that damages in lieu of rescission would be appropriate. They are clearly inappropriate given the fraudulent misrepresentation in example 1. **Section 2(2) MA 1967** should not therefore be considered.)

Step 2: Consider the remedy of damages for misrepresentation

Where there is additional loss (i.e. not recovered by rescission alone) or the parties are not put in their original position because rescission is unavailable, it is necessary to consider the remedy of damages for misrepresentation.

The type of misrepresentation is important in calculating the measure and ability to recover.

Practical example 1

Rescission will not wholly restore the parties to their original positions as Ranjit has incurred the cost of towing the cab to the garage when it breaks down on the first journey. Can he recover this? Scott's misrepresentation was fraudulent. (Note that this is a B2B contract.)

Fraudulent misrepresentation—damages in the tort of deceit

The object of the damages award in the tort of deceit is, not surprisingly, tortious, i.e. the aim is to restore the misrepresentee to the position they would have been in had the representation not been made (i.e. the amount the misrepresentee is out of pocket).

The test of **remoteness** is very wide indeed in that the misrepresentee may recover for **all the direct loss incurred as a result of the fraudulent inducement**, regardless of foreseeability. See *Doyle v Olby (Ironmongers) Ltd* (1969): Lord Denning MR:

> The person who has been defrauded is entitled to say: 'I would not have entered into this bargain at all but for your representation . . . '.

Smith New Court Securities Ltd v Scrimgeour Vickers (Asset Management) Ltd (1997)

This case concerned the purchase of shares in a company as a result of a fraudulent misrepresentation. The House of Lords (HL) held that the measure of damages would normally be based on the difference between the price paid for the shares (82.25p per share) and the market value of the shares at the date of the contract to purchase (78p). However, it was later discovered that the company had been the victim of a serious fraud by a third party so that the real value of the shares at the time of purchase was in fact only 44p per share. **Since the purchasers were 'locked into' the transaction as a result of the fraudulent misrepresentation, this subsequent loss was a direct loss flowing from the misrepresentation.** Therefore the HL allowed recovery of difference between 82.25p and 44p.

Tip

Where there is a fraudulent misrepresentation, if the purchaser has to retain the property in question until they can sell it, they are able to recover the difference between the purchase price and the eventual price they obtain on sale (*Doyle v Olby, East v Maurer, Downs v Chappell*) →

What remedies are available for the misrepresentation?

✳✳✳✳✳✳✳✳✳✳✳

➔ as this is a 'direct loss' (causal link) resulting from making the contract. There is, however, a duty to mitigate so that refusing a reasonable offer to purchase the business or property will break the chain of causation (***Downs v Chappell*** (1997)).

Loss of profits (if a direct loss) can be recovered for fraudulent misrepresentation but not on a contractual basis (i.e. not on the basis that the profit or turnover figures were correct). Recovery has to be on the tortious basis of restoring the parties to their original positions. This was interpreted to mean allowing recovery of the profit that would have been made had this contract not been entered into but another contract made instead.

East v Maurer (1991) **(CA)**

FACTS: The Ps bought one of the D's hair salons for £20,000 as a result of a fraudulent representation by the D that he had no intention of working in his other nearby salon, except in emergencies. The D continued to work full time at his other salon and this had an adverse effect on the Ps' business. The Ps eventually sold the salon for only £7,500.

HELD: In addition to recovery of damages in the tort of deceit, i.e. the difference between price paid and price on selling (£20,000 – £7,500 = £12,500 (plus the expenses of the sale)), the Ps could recover their lost profits as direct loss flowing from the fraudulent inducement to make this contract.

  However, this was not (as in breach of contract) to put the Ps in as good a position as they would have been in had the representation been true (i.e. the D had not worked in the other salon), but the profit they might have made had the representation not been made at all. This was calculated as the profit they would probably have made in another hairdressing business bought for a similar sum (calculated by the court as £10,000).

Practical example 1

Is the cost of towing a 'direct loss' caused by entering into this transaction? Yes, it is. The loss need not be foreseeable, although it clearly is on these facts. This is an easy example.

Damages for negligent misrepresentation

There are two types of damages claim for negligent misrepresentation:

Negligent misstatement at common law

Hedley Byrne & Co. Ltd v Heller & Partners Ltd (1964): *obiter* statement in this case that in certain circumstances damages may be recoverable in tort for a negligent misstatement causing financial loss. Until this case, damages could only be recovered in misrepresentation if the misrepresentation was fraudulent. See ***Esso Petroleum Co. Ltd v Mardon*** (1976) accepting that a negligent misstatement can arise from a representation made in pre-contract negotiations.

What remedies are available for the misrepresentation?

With this claim there is no requirement to establish the existence of a contract between misrepresentor and misrepresentee (compare s. 2(1) MA 1967), e.g. in *Hedley Byrne* there was no contract between Heller (misrepresentor) and Hedley Byrne (misrepresentee) but Heller's negligent statement (about the financial standing of Easipower) led HB to enter into a contract with a third party on behalf of Easipower and HB lost money as a result.

In such a claim, the claimant needs to establish the defendant's negligence (that a duty of care was owed, this duty has been breached, and loss caused). The remoteness test is the tort test of reasonable foreseeability.

Statutory damages claim for negligent misrepresentation: Misrepresentation Act, s. 2(1)

Tip

To use this section there must be a contract between the statement maker and the person to whom the statement was made.

---

s. 2(1) MA 1967

Where a person has entered into a contract after a misrepresentation has been made to him by another party thereto and as a result thereof he has suffered loss, then, if the person making the misrepresentation would be liable to damages in respect thereof had the misrepresentation been made fraudulently, that person shall be so liable notwithstanding that the misrepresentation was not made fraudulently, unless he proves that he had reasonable ground to believe and did believe up to the time the contract was made that the facts represented were true.

Tip

Due to its many advantages, **s. 2(1)** is the preferable claim in a situation where a contract has resulted between the statement maker and the person to whom the statement was made, i.e. a typical Contract exam problem scenario. You merely need to be aware of the *Hedley Byrne* claim as an alternative claim for damages where the statement was made negligently and its disadvantages when compared to **s. 2(1)**. You also need to be aware that it cannot be used in a B2C scenario where the consumer has a right to redress under the **CPRs 2008**. However, the extension of civil remedies (the rights to redress) in the 2014 Regulations refer only to 'misleading actions' under **Reg. 5 of the CPRs** and make no mention of 'misleading omissions' (**Reg. 6**) or silence. It may be that consumers may retain their ability to use **s. 2** damages because they fall outside the CPRs where their misrepresentation claim is based on inaction rather than action.

Advantages of the s. 2(1) claim

1. **Reversal of burden of proof**: under s. 2(1) the claimant has to prove an actionable misrepresentation and the D is deemed negligent. The D then bears the burden of showing that he had reasonable grounds for believing, and did believe, up to the time that the contract was made, that the facts represented were true, i.e. he has to disprove negligence.

What remedies are available for the misrepresentation?
✱✱✱✱✱✱✱✱✱✱✱✱

Howard Marine & Dredging Co. Ltd v A. Ogden & Sons (Excavations) Ltd (1978) **(CA)**

FACTS: During negotiations to hire out barges the owners' representative misrepresented their carrying capacity. He relied on the Lloyd's register but this was incorrect. The correct information was on file at the owners' head office.

HELD (Majority, Bridge and Shaw LJJ): The owners were liable to pay damages under **s. 2(1)** as they had not demonstrated that they had reasonable grounds to believe what they said about the carrying capacity. It was unreasonable not to refer to the shipping documents at the company's head office.

---

2. **The fiction of fraud**: damages are assessed on the same basis as if the misrepresentation had been fraudulent (although it is not fraudulent): *Royscot Trust Ltd v Rogerson* (1991). It follows that the remoteness test for recovery under **s. 2(1)** is extremely wide, namely 'all direct loss regardless of foreseeability' (see the discussion of recovery of damages in the tort of deceit and compare remoteness in a claim for damages for negligent misstatement—*Hedley Byrne*). Taken to its logical conclusion the case law principles on measure of damages in the fraud cases (*Smith New Court, East v Maurer* on profits) should also apply to **s. 2(1)** cases.

❶ Don't fall into the trap

Be careful with your terminology since **s. 2(1)** was not intended to cover fraudulent misrepresentations (tort of deceit). It is incorrect to state that it applies (on its wording) to fraud and negligence.

However, in practice it may be more straightforward to use **s. 2(1)** in cases which seem fraudulent rather than have to establish any state of mind (and rather than have to prove deceit) and it is for this reason that **s. 2(1)** is often pleaded in preference to deceit.

When applying **s. 2(1)** to determine whether particular losses are recoverable, the only question should be one of causation. Does the loss (particular expense) result from the misrepresentation? **Did the misrepresentation cause the loss? If it did, then it is recoverable.** Only if there is an unreasonable intervening action will this not be the case.

Naughton v O'Callaghan (1990)

FACTS: The Ps purchased a colt for 26,000 guineas but the pedigree was incorrectly described so that the actual value at the time of the sale was £23,500. Before the truth was discovered the Ps trained and raced the horse. It did badly and its value fell to £1,500.

What remedies are available for the misrepresentation?

※ ※ ※ ※ ※ ※ ※ ※ ※ ※ ※

> **HELD: Section 2(1)** damages were awarded for all direct losses flowing from the misrepresentation. The judge considered that the fall in the horse's value to £1,500 was caused by the misrepresentation rather than the intervening actions of the Ps. The fact that the Ps had trained and raced the horse was exactly the conduct which would have been expected in the circumstances. Therefore the Ps recovered the difference between purchase price and the value of the horse at date of judgment.

Practical example 2

Assuming that there can be no rescission, what would the damages award be in relation to the purchase of the bicycle business? Tamzin is also claiming for wasted expenditure in running the business and her loss of profits.

As there is a contract between Tamzin and Umar, if Tamzin relies on a claim for **s. 2(1)** damages, she need only establish Umar's actionable misrepresentation (see earlier). The burden of proof then moves to Umar to show that he had reasonable grounds to believe his statement as to turnover to be true. He will be unable to demonstrate this, i.e. he will not be able to prove that he was not negligent since he gave the accounts no more than 'a quick glance' and admits that he is not very good with figures.

Due to the fiction of fraud, Tamzin can now recover damages on the same basis as if Umar had been fraudulent, i.e. on the basis of 'lock in' she can recover the difference between the price paid for the business and the eventual sale price and sale costs, subject only to **mitigation** (*Smith New Court*). She can also recover additional wasted expenditure which is a direct loss (assuming causal link and reasonable expense to incur: *Naughton v O'Callaghan*). Loss of profits on a tortious basis are also recoverable (*East v Maurer*), i.e. loss of profits incurred on a similar business purchased for the same price.

Damages for innocent misrepresentation: s. 2(2) MA 1967

The misrepresentor in such a case will be able to discharge the burden of disproving negligence under s. 2(1) MA.

Damages **may not be claimed** at common law for a wholly innocent misrepresentation. However, s. 2(2) (damages in lieu of rescission) gives the court a **discretion,** where the injured party **would otherwise be entitled to rescind,** to award damages instead of that rescission based on the fact that rescission would be too drastic a remedy given the nature of the misrepresentation as innocent. (Remember that s. 2 MA will not apply to B2C contracts where the CPRs 2008 give a right to redress (s. 2(4) MA 1967, as amended by the Consumer Protection (Amendment) Regulations 2014, SI 2014/870).)

> Section 2(2) states that this discretion can be exercised if the court considers it equitable to do so having regard to:
>
> - **the type of misrepresentation**
> - **the loss upholding the contract would cause to the representee** (it is this loss that will need to be compensated for in damages) **compared to the loss rescission would cause to the representor.**

What remedies are available for the misrepresentation?

****

William Sindall plc v Cambridgeshire County Council (1994) (CA)

See also p. 165, Chapter 8, 'Risk allocation'.

FACTS: The purchaser sought to avoid a contract to purchase land for development when the market value of the land fell dramatically. The purchaser had discovered a sewer running across the land which required a six-foot maintenance strip.

HELD: On the facts there was no misrepresentation by the D Council and no negligence. *Obiter* the CA considered that even if there had been an actionable misrepresentation, on these facts it would have exercised its discretion under **s. 2(2) MA** and awarded damages in lieu of rescission. The representation was relatively trivial (costing £18,000 for the diversion) as compared to the value of the land (£5m). Rescission would have placed the risk of a fall in market value on the D Council.

The CA rejected the argument that **s. 2(2)** damages were the same as **s. 2(1)** damages and should compensate for losses caused by entering into the transaction (i.e. the fall in the market value of the land). Instead, **s. 2(2)** damages are limited to compensating the misrepresentee for the loss suffered if the contract is upheld (the cost of diversion of the sewer) and are unlikely to include any consequential losses.

✅ Looking for extra marks?

Identifying any contributory negligence on the part of the misrepresentee and assessing whether this impacts to reduce the damages award will demonstrate a thorough application.

Practical example 2

Umar had offered Tamzin the opportunity to inspect the accounts for the bicycle shop and she did not take up this opportunity. We saw earlier (*Redgrave v Hurd*) that this did not affect the existence of inducement in the form of any statement about the figures, e.g. turnover of £75,000. However, Tamzin is negligent. Should this reduce the damages which Umar has to pay Tamzin?

1. **If Umar (as misrepresentor) had been fraudulent, any contributory negligence by Tamzin (misrepresentee) can be ignored (*Standard Chartered Bank v Pakistan National Shipping Corp (Nos. 2 & 4)* (2002)).** But Umar was negligent.

2. **Both Umar and Tamzin were negligent. Can Tamzin's damages be apportioned (reduced) to take account of her contributory negligence?** If the claim for damages was based only on *Hedley Byrne* (negligent misstatement at common law), any damages payable to Tamzin would be reduced to take account of her contributory negligence (the **Law Reform (Contributory Negligence) Act 1945** applies). The same *should* be true where there are concurrent claims under *Hedley Byrne* and s. 2(1) MA (*Gran Gelato Ltd v Richcliff (Group) Ltd* (1992)) since the position should not be different where claims are pleaded as alternatives. However, if the claim for damages is formulated only under **s. 2(1)**, it is arguable that the fiction of fraud should apply and there would be no reduction in Tamzin's damages.

---

⑨ Key debates

---

1. The fiction of fraud in s. 2(1) and the resultant treatment of a negligent statement maker as if they were fraudulent

Poole and Devenney, 'Reforming Damages for Misrepresentation: The Case for Coherent Aims and Principles' [2007] JBL 269.

Academic opinion supports the view that the fiction of fraud relates only to establishing liability rather than the measure of damages being the same as for fraud. It is arguable that the remoteness rule for **s. 2(1)** should be the same as under *Hedley Byrne* (i.e. reasonable foreseeability) because these were alternative types of liability for negligent misrepresentation. By relying too heavily on the fiction of fraud, the CA has created a distinction between damages for negligent misstatements in tort and damages under **s. 2(1)** for negligent misrepresentation.

This can be criticized because:

- There is a failure to draw any distinction between fraud and negligence.

- An artificial distinction is created between negligent misstatement (*Hedley Byrne*) and negligent misrepresentation (**s. 2(1)**).

- It requires a very literal statutory interpretation of the wording of **s. 2(1)**.

---

2. Misrepresentation in the consumer context

The Law Commission consulted (*Consumer Redress for Misrepresentation and Aggressive Practices*, LCCP 199, April 2011) and reported (Law Com. No. 332, Cm. 8323, March 2012) recommending reforming the law on remedies to protect consumers in the event of misrepresentations and aggressive practices. The Law Commission pointed in particular to consumer problems in identifying the availability of rescission and the measure of damages where damages were available. It therefore proposed tiers of remedies designed to restore consumers to their original positions. Tier 1 remedies (available for all types of misrepresentations) related to 'unwinding' the contract through the return of goods and services within three months of delivery, and securing a refund of the price. If 'unwinding' was no longer possible, the consumer would still secure a discount on the purchase price. Tier 2 remedies would apply only if a consumer could prove they had suffered actual loss over and above their recovery through unwinding or discount on the price. It was recommended that these damages should cover consequential losses and also damages for distress and inconvenience.

The Consumer Protection (Amendment) Regulations 2014 (CP(A)R 2014) amended the **Consumer Protection from Unfair Trading Regulations 2008 (CPRs 2008)** to introduce consumer 'rights to redress' (**Part 4A**) in situations which would fall within actionable misrepresentations ('misleading actions' under **Reg. 5**), although not 'misleading omissions' so that omissions and silence would appear to be excluded from the CPR 'right to redress' regime.

Where the regime applies, the consumer has the right to unwind the contract by rejecting the product within 90 days, assuming that the goods or services have not been fully consumed or performed (**Reg. 27E**). This gives rise to a right to a refund for the consumer. Where the consumer has not exercised the right to unwind and has not made one or more payments due for the product, there may be a right to a discount on some or all of those payments in complex circumstances which, by their very complexity seem inappropriate for the consumer context. The circumstances turn on the seriousness of the 'misleading action' and the difference (if any) between the contract price and the market price of the product at the time of the contract (**Reg. 27I**). Finally, there is a right to damages where the consumer has suffered consequential financial loss or 'alarm, distress or physical inconvenience or discomfort' as a result of the 'misleading action'. Traders have a due diligence defence in respect of any right to damages. There is no further explanation of the basis on which these damages will be calculated. While the right to unwind seems clear, the right to a discount and the right to damages provisions under the CPRs appear more questionable—as does the omission of misleading omissions. By comparison, in its interpretation **s. 2(1) MA** has the advantage of being reasonably clear and generous to consumer claimants who seek to recover financial compensation for consequential losses.

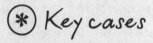 Key cases

Case	Facts	Principle
With v O'Flanagan (CA)	In January 1934, negotiations were entered into for the sale of a medical practice which the vendor represented as having an income of £2,000 per annum. However, by the time the contract was signed in May, the practice had declined due to the vendor's illness, but this was not disclosed. The purchasers sought rescission. Held: the representation was made to induce purchasers to enter into the contract and had to be treated as continuing until the contract was signed. Once it became false, to the knowledge of the representor, there was a misrepresentation if he failed to correct it.	A change of circumstances may give rise to a duty to speak so that silence constitutes a misrepresentation.
Smith v Land and House Property Corporation (CA)	Ps advertised property for sale, stating in the particulars that it was let to 'a most desirable tenant' when the tenant was in arrears with his rent at the time. Ps sued for **specific performance**. CA held this description was not a mere expression of opinion but contained an implied assertion that the vendors knew of no facts leading to the conclusion that the tenant was not 'a most desirable tenant'.	Statement of opinion will be treated as a statement of fact (and so an actionable misrepresentation) where it is made by a person in a better position to know the truth—since there is an implied representation that the statement is based on facts.
Redgrave v Hurd (CA)	P advertised for a partner in his solicitor's practice and to purchase his house. D was told that the practice brought in about £300 a year and that the evidence could be seen in certain papers which P showed to D. However, D did not examine them. If he had he would have discovered that the income figure was incorrect. D entered into the contract and then discovered the truth. He sought rescission and damages for misrepresentation. CA held that D had relied on the misrepresentation since he did not know of any facts establishing that the statements were not true.	If a party fails to take the opportunity to check the accuracy of a representation he will still be induced by it to enter the contract and have remedies in misrepresentation. However, there may now (post **Redgrave**) be a reduction in any damages to account for his contributory negligence. This depends on the state of mind of the statement maker and possibly also on the type of damages claim.

Case	Facts	Principle
Edgington v Fitzmaurice (CA)	The directors of a company issued a request for loans, stating that the money raised would be used to complete alterations in the buildings of the company and to develop the company's trade. The real object of the loans was to pay off company debts. P claimed to have relied on these statements but also admitted to have mistakenly thought that there was security for the loan and that he would not have lent money if he had known that there was none. CA held that the misstatement of the company's intentions amounted to a misstatement of fact which had induced the contract.	A statement of future intention which is made knowing it is a false intention is a false statement of fact (misrepresenting the state of a man's mind). The false statement of fact does not need to be the only reason inducing the contract as long as it was one of the reasons.
Smith New Court Securities Ltd v Scrimgeour Vickers (Asset Management) Ltd (HL)	Purchase of shares in a company as a result of a fraudulent misrepresentation. HL held that the measure of damages would normally be based on the difference between the price paid for the shares and their market value at the date of the contract to purchase. However, it was later discovered that the company had been the victim of a serious fraud by a third party so that the real value of the shares at the time of purchase was in fact much less. Since the purchasers were 'locked into' the transaction as a result of the fraudulent misrepresentation, HL allowed recovery of this full loss.	Measure of damages in tort of deceit: all direct loss so that if the fraud locks the innocent party into the transaction he can recover for his losses down to the point of sale or judgment.
East v Maurer (CA)	Ps bought one of D's hair salons as a result of a fraudulent representation by D that he had no intention of working in his other nearby salon, except in emergencies. D continued to work full time at his other salon and this had an adverse effect on Ps' business. They sought their loss of profit. CA held that they could recover lost profits on a tortious basis as a direct loss flowing from the fraudulent inducement. This was calculated as the profit they might have made had the representation not been made at all and they had bought another hairdressing business for a similar sum.	Loss of profits can be recovered in a claim based on the tort of deceit but on a tortious, not a contractual, basis.

#10
Undue influence

- An agreement may be avoided where it was entered into as a result of unfair influence resulting from the parties' relationship.

- **Undue influence** is an equitable doctrine which can arise in two ways—actual undue influence (which is similar to **duress** because it arises from illegitimate pressure and abuse exerted by one party over the other) and circumstances where there is an evidential presumption that influence has been exercised which may become an evidential presumption of **undue** influence where there is something in the transaction 'which is suspicious or calls for an explanation' (i.e. of such a size, nature, or context as to raise suspicions).

- In the case of presumptive undue influence, the conclusion of influence may arise automatically in the case of certain types of protected relationships but needs to be established on the facts in other cases on the basis that there is a relationship of trust and confidence between the particular parties.

- Where undue influence is established as between the contracting parties, the victim can have the transaction set aside.

- Where a wife gives security in order to support the debts of her husband (i.e. her contract is with the lender—someone other than the person exercising the influence), the lender will be affected by the actions of the person exercising the undue influence (e.g. her husband) where that lender is fixed with constructive notice of the other's undue influence. This will occur where the lender is 'put on inquiry' (and may occur in all cases where a wife stands surety for her husband's debts and not for any joint purpose). A lender is required to take precise steps (involving ensuring that the practical implications of the proposed transaction have been explained to the wife) or that lender risks losing its security.

Introduction

This chapter is concerned with instances where the agreement cannot stand in light of the fact that, in making the agreement, one party has taken advantage of the relationship existing between the parties (undue influence) or one party had notice of the existence of undue influence exercised by a third party in ensuring the agreement was concluded. If undue influence (and notice in the case of third party undue influence) is established, the agreement will be **voidable** (liable to be set aside).

Think like an examiner

This topic is invariably set as a problem question with all of the traditional ingredients, i.e. husband persuading his wife to secure the matrimonial home to cover the debts of the husband's company in favour of that company's lender. The question is whether the wife can avoid this contract due to her husband's undue influence. Such a question can be combined with misrepresentation since the husband might well misrepresent the effect of the security or purpose of the loan. (Note that the **Consumer Protection from Unfair Trading Regulations 2008 (CPRs 2008)** have no application to this scenario, **Reg. 27D.**)

Equally, undue influence can be part of a mixed problem involving economic duress (financial pressure or threats) to secure agreement and undue influence (taking advantage of the parties' relationship). Duress and undue influence are closely linked although they are separated in this book because of the very clear practical association (and applicable legal principles) that now exists between enforcing alteration promises (changes to existing contractual **terms**) and allegations of duress (see Chapter 3).

✅ Looking for extra marks?

Examiners want to know that you understand the context for the allegation of undue influence and whether you are faced with a case involving two parties. If so, you simply need to establish the undue influence—and its type—with supporting authority, and appreciate the consequences of the finding of undue influence for the parties' positions.

Alternatively, you may be faced with a claim that a contract between two parties should be set aside as a result of the undue influence of a third. Can you appreciate this distinction—and identify each party's role in this scenario? If so, are you then also able to apply the applicable principles and appreciate the balancing act being attempted by means of these principles?

Technical knowledge of principles and appreciation of context are key.

Undue influence

Definition

The doctrine of **undue influence** is an equitable doctrine allowing a contract to be set aside (the remedy of **rescission**) at the court's discretion where there has been a wrongful (undue) exercise of influence by one party over the other. There are different types of undue influence – actual and presumed, see Table 10.1.

Undue influence

✳✳✳✳✳✳✳✳✳✳✳

Table 10.1 Types of undue influence

Actual undue influence	Claimant has to prove that undue influence was exercised at the time of the transaction so that it was not the product of the exercise of free will.	
Presumed undue influence: 2A	Claimant only has to show that there was a special relationship between the claimant and the wrongdoer. This leads to a presumption of influence in law. The presumption of *undue* influence arises if there is something suspicious about the transaction which calls for an explanation. The burden then falls on the other party to show that in fact there was no undue influence exercised, e.g. it may be possible to achieve this by showing that the transaction was entered freely following independent advice.	Protected relationships: religious adviser and disciple (*Allcard v Skinner* (1887)), parent and child (*Bainbrigge v Browne* (1881)), and solicitor and client (*Wright v Carter* (1903)), **BUT NOT** husband and wife relationship (*Bank of Montreal v Stuart* (1911)), or bank and customer (*National Westminster Bank Plc v Morgan* (1985)).
Presumed undue influence: 2B	Claimant is able to establish the existence of a relationship of trust and confidence on the facts. This raises a presumption that influence has been exercised and that presumption will be 'undue' where there is something in the nature of the transaction which calls for an explanation. (A small gift between relatives might be easily explicable; a large gift may call for an explanation.) The burden then falls on the other party to show there was no undue influence exercised.	*Lloyds Bank Ltd v Bundy* (1975): bank customer placed trust and confidence in bank manager for financial advice. A wife may place trust and confidence in her husband with regard to financial affairs.

Examples of presumed undue influence (2B) to illustrate the scope of this category

Goodchild v Bradbury (2006)

FACTS: There was a gift of land by a frail and elderly gentleman (while in hospital suffering from a stroke) to his great-nephew and the subsequent sale of that land by the great-nephew to a property developer for only £1,800. The evidence was that the property developer had arranged for the solicitor who acted for the great-nephew in the transfer of the land from the great-uncle.

HELD: Both transfers would be set aside for undue influence. The presumption of influence was shown to exist between the great-uncle and the great-nephew and the sale was not in the interests of the great-uncle (property development devalued his remaining land). The great-nephew was unable to show that the great-uncle had acted freely in the transaction or with independent advice.

Hammond v Osborn (2002)

FACTS: An elderly donor had made a number of sizeable gifts (nearly £300,000) to the D, his neighbour, who had been taking care of him. These gifts represented over 90 per cent of the donor's liquid assets and exposed him to a considerable tax liability.

HELD: A relationship of trust and confidence was shown to exist on the facts and there was clearly something suspicious about gifts of this size in these circumstances. The D had not been able to rebut the presumption of undue influence since the donor had received no advice concerning the wisdom of his actions and the implications. Therefore the gifts could not be the result of full, free, and informed thought.

Can a transaction be set aside on the ground that undue influence was exercised by a third party?

For example, a wife gives a guarantee and charge over the matrimonial home to a bank as security for the debts of her husband's company but later wishes to have that contract with the bank set aside on the basis that she entered into the contract only because of her husband's undue influence (see Fig. 10.1).

Figure 10.1 Exercise of undue influence by husband upon wife

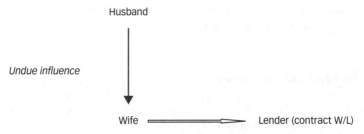

The wife argues that her contract with the lender should be set aside due to her husband's undue influence since this had persuaded her to make the contract with the lender (i.e. contract W/L). Can she succeed?

1. **Undue influence by the third party needs to be established.** In the case of husband and wife this will need to be either actual undue influence, or presumed undue influence (2B) where the transaction is based on a relationship of trust and confidence but calls for an explanation in the circumstances—and that the presumption of undue influence has not been rebutted.

Undue influence
✱✱✱✱✱✱✱✱✱✱✱✱✱

2. **The lender will only be affected by this undue influence** (and lose its security) if either:

   - the husband could be shown to be acting as agent for the lender in obtaining his wife's signature to the charge or other security document; or

   - **if the lender knew of the husband's undue influence (actual or constructive notice).**

Lord Bingham in *Royal Bank of Scotland plc v Etridge (No. 2)* (2001), at [2] explained the need for the law to achieve a balance of interests:

> It is important that a wife (or anyone in a like position) should not charge her interest in the matrimonial home to secure the borrowing of her husband (or anyone in a like position) without fully understanding the nature and effect of the proposed transaction and that the decision is hers, to agree or not to agree. It is important that lenders should feel able to advance money, in run-of-the-mill cases with no abnormal features, on the security of the wife's interest in the matrimonial home in reasonable confidence that, if appropriate procedures have been followed in obtaining the security, it will be enforceable if the need for enforcement arises. The law must afford both parties a measure of protection. It cannot prescribe a code which will be proof against error, misunderstanding or mishap. But it can indicate minimum requirements which, if met, will reduce the risk of error, misunderstanding or mishap to an acceptable level. The paramount need in this important field is that these minimum requirements should be clear, simple and practically operable.

When will a lender have constructive notice of the husband's undue influence?

- The lender is put on inquiry by the circumstances—and this will occur whenever a wife stands surety for her husband's debts (or vice versa, or in the case of any other unmarried relationship of which the lender is aware).

✓ *Looking for extra marks?*

Where the loan is made to husband and wife jointly (or the paperwork indicates this) the lender is *not* put on inquiry unless the lender is aware that the real position is that the loan is solely for the husband's purposes: *CIBC Mortgages plc v Pitt* (1994).

However, the lender is put on inquiry where the wife is named as a shareholder, director, or secretary of the husband's company for whose purposes the loan is being advanced. Examiners are fond of these cases!

- Having been put on enquiry, the lender will be deemed to have constructive notice if it then fails to take reasonable steps to satisfy itself that the wife's agreement to act as surety has been properly obtained.

What are these steps?

In general terms, the lender only needs to take reasonable steps to satisfy itself that the practical implications of the proposed transaction have been explained to the wife and can rely on confirmation from the lender's solicitor that this advice has been given, unless the lender knows or ought to realize that the appropriate advice was not received.

The effect of undue influence

The contract is voidable so that both parties are to be restored to their original positions. *Dunbar Bank plc v Nadeem* (1998): the victim of the undue influence needs to make **restitution** of all that they have obtained from the transaction.

What if that restitution cannot be achieved due to a fall in the value of the property?

Cheese v Thomas (1994) (CA)

FACTS: The 86-year-old P had contributed £43,000 to the purchase of a property for £83,000, with his great-nephew, the D, contributing £40,000 by means of a building society mortgage. The P was to live in the property until his death. The property was in the D's name but he defaulted on the mortgage payments. The P succeeded in having the transaction set aside for undue influence and sought to recover his £43,000. However, the property's value had fallen and it sold for £55,000.

HELD: It was not possible to restore the parties to their exact original positions, so the court would do what was fair and just in practical terms. Since the purpose of the transaction had been to benefit both parties, it would not be just for the D to suffer the entire loss of market value. Each party was therefore to receive a proportionate share of the net proceeds (i.e. 43:40) of £55,000.

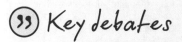 Key debates

The nature of undue influence and whether it is based on the defendant's wrongdoing or is a 'claimant-sided doctrine' (see Birks and Chin, 'On the Nature of Undue Influence' in Beatson and Friedmann (eds.), *Good Faith and Fault in Contract Law* (Oxford University Press, 1995)).

For a summary of the arguments, see Morgan, *Great Debates: Contract Law*, 2nd ed (Palgrave, 2015), pp. 205–10.

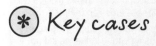 Key cases

You need to be careful with the case examples for undue influence since the law has developed over the years and cases pre-*Etridge* might not be explained in the same way now due to the rejection of any requirement to establish manifest disadvantage.

Key cases

****

Case	Facts	Principle
Royal Bank of Scotland plc v Etridge (No. 2) (HL) (known as *Etridge*)	Eight joined appeals. Wife provided security on home for loan by bank to her husband's business. Home was being repossessed and wife alleged she had not understood the legal advice.	*Latest statement of principles that apply to establishing undue influence and should be discussed in all answers on this topic. Bank will be put on inquiry where wife stands surety for her husband's debts. Once on inquiry the bank will avoid being fixed with constructive notice of husband's undue influence by ensuring the wife receives independent advice.
Allcard v Skinner (CA)	A had inherited her family's wealth. She became a member of the 'protestant sisters of the poor' (religious order with oaths of poverty and obedience) and this involved giving up her property. She gifted her property to the sisterhood. She left the order but it was a further six years before she sought to reclaim her property. The Court of Appeal (CA) held that although she had been unduly influenced, she could not recover due to delay (laches) and acquiescence since leaving the sisterhood.	The judgment involves distinctions of actual and presumed undue influence. It is important for Lindley LJ's test of the types of gifts which will be set aside (raising suspicions) which later became the test adopted more expressly in *Etridge* and for the fact that it is not necessary to prove 'wrongdoing' (or a motive to abuse the relationship) in order to establish undue influence based on the parties' relationship.
CIBC Mortgages plc v Pitt (HL)	Husband persuaded his wife to provide security over the matrimonial home for a bank loan. The stated purpose of the loan was to purchase a holiday home and pay off the mortgage. The husband in fact intended to purchase shares with this money and did so. The House of Lords (HL) held that this was a case of actual undue influence by the husband but that the bank was not put on inquiry due to the joint benefit statement in the loan application. It followed that the bank was not fixed with constructive notice and the security could not be avoided.	Actual undue influence. A bank will not be put on inquiry (and so in danger of being fixed with constructive notice of the undue influence of husband) where the loan is for joint purposes so that there is nothing suspicious in the transaction.
Lloyds Bank v Bundy	Mr Bundy placed trust and confidence in bank manager with regard to his financial affairs. He was persuaded to charge his home as security for the debts of his son's company. CA set this aside for undue influence by the bank.	Presumed undue influence because a relationship of trust and confidence arose on the facts. A case involving a bank as the party exercising undue influence (so not a third party case).

Glossary

Acceptance: Acceptance is the *final* and *unqualified* agreement to all the terms contained in the **offer**.

Actionable misrepresentation: An actionable misrepresentation is a false statement of fact (not opinion, not future intention, and not abstract law) made by one party to the other which induces the other to enter into the contract, rendering the contract **voidable** (liable to be set aside)—and giving rise to other possible remedies for misrepresentation.

Affirmation: Affirmation occurs when a party, with full knowledge of its ability either to **terminate** a contract for **repudiatory breach** or to **rescind** for **actionable misrepresentation**, continues performance of the contract or acts in such a way that an unequivocal intention to continue performance can be implied from conduct. Affirmation preserves the contract and therefore the parties' performance obligations.

Agreed damages clause: The parties may provide in their contract for the amount of damages to be paid upon **breach**. Where these clauses were designed to reflect the compensatory aim of damages for breach, they are enforceable (liquidated damages clauses). However, if the intention is punitive and the clause is merely a threat to compel performance, it will be an unenforceable penalty clause.

Anticipatory breach: An anticipatory breach occurs where before the time fixed for performance one party indicates that he will not be performing, i.e. rejects the contract. The innocent party has the usual election to **terminate**, in which event he need not wait until the date for performance before claiming **damages**, or to **affirm**.

Bilateral agreements: Bilateral agreements consist of a promise in exchange for a promise. Bilateral means that both parties are bound on the exchange of promises, although it may be that there has yet to be any performance of those promises.

Breach: A breach of contract occurs where, without lawful excuse (e.g. frustration), a party either fails or refuses to perform a performance obligation imposed upon it under the terms of the contract or performs that obligation defectively, in the sense of failing to meet the required standard of performance.

Common mistake: Where both parties enter into a contract based on the same fundamental mistake relating to a contractual **term**, e.g. that the subject matter exists, and where there is no express or implied provision allocating the risk of this mistake to one party, the contract will be **void** at common law for mistake.

Condition: A condition is an important term going to the root of the contract so that its **breach** is considered **repudiatory** and justifies the option to **terminate** the contract (so discharging the parties' future obligations). Condition is sometimes used in other senses, e.g. in a generic sense to mean a '**term**' of the contract.

Consideration: Consideration means an act or a promise given in exchange for the promise (i.e. the price for which the other's promise was bought). Unless a promise is contained in a deed it is generally only enforceable if supported by consideration. Some enforceability of alteration promises may be achieved via the doctrine of **promissory estoppel**.

Counter-offer: A counter-offer purports to be an **acceptance** but has either added a new term or, more usually, amended an existing term. It can be compared with a request for further information which is merely *asking* for more information or whether a particular means of performance will be possible before finally committing via acceptance.

Damages: Damages are a financial remedy which aims to compensate the injured party for the loss it suffers as a consequence of the **breach** or **actionable misrepresentation**.

Duress: Duress is an equitable doctrine allowing a contract to be set aside because it was

Glossary

✱✱✱✱✱✱✱✱✱✱✱

entered into as a result of illegitimate pressure or threats such that the other party had no realistic choice other than to agree.

Entire agreement clause: An entire agreement clause provides that all the **terms** of the parties' agreement are contained in the written document and there are no other terms. This prevents a party from alleging that there are separate oral terms or an oral or written collateral contract.

Exemption clause: An exemption clause is a particular **term** which purports to exclude or limit the liability or the remedies which would otherwise be available to the injured party.

Frustration: In the absence of a contractual provision allocating the risk of the event in question, frustration occurs when, during the performance of the contract, and **without the fault of either party**, some event occurs which renders further performance either impossible, illegal, or radically different so that the purpose of both parties is no longer possible and the contract becomes essentially different. Frustration automatically discharges the contract (**terminates** both parties' obligations for the future).

Innominate term: An innominate term is a **term** which can be broken in a number of different ways, not all of which would be serious. The courts look at the effect of its breach when deciding whether the injured party should be able to **terminate** for its **breach** or should be limited to a remedy in **damages**. Only if the effects of the breach deprive the injured party of substantially the whole benefit it was intended to obtain by the contract will the breach of this term be repudiatory.

Invitation to treat: An invitation to treat is an invitation to others to make **offers** as part of the negotiating process.

Mitigation: The injured party has a 'duty' to minimize the losses it suffers following breach or misrepresentation so that it cannot recover for any losses which it failed to mitigate by taking 'reasonable steps' to minimize its loss.

Mutual mistake: A mutual mistake occurs where each party is fundamentally mistaken but each makes a different mistake, i.e. the parties are at cross-purposes as to a **term**. This mistake will prevent agreement where it is not possible for the reasonable man to say which party's interpretation is the more reasonable (using the objective test for contract formation) because of the ambiguity in the **offer** terms. Such a 'contract' is **void**, i.e. of no effect from the very beginning.

Offer: A definite promise to be bound on the **terms** proposed, made with the intention that it is to become binding as soon as the person to whom it is addressed (the offeree) accepts the offer terms.

Privity of contract: The doctrine of privity of contract provides that only the parties to a contract may enjoy the benefits of that contract or suffer its burdens. In other words, only the parties can enforce the contractual obligations, rely on its protections, or be subjected to its restrictions.

Promissory estoppel: Promissory estoppel is an equitable doctrine designed to prevent the promisor going back on his promise or representation that he would not insist on his strict legal rights under an existing contract where this would be inequitable (unfair) because the promisee has relied on this promise or representation.

Quantum meruit: An injured party may recover on a *quantum meruit* (as a restitutionary remedy) for the reasonable value of a non-financial benefit which the innocent party has provided and which is not otherwise recoverable since there is no express contractual provision for remuneration. The basis of recovery is that the guilty party would otherwise secure a benefit that it did not have to pay for.

Remoteness: Remoteness determines the scope of losses for which a party can be held responsible and so be liable to compensate the injured party in the event of **breach** or **actionable misrepresentation**. Some losses are considered too remote a consequence of the contractual wrong.

Representation: A representation is a statement which induces the contract but which does not involve any binding promise as to truth. If a representation turns out to be false it may be an **actionable misrepresentation**.

Repudiatory breach: Every breach of contract will give rise to a right to claim **damages**. However, unless the breach constitutes a repudiatory breach, the contract will remain in force. If the breach is repudiatory the non-breaching party will have the option either to accept the breach as **terminating** the contract or to **affirm** the contract.

Rescission: Where a contract is **voidable**, e.g. for **actionable misrepresentation**, **duress**, or **undue influence**, the remedy of rescission is available to the injured party (unless barred) in order to set aside the contract, involving handing back the property received under the contract and the return of the price paid.

Restitution: Restitution allows for the recovery of money paid to the guilty party or the value of benefits conferred on the guilty party (via a *quantum meruit*) on the basis that the guilty party should not be unjustly enriched at the injured party's expense.

Revocation of offer: Revocation of an offer involves the withdrawal of an **offer** previously made

Specific performance: This is an equitable (and hence discretionary) remedy (or order) which compels the party in **breach** to perform its obligations

Term: A term is a statement, pre-contractual and/or included in a written contract, which constitutes a binding contractual promise as to truth. If the term/promise is broken it amounts to a **breach** of contract, giving rise to remedies for breach of contract.

Terminate: Future performance of both parties' obligations may be discharged (terminated for the future) where a **repudiatory breach** occurs and the injured party exercises its option to accept that repudiatory breach as **terminating** the contract, rather than affirming the contract.

Undue influence: The doctrine of undue influence is an equitable doctrine allowing a contract to be set aside (the remedy of **rescission**) at the court's discretion where there has been a wrongful (undue) exercise of influence by one party over the other.

Unilateral mistake: A unilateral mistake occurs where one party is mistaken as to a **term** of the contract and the other knows or ought to know of this mistake and cannot be allowed to take advantage of it. Such a mistake will prevent agreement so that any 'contract' is **void**.

Unilateral agreements: Unilateral agreements consist of a promise in exchange for an act. It follows that only one party is bound at the outset by a promise. The other's **acceptance** is the performance of the requested act.

Void: Where a contract is **void** it is automatically of no effect from the very beginning. There is, and never was, agreement (and hence there is no contract). This effect is automatic and has nothing to do with action being taken by either of the parties.

Voidable: Where a contract is **voidable** it is liable to be set aside by one party using the remedy of **rescission**. Once it is set aside the contract is treated as never having existed. However, there are bars to rescission and where any of these applies the voidable contract must remain valid and binding

Warranty: A warranty is a less important **term** of the contract (not going to the root of the contract) so that if it is breached the injured party would be adequately compensated by the payment of damages. If this term is broken it is not therefore a **repudiatory breach**. The word warranty is also sometimes used in a more general sense to mean 'a term'.

Index

acceptance
actual communication of 1,
8, 12–13, 15–17
bilateral agreements 5–19
counter-offers 1, 8–10, 26–7
cross-offers 11–12
definition A1
dispatch rule 13
electronic contracting 11–12,
16–18
emails, contracts by
exchange 11–12, 16–18
factual acceptance 8, 11
fax communications 8,
11–12, 15–16
instantaneous
communications 1–2, 8,
12–13, 15–17
mandatory methods 11
mirror-image rule 8, 10
non-instantaneous
communications 2,
15–16, 20
offer 1–44, 49–51, 56–7,
126
office hours 16, 17
postal rule 11, 12–14, 17–19,
26–7, 82
prescribed methods 8, 11
receipt rule 12, 15–18
response to offer, must be
in 8, 11, 19
revocation of offer 2, 4, 8,
13–14, 18–19, A3
silence 12, 25
telephone answering
machines 17
telephone
communications 8,
14–15, 17
unilateral agreements 5, 7,
11, 19–25
website trading 17–18
actionable misrepresentation
belief or opinions 190–2,
195

claimant's reliance on
own judgement/
investigations 193–4
conduct 190–2
definition A1
fact, statements of 190–2,
195
false statements 100, 190–5
future conduct or
intention 190, 192
inducement 192–4
knowledge of
statements 193–4
materiality 191, 194
omissions 192–4
silence 191, 200, 201, 205
statements of law,
abstract 190, 192
actual communication 1–2,
7–8, 12–13, 15–17, 19, 22
advance payments 178–80
advertisements
advertising gimmicks 51
bilateral agreements 7
mere puffs 100
unilateral advertisements 7,
19–20, 27
affirmation
damages 115–16
definition of A1
duress 53, 55
limitations 115–16
repudiatory breach 98–9,
100, 110–16, 119, 143, A3
rescission, bar to 197
agency and privity 73–4,
83–5, 95
agreed damages clauses
definition 155–6, A1
discharge of a contract
61–3, 111, 142, 145,
155–60, 162, A1
liquidated damages clause
142, 145, 156–9, 162
penalty clauses 61–3, 142,
145, 156–60, 162

agreement 1–28
bilateral agreements 5–19,
22–5, A1
breach of *see* **breach**
certainty of terms 29–36,
51–2
commercial *see*
commercial
agreements
composition agreements
65
contract, definition of 3
domestic or social
agreements 46, 48,
51–2, 57
mistake 36–43
non est factum, plea of 29,
43
problems 29–45
promises 46–7, 48–50, 52–3,
55–60, 66–7
quantum meruit 29–30
rectification 29, 42–3
terminology 3–4, 30–1
terms sufficiently
certain 29–36
two-contract analysis 19,
22–5
unilateral agreements *see*
unilateral agreements
void for uncertainty 29,
30–2, 34–5
voidable for mistake 29–30
agreement promises
alteration promises 47,
48–50, 52–3, 55, 57
consideration 46, 47, 48
duress 47, 48–9
enforceability 49–50
factual benefits 47
formation 46–8, 50, 55–60,
66–7
intention to be legally
bound 46, 48–9, 51–2
promissory estoppel 47,
48–50

Index

****

alteration promises 60–71
agreement promises 47,
48–50, 52–3, 55, 57
consideration 47, 60–9
definition 50
duress 48, 53
enforceability 47, 55–68
formation promises,
distinguished 50
promissory estoppel 60, 65
anticipatory breach
affirmation of
contract 114–16, 119
definition 98, 114, A1
limitation on ability 116
remedies 99, 115
repudiation 98–9, 100,
110–16, 119, 143, A3
'wholly unreasonable'
to 115–16
attributes mistake 29–30,
39–42
auctions 7, 24–5

bad bargains 150
battle of forms 10, 26
beliefs or opinions 190–2,
195
bids 7, 23–4
bilateral agreements 5–19
acceptance 5–19
actual communication 7–8
advertisements 7
auctions 7
battle of the forms 10, 26
brochures and circulars 7
consideration 55–6
counter-offers 8–10
cross-offers 11–12
definition of 5, A1
invitations to treat 6–7
mirror-image rule 8, 10
offer 6–12
sale of goods 5, 113–14
two-contract analysis 19,
22–5
unilateral agreement
distinguished 5–6
withdrawal of offers 8
binding promises 100–2

**black hole problem and
privity** 73, 77, 89–90
blackmail 54
breach 99, 109–19
agreed damages clause
61–3, 111, 142, 145,
155–60, 162, A1
anticipatory breach 98–9,
114–16, 119, A1
Consumer Rights Act
2015 113–14
conditions, of 98, 111–13,
117–18
consequences 109–12
continuation in force 98
definition 98, A1
enforceability 50
exemption clauses 110–11
frustration 98, 109
fundamental breach 128–9
good/bad reasons 117
implied obligations 124,
132–3
innominate terms 98, 111–13,
117–18
option to terminate or
affirm 98–9, 111–16,
143
performance obligations,
strict and qualified 110
remedies for breach *see*
remedies for breach
repudiatory breach 98, 100,
110–11, 112, 114, 119,
143, A3
sale of goods 113–14
warranties 112–13, 117
brochures 7
business contracts *see*
commercial contracts

cancellation 82–3, 147
certainty 29–36
agreements to negotiate 30,
32–3
Consumer Rights Act
2015 33
consequences of
uncertainty 30, 35–6
incomplete terms 32

meaningless clause,
severing 32
performance, significance
of 34–5
price-fixing mechanism
33–4
quantum meruit 29–30,
35, 44
reasonable price, statutory
provision for 33
relatives, promises by 48,
51–2
terms sufficiently
certain 29–30
uncertainty, meaning of 31
vague terms 31
void agreements 29
circulars 7
coercion of will 53–4
collateral contracts 86–7
commercial contracts
advertising gimmicks 51
conditions, identification
of 106
consumer contracts 139
damages 154–5
non-pecuniary losses 152–3
presumption to be legally
bound 49
sale of goods 105–6
trade usage/business
practice 97, 104
unfair terms 134, 136, 139
commercial lenders
duress 53
undue influence 208–13
common mistake
compromise
agreements 171–2
definition A1
existence of subject
matter 167, 175, 183–4
frustration 175, 183–5
initial impossibility of
performance 166–72,
183–4
ownership of subject
matter 167–8
quality, as to 167, 169–71,
183

res extincta 167, 175, 183–4
res sua 167–8
rescission 183
void, renders
contract 167–71
composition agreements 65
compromise
agreements 171–2
compulsion/coercion of
will 53–4
conditions
breach 98, 111–13, 117–18
definition of 111, A1
identification, difficulties
with 123
oral statements, as 112
repudiatory breach 98,
111–13
subject to conditions 126,
140
term as, conclusiveness
of 113
unfair terms 136
conduct, acceptance by 191–2
consequential losses,
damages for 101
consideration
adequacy 46, 56, 62
agreement promises 46,
47, 48
alteration promises 47,
60–9
bilateral agreements 55–6
composition agreements 65
definition of 46, 55, A1
duress 53
duty imposed by law as and
going beyond 58
formation promises 48, 50,
55–68
good consideration 46,
49–50, 57–60, 63–4
invented consideration 70
part payment 64
past consideration 46, 48,
56–7, 70
payment in kind 65
privity of contract
57–60, 73–7, 81–5,
87, 94–5

promisee , move from 70,
73, 75
promissory estoppel 47–50,
65–9, 72
reliance 66–7, 69–71
restitution 143–4
sale of goods 147
sufficiency of 49, 56–7
supported by consideration,
definition of 47–60
third party, performance of
duty owed to 57–60
total failure 143–4, 171
unfair terms 120–1, 122–4,
128, 130–1, 134, 136–40
unilateral agreements 56–7
Consumer Rights Act 2015
breach 113–14
care and skill 107
certainty 33
consumers 107, 130
good faith 120, 137–8
implied terms 97, 105–7,
110
information, provision
of 107, 169
price fixing 143
price reductions or
refunds 113–14
qualified obligations 110,
123–4
rejection
partial right to reject 113
short-term right to
reject 113
remedies 98–9, 113–14, 143,
149, 169
repair or replacement 113,
149
repeat performance, right
to 114
satisfactory quality 106,
110, 169
standard of service 107
strict obligations 110,
123–4
supply of goods 105–7
supply of services 105,
107
trader, definition of 130

unfair terms 93, 120–4,
130–1, 136–9
consumers
commercial contracts,
different treatment
of 139
Consumer Protection
Amendments
Regulations 2014 188,
203, 205
Consumer Rights Act 2015
see **Consumer Rights**
Act 2015
consumer, definition of 130
exemption clauses 120–1,
122–4, 128, 130–1, 134,
136–40
misrepresentation 205–6
unfair contract terms 120–
1, 122–4, 128, 130–1,
134, 136–40
contract, definition of 3
contracting parties 73, 87–94
contractual obligations, trust
of 87
contributory negligence 142,
145, 151, 193–4, 204, 206
counter-offers 1, 8–11, 26–7,
A1
course of dealing 128
cross-offers 11–12
cross purposes, parties at
30–1, 36, 44, 166
custom, terms implied
by 117

damages 145–62
actual loss 135, 141, 145–6,
153, 156–8
affirmation 115–16
agreed damages
clauses 111, 142, 145,
155–60, 162, A1
cancellation 147
commercial
contracts 154–5
common law remedy,
as 143
compensatory 141, 145–6,
156

Index

****

damages (*Cont.*)
consequential losses,
recovery of 101
Consumer Protection
Amendments
Regulations 2014 203
contributory
negligence 142, 145,
151, 194, 204, 206
deceit 187, 199–200, 202,
207
defective
performance 147–8
definition 143, A1
delivery 147
disappointment and
distress 152–5
exemption clauses 110
expectation loss 141,
145–55
fiction of fraud 187, 202–5
fraudulent
misrepresentation 100–
1, 187, 199–200, 202, 207
liquidated damages
clause 142, 145, 156–9,
162
loss of profits 200, 207
misrepresentation 101,
188–9, 194–207
mitigation 114, 142, 143,
145, 147, 151, 155
nominal damages 73, 88,
90–2, 145, 147, 151
non-pecuniary losses 141,
152–5, 160
non-performance, damages
for 146–7
'party convenience'
cases 89, 155
penalties 61–3, 142, 145,
156–60, 162
privity 73–4, 78, 83, 87–92,
95–6, 155
property development
cases 88–92
remoteness 100, 142, 145,
151–3, 155, 160–1, 199
repair, costs of 141, 147–8,
160

repudiatory breach 110,
143
rescission 196
supply services,
cancellation of
contracts to 147
terms, remedy for breach
of 73, 98, 100
warranties 112–13
wasted expenditure 141,
149–51, 196, 203
**death or personal injury,
exemption clauses
relating to** 132, 138
debt claims 143
deceit 187, 199–200, 202, 207
deeds 55, 90–1, 96
**defective performance,
damages for** 147–8
**delivery, damages for
non** 147
description, sale by 104–7,
133, 149, 169
**disappointment and distress,
damages for** 152–5
dispatch rule 13, 18
**domestic and social
agreements** 46, 48,
51–2, 57
duress
affirmation 53, 55
agreement promises 46,
48–9
alteration promise 48, 53
blackmail 54
coercion of will 53–4
commercial lenders 53
consideration 53
definition A1–A2
deed, promise contained
in 55
economic duress 63–4,
209
enforceability 47–9, 52–5
pressure/threats,
illegitimate 47, 49,
52–4, 209
promissory estoppel
defence 72
rescission 55

voidable, agreements
rendered 47–9, 53–5, 61
duty of care deed 90–1, 96

economic duress 63–4, 209
**emails, contracts by
exchange of** 11–12,
16–18
**employment contracts,
specific performance
of** 144
enforceability 46–72
advertising gimmicks 51
agreement promises 49–50
alteration promises 47,
55–68
breach of agreements 50
consideration *see*
consideration
criteria 46–72
domestic and social
agreements 46, 48,
51–2, 57
duress 47–9, 52–5
extinguishing liability 49
formation promises 46, 60
good consideration 49
identifying promise
see king to be
enforced 49–50
intention to create legal
relations 46, 49, 51
privity of contract 73–91,
96–7
promise, reasonable
person's understanding
of 49–50
promissory estoppel,
doctrine of 47–50
relatives, promises by 51–2
supported by
consideration 47–60
unfair terms 120–1, 122–4,
128, 130–1, 134, 136–40
voidable agreements 47–9,
53–5, 61
**entire agreement
clauses** 103–4, A2
estoppel *see* **promissory
estoppel**

'*Eurymedon*' device 59, 74, 85–6, 95
exemption clauses
  breach 110–11
  damages 110
  definition 120, A2
  Himalaya clause 59, 80, 84, 86
  oral statements 103–4, 118
  third party's reliance 73, 74–5, 78–80, 84–6, 95
  unfair terms *see* **unfair contract terms and exemption clauses**
  validity after discharge 110–11
  who may rely on 74
expenses 141, 149–51, 178–80, 196, 203

fact
  implied terms 107, 108–9, 117
  statements of fact 190–2, 195
fair dealing, definition of 138
false statements 100, 190–5
fax, communications by 8, 11–12, 15–16
fiction of fraud 187, 202–5
fitness for purpose 106, 124, 133, 135, 147, 149
force majeure **clause** 165–6, 172
foresee ability 176–7, 185
formation promise 46, 48, 50, 55–68
fraud
  fiction of fraud and damages 187, 202–5
  misrepresentation *see* **fraudulent misrepresentation**
fraudulent misrepresentation
  contributory negligence 204
  damages 100–1, 187, 199–200, 202, 207
  definition 194

fiction of fraud and damages 187, 202–5
mistake as to identity 29, 38–44
remedies 187, 202–5
voidable agreements 29, 39, 40–1
frustration 172–86
  advance payment obligations prior to 178–80
  automatic discharge for future 172, 178, 180
  breach of contract 98, 109
  common purpose, ending of 175, 185
  definition 163, A2
  effect on contract and parties' obligations 172
  expenses 178–80
  force majeure 165–6, 172
  frustrating event 163–85
  illegality 172, 174–5, 180, 182
  impossibility 163–85
  limitation on 176–7
  mistake 175, 183–5
  pre-frustration performance 190, 194
  risk allocation 178
  statutory provision on discharge 164, 172, 178–81, 183–4
  subsequent impossibility 163–4, 172–86
  tangible benefit to recipients 180–1
  unjust enrichment 181–2, 184, 186
  valuable benefit, performance conferring a 181–3
fundamental breach 128–9
further information, requests for 1, 9

good faith
  meaning 135
  negotiation 30, 33, 44

third parties 198
unfair terms 120, 137–8

Himalaya clause 59, 80, 84, 86
hire of goods 105–7
honour clauses 51

identity, mistake as to
  face-to-face cases, presumption in 39–42, 44–5
  fraudulent misrepresentation 29, 38–44
  identity theft 40
  third parties 39–41, 53
illegality 172, 174–5, 180, 182
implied terms
  breach 124, 132–3
  Consumer Rights Act 2015 97, 105–7, 110
  courts, implied by 97, 99, 104, 107–9, 117
  customary 117
  fact, in 107, 108–9, 117
  fitness for purpose 106
  hire of goods, contracts for 105–7
  information about trade or service 107
  law, in 107, 109, 117–18
  parol evidence rule 103–4
  qualified obligations 110
  risk allocation 166
  sale of goods, contract for 97, 104–5, 113, 132, 169
  satisfactory quality 106, 110, 169
  standard of service 107
  statutory 97–8, 104–7, 110
  strict obligations 110
  supply of services, contracts for 105–7
  trade usage/business practice 97, 104
importance attached to the statement test 101–3, 112, 117

Index

****

impossibility 163–85
force majeure
    clauses 165–6
    frustration 163–4, 172–86
    initial impossibility 166–72,
      183–4
    mistake 166–72, 183–5
    risk allocation 165
    subsequent impossibility
      163–4, 172–86
incorporation of terms 120,
    122, 124–8
information 1, 107, 169
injunctions 144, 154
innocent misrepresentation
    194–8, 203
innominate terms 98, 111–13,
    117–18
instantaneous communications
    1–2, 8, 12–13, 15–17
intention to create legal
    relations 46, 48–9, 51–2
invitation to treat 1, 6–7, 17,
    19–20, 23–4, 26, A2

land and specific performance
    69, 144, 206
lenders *see* **commercial**
    lenders
limitation of liability 90–3,
    116, 120, 122, 128–9, 133
liquidated damages
    clauses 142, 145,
      156–9, 162
loss of profits, damages
    for 200, 207

mirror image rule 8, 10
misrepresentation 187–207
    actionable *see* **actionable**
      misrepresentation
    consumer context 205–6
    Consumer Protection
      Amendments
      Regulations 2014 188,
      205
    contributory
      negligence 193–4, 204,
      206
    damages 188–9, 194–207

fraudulent *see* **fraudulent**
    misrepresentation
innocent *misrepresentation*
    194–8, 203
negligent misrepresentation
    187, 193–6, 198, 200–3
remedies 97, 188–9,
    194–207
rescission 100, 187, 195–9
sale of goods 198
statements as
    representations and not
    terms 190
voidable agreements 187,
    189–90, 196
wasted expenditure,
    damages for 196, 203
mistake
    agreement mistakes 36–43
    attributes 29–30, 39–42
    common *see* **common**
      mistake
    Consumer Protection
      Amendments
      Regulations 2014 188
    fundamental mistake
      29–30, 38–9, 41–2, 163
    identity 29, 38–44, 53
    impossibility 167–72,
      184–5
    mutual mistake 30–1, 36–7,
      44, 163, 166, A2
    non est factum, pleas of 30,
      43
    rectification 29, 42–3
    sale of goods 167
    unilateral *see* **unilateral**
      mistake
    void agreements 37, 163
    voidable agreements 29–30,
      39–42
mitigation 114, 142, 143, 145,
    147, 151, 155, A2
mutual mistake 30–1, 36–7,
    44, 163, 166, A2

negligence
    contributory
      negligence 142, 145,
      151, 193–4, 204, 206

damages 142, 145, 151, 194,
    204, 206
misrepresentation
    see **negligent**
    misrepresentation
unfair terms 122–4, 128–30,
    132, 135, 138, 142
negligent misrepresentation
contributory
    negligence 193–4, 204,
    206
damages 101, 187, 193,
    195–6, 198, 200–3
definition 195
fiction of fraud 202
remedies 187, 195–6, 198,
    200–3
rescission 196
negotiations 30, 32–3, 100–1
nominal damages 73, 88,
    90–2, 145, 147, 151
non est factum, **plea of** 29, 43
non-molestation
    injunctions 154
non-pecuniary losses 141,
    152–5, 160

offer
    acceptance 1–44, 49–51,
      56–7, 126
    actual communication 7–8,
      13, 19, 22
    bilateral agreements 6–12
    counter-offers 1, 8–10,
      26–7, A1
    cross-offers 11–12
    definition of 6, A2
    invitation to treat 1, 6–7,
      17, 19–20, 23–4, 26
    revocation 2, 4, 8, 13–14,
      18–19, 27, A3
    unilateral offers, special
      principles for 19, 21–2
omissions 192–4
onerous or unusual
    clauses 127
openness and unfair
    terms 136–8
oral statements
    conditions 112

exemption clauses 103–4,
118
importance attached
test 103–4
mistake 42
unfair terms 127–8
writing 102–4, 118, 127

parol evidence rule 103–4
part payment 64
'party convenience' cases 89,
155
payments in kind 65
penalty clauses 61–3, 142,
145, 156–60, 162
performance
certainty 34–5
damages 92, 146–8
defective performance,
damages for 147–8
illegality 172, 174–5,
180, 182
impossibility 163–85
qualified contractual 110
strict contractual 110
valuable benefit 181–3
postal rule 1, 12–14, 17–19,
26–7, 82
prices
fixing 33–4, 143
reductions or
refunds 113–14
privity and third party
rights 73–96
agency, use of 73–4, 83–5, 95
basic principle 74
black hole problem 73, 77,
89–90
broad ground 92
collateral contracts 86–7
common law devices to
avoid 74, 77, 83–7
consideration 57–60, 73–7,
81–5, 87, 94–5
contracting parties
distinguished 74
contractual obligations,
trust of 87
damages 73–4, 78, 83,
87–92, 95–6, 155

definition of privity 73,
75, A2
enforceability 73–87
'Eurymedon' device 59, 74,
85–6, 95
exemption clauses 73, 74–5,
78–80, 84–6, 95
good faith 198
Himalaya clause 59, 80,
84, 86
mistake as to identity
39–41, 53
narrow ground
principle 89–91
party convenience
cases 89, 155
property development
cases 88–93
remedies 74, 78, 87–95, 198
rescission 198
revocation 19
specific performance 74,
78, 88, 95
statutory reform of third
party rights 73–4,
77–91, 94, 96–7
trusts of contractual
obligations 87
undue influence 209,
211–13, 214
promises
agreement promises 46–7,
48–50, 52–3, 55–60, 66–7
alteration promises 47, 50,
60–71
binding promise 100–2
deed, contained in 55
duress 55
estoppel see promissory
estoppel
formation see formation
promise
relatives, by 52
promissory estoppel
agreement promises 47,
48–50
alteration promises 60, 65
Australian approach 69
consideration 47–50, 65–9,
72

defence only 66–7, 69, 71–2
definition of 66, A2
duress 72
effect 68
ending by reasonable
notice 68
enforceability 47–50
English law, limitations on
in 66–7
equitable remedy, as 47, 66
operation of 67
'suspensory effect' of
estoppel 49, 68
unconscionability 69–70
property development
cases 88–92, 96

qualified obligations 110,
123–4
quality
mistake 167, 169–71, 183
possess a certain quality,
where goods do not 169
satisfactory quality 105–6,
110, 124, 132–3, 135,
147, 149, 169
quantum meruit 29–30, 35,
44, 144, 185, A2

reasonableness of unfair
terms 120, 127, 130,
132–6, 139
receipt rule 12, 15–18
recovery of money
paid 143–4
rectification 29, 42–3
rejection 113
remedies for breach 141–62
anticipatory breach 99, 115
Consumer Protection
Amendments
Regulations 2014 188,
201, 205
Consumer Rights Act
2015 98–9, 113–14, 143,
149, 169
contracting parties 87–94
damages see damages
debt claims 143
injunctions 144, 154

Index

****

remedies for breach (*Cont.*)
  misrepresentation 97,
    187–9, 194–207
  price reduction or
    refunds 113–14
  privity 74, 78, 87–95, 198
  promissory estoppel *see*
    promissory estoppel
  quantum meruit 29–30, 35,
    44, 144, 185, A2
  recovery of money
    paid 143–4
  rejection 113
  repair or replacement 149
  rescission *see* **rescission**
  restitution *see* **restitution**
  specific performance 69,
    74, 78, 88, 95, 144, 206,
    A3
remoteness
  abnormal loss 152–3, 161
  damages 100, 142, 145,
    151–3, 155, 160–1, 199
  definition A2
  normal loss 152–3, 161
  reasonable contemplation,
    loss within 151–2, 155,
    161
repairs
  damages 141, 147–8, 160
  repair or replacement 113,
    149
repeat performance, right
    to 114
representations 97, 99, 101–2,
    190, A3
repudiatory breach
  affirmation 98, 100, 110–11,
    112, 114, 119, 143, A3
  anticipatory **breach** 98–9,
    100, 110–16, 119, 143,
    A3
  conditions 98, 111–13
  damages, right to
    claim 110, 143
  definition A3
  innominate terms 98,
    111–13, 117
  recognising breach 111–12
res extincta 167, 175, 183–4

res sua 167–8
rescission
  affirmation 197
  bars 55, 187, 196–8
  damages 196
  definition A3
  duress 55
  lapse of time 197
  misrepresentation 100, 187,
    195–9, 203
  mistake 183
  restitution, impossibility
    of 55, 197
  third parties 198
  undue influence 209, A3
  voidable contracts 30,
    55, A3
restitution 55, 143–4, 197, A3
retailers' websites 7
revocation
  acceptance 2, 4, 8, 13–14,
    18–19
  actual communication
    requirement 2, 13,
    19, 22
  definition A3
  offer 2, 4, 8, 13–14, 18–19,
    27, A3
  postal rule 27
  third parties 19
  unilateral offer, special
    principles 19, 21–2
rewards 5, 6, 11, 19–20, 22,
    27, 57
risk allocation 165–6, 172,
    178

sale of goods contracts
  bilateral agreements 5,
    113–14
  breach 113–14
  collateral contracts 87
  commercial
    contracts 105–6
  consideration 104
  Consumer Rights Act
    2015 113–14, 143, 169
  damages 147
  delivery, damages for
    non 147

description, sale by 104–7,
    133, 149, 169
  fitness for purpose 106,
    124, 133, 135, 147, 149
  implied terms 97, 104–5,
    113, 132, 169
  misrepresentation 198
  mistake 167
  model, correspondence
    with a 149
  price-fixing 33
  quality, where goods
    do not possess a
    particular 169
  sample, sale by 106–7, 133,
    149
  satisfactory quality *see*
    satisfactory quality
  statutory definition 104
  title 105
  unfair terms 132–3
  warranties 113
sample, sale by 106–7, 133,
    149
satisfactory quality 105–6,
    110, 124, 132–3, 135,
    147, 149, 169
severance 32
shop window displays 7
silence 12, 25, 187, 191, 200,
    201, 205
social and domestic
    agreements 46, 48,
    51–2, 57
specific performance 69, 74,
    78, 88, 95, 144, 206, A3
standard forms 10, 26, 32, 133
standard of services 107
strict obligations 110, 123–4,
    129–30, 132–3
subject to conditions 126, 140
supply of goods 105–7
supply of services 105–7,
    110, 147

telephone communications 8,
    14–15, 17
tenders 7, 23–4
terminate, option to 98–9,
    111–16, 143, A3

terms 99–109
  advertising statements 100
  binding promise 100–2
  breach, remedies for 73,
    98, 100
  certainty 29–36
  conditions *see* conditions
  definition of 97, A3
  entire agreement
    clauses 103–4, A2
  exemption clauses *see*
    exemption clauses;
    unfair contract
    terms and exemption
    clauses
  honour clauses 51
  implied *see* implied terms
  importance attached
    test 101–3, 112, 117
  incomplete terms 32
  innominate terms 98,
    111–13, 117–18, A2
  mistake 29, 30
  offer 3
  oral statements 103–4, 118
  parol evidence rule 103–4
  pre-contractual
    negotiations 100–1
  representations
    distinguished 97, 99,
    101–2
  severance 32
  standard forms 10, 26, 32,
    133
  unfair terms *see* unfair
    contract terms and
    exemption clauses
  vague terms 31
  warranties 111–13, 117, A3
  writing 10, 29, 32, 97, 99,
    102–9, 126–7, 133
third parties *see* privity and
    third party rights
tickets 125–6, 139–40
title 105
trade usage/business
    practice 97, 104
trader, definition of 130
transparency 136–8
'two-contract analysis' 19, 22 5

uncertainty *see* certainty
unconscionability 69–70,
  156
undue influence 208–14
  actual 208, 210–11, 214
  constructive notion
    212–13
  definition 208, 209, A3
  economic duress 209
  effect of 213
  husbands and wives 208–
    12, 214
  lenders 208–13
  presumed 208, 210–11, 214
  rescission 209, A3
  special protected
    relationships 208–12,
    214
  third parties 209, 211–13,
    214
  voidable contracts 209, 213
unfair contract terms
    and exemption
    clauses 120–40
  ambiguity 128
  ancillary terms 137, 139
  burden of proof 136
  commercial contracts
    130–1, 134, 139
  conditions 136
  consequences of
    unfairness 138–9
  construction 120, 122,
    128–30, 132, 135, 140
  Consumer Rights Act
    2015 93, 120–4, 130–1,
    136–9
  consumers 120–1, 122–4,
    128, 130–1, 134, 136–40
  core terms 137, 139–40
  course of dealing 128
  death or personal
    injury 132, 138
  duty to consider
    fairness 139
  enforceability 120–1, 122–4,
    128, 130–1, 134, 136–40
  fair dealing 138
  fundamental breach
    128–9

good faith 120, 137–8
  guidance 137–8
  identification of clause 123
  indicative list of terms 137
  incorporation of terms 120,
    122, 124–8
  individual negotiation 133
  injunctions 144
  liability 120, 123–30
  limitation clauses 93, 120,
    122, 128–9, 133
  negligence liability 122–4,
    128–30, 132, 135, 138,
    142
  non-consumer 132
  onerous or unusual
    clauses 127
  openness 138
  oral statements 127–8
  prominence 136–7
  qualified obligations
    123–4
  reasonable notice 120, 125,
    127
  reasonableness,
    assessing 120, 127, 130,
    132–6, 139
  regulations 120–1, 131, 133,
    136–40, 144
  sale of goods 132–3
  signed contractual
    documents, terms
    in 125
  significant imbalance 121,
    137–8
  statutory regulation 120,
    130–1, 136, 138–9
  strict contractual
    obligations 123–4,
    129–30, 132–3
  subject to conditions 126,
    140
  total exclusion clauses 120
  transparency 136–8
  UCTA 1977 93, 120, 122,
    124, 130–6, 138–9
  unenforceable terms 120,
    130–1
  work and materials,
    contracts for 132–3

Index

****

unilateral agreements 19–25
  acceptance 5, 7, 11, 19–25
  advertisements 7, 19–20, 27
  bilateral agreement
      distinguished 5–6
  consideration 56–7
  definition of 5, 19, A3
  implied waiver of need
      to communicate
      acceptance 19–20
  offer 19, 21–2
  revocation, special
      principles of 19, 21–2
  rewards 5, 6, 11, 19–20, 22,
      27, 57
  two-contract analysis 19,
      22–5
unilateral mistake
  attributes 29, 30, 39–42
  carelessness by party
      signing 43
  collateral matters 38
  definition 37, A3
  generally 30, 37–9
  identity 29, 38–44, 53
  mistake as to terms 29, 30
  non est factum, plea of 43
  rectification 29, 42–3

risk allocation 166
unjust enrichment
  frustration 181–2, 184, 186
  prevention 35, 181–2, 184,
      186
  restitution 143

vague terms 31
void agreements
  definition 30, A3
  mistake 30, 37, 39–40, 163,
      167–71
  uncertainty 29
voidable agreements
  attributes mistake 29, 30,
      39, 40
  definition 30, A3
  duress 47–9, 53–5, 61
  enforceability 47–9, 53–5,
      61
  misrepresentation 29, 39,
      40–1, 187, 189–90, 196
  mistake 29–30, 39–42
  rescission 30, 55, A3
  undue influence 209, 213

warranties
  breach 112–13, 117

collateral 111, 117
  damages for breach 112–13
  definition 112, A3
  sale of goods 113
wasted expenditure
      damages
  'bad bargains' 150
  burden of proof 151
  expectation loss 141
  misrepresentation 196, 203
  recovery 149–51
website trading 7, 17–18
works and materials,
      contracts for 92–3,
      105–6, 132–3
writing
  incorporation 125
  information, provision
      of 107
  mistake 31, 40–4
  oral statements 102–4, 118,
      127
  rectification 29
  standard forms 10, 26, 32,
      133
  terms 10, 29, 32, 97, 99,
      102–9, 126–7, 133
  unfair terms 126–7